Apple Betty & Sloppy Joe

Apple Betty & Sloppy Joe

Stirring Up the Past with Family Recipes and Stories

Susan Sanvidge

Diane Sanvidge Seckar

Jean Sanvidge Wouters

Julie Sanvidge Florence

Note: No garlic was harmed in the production of this book.

Wisconsin Historical Society Press

Published by the Wisconsin Historical Society Press
Publishers since 1855

wisconsin history.org

Printed in Canada

Cover designed by Sue Ellibee
Interior designed by Jill Bremigan
Illustrations on front cover and page 230 by Cloo Stevenson
Back cover photographs: Mom in the Bowen Street kitchen in Oshkosh; Susan, Jean, Diane, and Julie with Grandma Great

All photographs are from the authors' collections
Other art credits appear on page 366

12 11 10 09   5 4 3 2

Library of Congress Cataloging-in-Publication Data

Sanvidge, Susan.
   Apple Betty & sloppy Joe : stirring up the past with family recipes and stories / Susan Sanvidge ... [et al.].
      p. cm.
   Includes index.
   ISBN 978-0-87020-386-2 (pbk. : alk. paper) 1. Cookery, American—Midwestern style. 2. Cookery—Wisconsin. 3. Wisconsin—Social life and customs. 4. Oshkosh (Wis.)—History—20th century. I. Title.
   TX715.2.M53S36 2007
   641.5977—dc22

                         2007026320

Our Two Cooks
Helen Noffke Sanvidge and Neil Sanvidge

Our very own salt and pepper shakers,*
before kids . . .

and after kids.

It does look like Dad tore some of his hair out, and Mom needs glasses now after all those years of "seeing what we were up to." We couldn't have been too bad, because they still look good.

*One of our favorite salt and pepper shakers in Grandma Sanvidge's collection was the bride and groom—before and after the wedding.

This cookbook is dedicated to Mom, as a small
thank you for the big job of getting meals on the
table for four kids all those years, and to Dad,
for working so hard and for making breakfasts,
Sunday night suppers, and popcorn.

This book was Diane's idea, but as Mom would
say, "We all put our two cents in."

Contents

"Girls! Time to come in!"

The bell Mom used to call us in to eat is on the shelf above her head, and the cups from our play tea set are sitting on the counter behind her, in front of the cake saver.

Our summer began when the freezer was stocked with Reimer's hot dogs and brats and the old basement fridge was crammed with grape pop, cream soda, root beer, Pepsi, 7UP, and beer. We went strawberry picking—and hulling and eating— and Mom made jam with what was left. We bought corn from roadside stands. We had beets, tomatoes, carrots (rubbed on the grass and eaten on the spot), peas, and beans from our own garden. We ate wild asparagus from Grandma Sanvidge's ditch and raspberries from Grandma Noffke's garden. Summer was watermelon with salt, ice cream cones at the Sunlight Dairy on Main Street, the single piece of rhubarb pie Grandma brought over for Mom (because she was the only one who liked it), and the dreaded berry-picking with Grandpa Noffke. (How come he never needed a bathroom?)

In the fall, we went to Rasmussen's for bushels of apples, cheese, and maple sugar candy and headed out on leisurely Sunday afternoon drives to gather hickory nuts. I remember the dim root cellar at Grandma Noffke's with a dusty ray of sunlight that made the green beans, red tomatoes, and yellow beans in the Mason jars glow.

We ate oranges that Grandma Noffke brought back from Florida, Georgia pecans from Uncle Cliff and Aunt Millie, cheese from local cheese factories, smoked sturgeon and chub, deer sausage, venison passed off (unsuccessfully) as beef, elk, partridge, pheasant, duck, trout, and, in good years, lobster.

We all remember the fragrance of Mom's bread baking in the oven, the chewy brownies, and the beautiful birthday cakes. We remember meals with our grandparents: Grandma Sanvidge's Blue Willow dishes, Grandpa Sanvidge saying, "I ate quite freely of it," Grandma Noffke's yellow and brown plaid dishes, and Grandpa Noffke *definitely* eating quite freely of it. We remember Grandma Great teetering in with her little cloth-covered pan of Suet Pudding at Christmas, the sound of the mixer in the mashed potatoes, the cranberry sauce that ran into the potatoes, turning them pink, the rice in Cile's pale green glass salt shaker with the dented top, the falling-apart-tender pork roast, the clown cookie jar, the cocoa pitcher and the sighing percolator . . . *I'm hungry. When's supper ready?—Susan*

The Big Kitchen on Bowen Street in Oshkosh . . .

The rippled-glass picture window between the kitchen and the added-on den, and the morning sun filtering through during breakfast . . . the green linoleum floor, the brown Formica table and patterned vinyl chairs . . . the utility table with the Old Spice cup filled with bus tokens and spare change . . . the old-fashioned black iron trivets flanking the clock on the papered wall . . . the toasty register next to the "fridge" . . . the summer we ordered milk in spigotted boxes and doubled our milk consumption . . . the mangle (a big appliance with a padded roller for ironing sheets and tablecloths) and how Mom could make it work by magic! (The foot pedal!) . . . the red plastic tumblers and steak knife set that came free with our new green hide-a-bed . . . the aluminum milk box on the back stoop . . . the blessed KitchenAid

Susan, Diane, and Jean in front of the kitchen's east windows before "the addition." The ceramic figures on the windowsill were painted by Mom. (She took a class.)

dishwasher . . . the restaurant dishes with the cocoa brown and pale aqua crescent pattern . . . trying to hatch the quail egg on the counter and Duck Duck's cardboard box in the corner . . . the Westinghouse range with two ovens . . . the intercom that issued "Beautiful Music" and wake-up calls throughout the house . . . the wonderful smell of turkey when we woke up Thanksgiving morning . . . the white-flocked and bejeweled candleholder that the Noffke boys thought was "cozzy" . . .

Julie sitting in front of the wallpapered south kitchen wall (just under the two trivets and the wall clock with the red nail polish hands, which are not shown in the photo). This highchair saw a lot of smeared food over the years.

Mom waxing the floor every week and the smell of ammonia when she stripped it . . . card club nights with the Sawickis, Martins, and Kelleys . . . the green metal picnic basket and cooler . . . Mom's dressy organdy aprons for holidays and dinner parties . . . Homemakers Club meetings at our house and the time they had a luau and all the women had to leave their girdles in a box by the door! . . . the time we grew an avocado plant from a pit . . . the black and white Mixmaster . . . the black wall phone (BEverly 1-5604) . . . the plastic bags of white margarine with the little orange dots of food coloring, or, if you were lucky, yellow margarine in sticks from whoever just got back from Michigan . . .

. . . Those big kitchen shears that were often the only scissors we could locate in the whole house . . . dinner parties in the den—we would be waitresses . . . bachelor friends like Fritz Buettner and Tony Peters coming for a weeknight dinner . . . SOS pads, Ajax cleanser, Joy detergent . . . Food Club everything, Apple-Tru canned sliced apples, Graf's 50/50, LaFontaine's bread and peanut squares, Reimer's wieners, Kraft mac and cheese with tuna, "blue" milk, Kaukauna Klub cheese spread in little brown crocks . . . *The Settlement Cook Book* . . . the little cardboard disks that Mom used on angel food cakes to cover up the hole and how extra good the frosting tasted on them . . . pie crust scraps baked with cinnamon sugar . . . yummy strips of apple peelings . . . buying apples by the bushel, beef by the side, potatoes by the 50- and 100-pound sacks . . . opening our birthday presents at the breakfast table the minute we woke up and could get someone else to wake up and watch us!—*Julie*

This is Julie in the kitchen after the addition. Can you find some of the things she mentions in this picture?

Breakfast

"Time to get up!"

The percolator has breathed its final sigh, and the coffee is ready. Mom's favorite Big Band music is coming from the boxy ivory radio next to the toaster on the utility table, and the sun is streaming through the window. The scrambled eggs in the cast-iron pan on the stove are almost done, and the glass carafe with oranges and green leaves printed on it is filled with icy-cold orange juice, foamy from the blender. One by one, we stumble into the kitchen, still in our pajamas. Julie heads for her favorite spot on the floor by the heat register. Somebody (could it be me?) is about to whine about the Big Band music . . .

In our Breakfast section you will find the food for: "The sun is shining and the birds are singing! Time to get up!"; Grandpa Noffke coming over again to talk about the shopping center he wants to build; the "Cleaning Lady" (who didn't last long) wants her morning beer break; and waking your kids up at 6 a.m. (even if they stayed up really, really late doing a jigsaw puzzle).—*Susan*

Banana Nut Bread (Mom)

Nobody wants toast when there's Banana Nut Bread on the breakfast table. If you happen to have two brownish bananas that nobody wants, you can transform them into this lovely loaf of moist and fragrant bread. (Mashed bananas can be frozen and used later.) Cut a half-inch-thick slice, spread on a little smear of butter . . .—*Susan*

2 cups flour

2 teaspoons baking powder

½ teaspoon baking soda

½ teaspoon salt

½ cup sugar

¼ cup (4 tablespoons) butter, softened

2 eggs

2 medium-size ripe bananas, mashed

½ cup sour milk*

1 cup chopped pecans or walnuts (optional, sort of)

Preheat oven to 350° and butter a loaf pan. (An 8½-inch glass loaf pan works best for this recipe, but a 9-inch metal pan works, too.) In a large bowl, sift together flour, baking powder, baking soda, and salt. In another bowl, cream sugar and butter with a mixer. Beat in eggs, mashed bananas, and sour milk. Gradually beat the dry ingredients into the banana mixture. Stir in the (optional) nuts. When well blended, pour batter into greased pan and bake for 1 hour. (A handsome "crack" in the top of the bread is a good thing.)

If Mom's Housekeeping Rules are being followed, you won't have sour milk languishing in your refrigerator. To make it: Put 1½ teaspoons of lemon juice or white vinegar (either works fine) in a measuring cup and pour in whole or 2% (not skim) milk until you have ½ cup.

I've found this bread keeps best in the refrigerator. It freezes well, too. (Mom's never lasted long enough to need refrigerating.) I haven't made banana bread as much since I started taping quarters to the ripe bananas. Eat that awful brown banana and you get a quarter.—Susan

Scrambled Eggs (a.k.a. Slime Eggs when Dad makes them and Crumbled Eggs when Mom does)

Break as many eggs as you need into a bowl. Whip them up vigorously. Heat up the cast-iron frying pan with a goodly blob of butter or margarine in it. Pour in the eggs. Salt and pepper to taste.

For Dad's Slime Eggs: *Stir once. Pour them out right away!*

For Mom's Crumbled Eggs: *Stir a few more times. You still have time to fit in that load of laundry. By the time the laundry's done, the eggs will be, too!—Susan*

"Hey, Diane brought donuts. Get out the butter."

Side Orders for Breakfast

Side pork, bacon, and pork sausage usually came from a butcher shop when we were growing up. Don't forget to put your "side order" on to fry before you start the eggs—they take a lot longer to cook.—*Susan*

> side pork (Pull out the bristles first, so you can enjoy this.)
>
> bacon from the slab (Peroutka's bacon is very good.)
>
> pork sausages (Yum!)
>
> pork patties (Yum!)
>
> smoky links (Some people like these and some people don't.)
>
> fried Spam slices (Hmmm.)

Hey! Put your shirt down. Don't show your fried eggs!

–Julie

Fried Eggs

Get out your cast-iron frying pan. Heat it up and melt a good gob of butter or margarine. Crack eggs, one by one, and drop them into the sizzling pan. The edges on an Authentic Sanvidge Fried Egg (the food kind) are brown and slightly curled.

Pancakes

Usually it's Dad who makes the pancakes. When we were kids, he would sometimes serve up "picture pancakes" (snowmen, turtles, Mickey Mouse). He also made chocolate pancakes and buckwheat pancakes from a mix. Dad always uses eggs and milk (not water) when he makes pancakes with Bisquick. If you want bacon with your pancakes, the first thing you should do is put it in the pan and get it started.—*Susan*

MAKES 12 TO 13 MEDIUM-SIZE PANCAKES

Crisco (or vegetable oil) for griddle

2 cups Bisquick

1 cup whole or 2% milk

2 eggs

"You sit down. Let me finish making those pancakes."—Mom

"No. You sit down! I'll make them."—Dad

"Let me finish making those. You sit down and eat."—Mom

"Jeeze!"—Dad

(Result: Mom always sits down and eats; Dad always makes all the pancakes.)

Beat Bisquick, milk, and eggs until smooth. (Pancake batter is best when it sits for a little bit.) Heat griddle until hot (over medium-high heat) and grease with Crisco. Put a drop of batter on the griddle to see if it is ready to use. If little bubbles form around the batter, the griddle is ready. For each pancake, pour a scant ¼ cup of batter onto hot griddle. Fry until edges look dry. Flip and fry until golden. Serve with maple syrup and butter or margarine.

French Toast

Mom always makes the French toast. The amounts below are very flexible. Basically, you need enough egg mixture to cover the bread. We loved French toast. On the rare occasions when we went out for breakfast, that's what we would always order.—*Susan*

Crisco or vegetable oil for griddle
5 or 6 eggs
a little milk
a little salt
12 slices of bread (better if it's a little stale, so it won't get
    soggy)

In a shallow bowl, using a fork, mix the eggs with the milk and a little salt. Beat ingredients until well blended. Heat griddle (medium-high) until hot and grease with Crisco or vegetable oil. Dip bread quickly, both sides, into egg mixture. Fry both sides until golden. Serve with butter (okay, sometimes margarine) and maple syrup.

Good bread makes good French toast.—Susan

It's Toast!

Toast was a staple at the Sanvidge breakfast table. We spread it with soft butter (Mom always left the butter dish out, so it would be room temperature) and raspberry jam, or sprinkled it with cinnamon sugar.

Often we had raisin bread to toast. It had white frosting on it that gunked up the toaster, dripped off, and scalded your hand . . . and then your lips. It was worth all the trouble. It was delicious.

Sometimes the toast would fail to pop up, probably due to frosting buildup. Mom would take out the toast, all stiff and plenty black, and scrape the burnt part off. Scr-r-itch, scr-r-itch, scr-r-itch. It sounded worse than Velcro.

Little flecks of black ash mixed in with the butter. Even jam couldn't hide it.

Optimistic Mom handed it to the closest daughter . . . "You can't even tell it was burned."—*Diane*

Scr-r-itch, scr-r-itch, scr-r-itch . . .

"There's no butter out!"

—Susan or Diane or Jean or Julie

Frozen Strawberry Jam

This jam tastes like fresh strawberries. (The recipe came from Joyce Peters, who is a great cook and one of Mom's best friends.)—*Jean*

I made this in 20 minutes!!—*Diane*

Diane is a fast cook.—*Susan*

1 box (1.75 ounces) Sure-Jell (powdered fruit pectin)
1 cup water
3 cups crushed strawberries
6 cups sugar
You will also need: seven 8-ounce jars with lids, all very
  clean

Boil Sure-Jell and water for 1 minute and mix into berries and sugar while still hot. (Berries will not be cooked more than this.) Pour into very clean jars, put on lids, and let stand overnight. After no more than 24 hours, put in freezer. This jam will keep for up to one year in the freezer, but no more than three weeks in the refrigerator.

Cinnamon Toast (an Unsupervised Breakfast)

While my sisters discovered television when they were a little bit older, I was weaned on it. *Captain Kangaroo, Colonel Caboose, Romper Room* . . . I was a television junkie from birth! With just three channels, there wasn't always children's programming on, so I'd watch the news, polka shows, hunting and fishing shows, and whatever the rest of the family was watching. But Saturday morning was all mine, as cartoons filled all three channels and my teen sisters slept in. I remember waking up about 5:30 and watching crummy cartoons until *Mighty Mouse* came on and I knew the good shows were ahead! While everyone else slept, I made a big stack of cinnamon toast and ate it all morning.
—Julie

6 to 8 slices of LaFontaine's white bread
Blue Bonnet margarine or real butter, if available
cinnamon and sugar, mixed in a cereal bowl

Toast the bread in the toaster that takes forever. Spread with oleo or butter you find in a dish on the counter. Sprinkle heavily with cinnamon sugar. Pile it up on a plate and take a dish towel into the living room with you. It's messy! Enjoy your solitude—it won't last long. Adjust the vertical and horizontal controls on the TV whenever it rolls, snows, or zigzags. Adjust the antenna rotor to perfection. Congratulate yourself on being the only person in the household who has these skills down pat. When *George of the Jungle* comes on, your sisters will come in to watch and ask for some cinnamon toast. Tell them it's yours and they can make their own!

Cereal in a Bowl

I hold the Sugar Jets record: six bowls for one breakfast.
—*Susan*

Buy a selection of the following: Sugar Jets, Post Toasties, Rice Krinkles, Rice Krispies, Cocoa Puffs, Kix, Trix, Frosted Flakes, Sugar Crisp, Sugar Smacks, Sugar Corn Pops (*sugar* was not a bad word then), Raisin Bran, Shredded Wheat (which used to come in a stubby little box with the biscuits sitting on cardboard layers printed with Niagara Falls lore), Puffed Wheat, Puffed Rice, Cheerios, Life, or Special K. Make sure there's milk in the refrigerator. That's all you have to do.

Cereal is Gr-r-r-r-reat!!!

On school day mornings, we almost always had cold cereal with milk for breakfast. Sugar-coated cereals were our favorites, but we also ate cereal that wasn't sugar-coated—and piled on the sugar. We liked cereal so much that we ate it after school, and at bedtime, too. Even better than the cereal were—

The Box: You put the box right in front of your face while you ate your cereal and read every single word off the back. Then, when the box was empty, you could:

- Test Mr. Peabody's optical illusions.
- Cut out and put together your Mighty Mouse Action Toy.
- Play a Go-Go Gophers carnival game.
- Cut out the Yogi Bear Mystery Message De-coder and write a secret message.
- Cut out the circus animals and put on a circus show.
- Cut out the real record on the back of the Wheaties (which you eat even if you don't like them—to get the record). Play it on your record player and sing along. "Pony boy, pony boy, won't you be my pony boy . . ."

The Prize Inside: You always wanted to be the one to open the new box of cereal if there was a prize inside. Open the waxed paper liner and slide your arm in all the way to the bottom . . . listen to the cereal crunching. Watch as your elbow pushes the cereal out of the top of the box. Dig, dig, dig. Tah-dah! Pull out:

- A Nautilus submarine to fill with baking soda and watch as it maneuvers by itself in the bathtub
- A little squirt-camera to fill with water and fool everyone
- A gold plastic airline wings pin so you can pretend you're a pilot
- Plastic sea divers (baking soda again), cartoon statues, rings, games, Roy Rogers buttons . . .

The Offer: Save the box tops and you can get cool stuff in the mail. Send check or money order (even if it costs only 25 cents). Allow 4 to 6 weeks for delivery.

- Two box tops and two dollars for a Valerie doll (I sent for one), and for only two dollars more you could get a wardrobe for her, too!
- Color a picture of the Sugar Smacks seal and enter a contest to win an Admiral transistor radio!
- Get a Wild Bill Hickok treasure map for only 25 cents and one Sugar Pops box top!
- Send for a walkie-talkie with a pair of two-way phones and 50 feet of cord!

Who wouldn't eat cereal three times a day?—*Diane*

Graham Cracker Mush

With four kids in the house, it must have been hard to keep enough cereal on hand. It was our weekday breakfast, home-from-school snack, and bedtime comfort food. When we ran out of cereal, we could have a bowl of mush.—*Julie*

Break several graham crackers into a cereal bowl. One-inch-square pieces are just about right. Pour 2% ("blue") milk over crackers to one-half the depth of crackers. Mix it around just a bit to moisten the crackers and eat real soon, or the crackers will become too mushy and you just don't like that very much.

Variation: Pour milk in a glass and dunk the crackers 'til the milk's almost gone. Refuse to drink the cracker milk because it's nasty!

Hot Cereal in Winter

Winter didn't stop us from eating cold cereal, but when it was really cold, Mom made hot cereal. We just put milk and sugar on ours, but Dad also added butter and salt.—*Susan*

Choose from the following list of hot cereals (but you will all have to agree on what kind because individual packets have not been invented yet): oatmeal (again!); Hot Ralston (so grainy, it has to be good for you); Cream of Wheat ("It's Cream of Wheat weather!"); Malt ... O ... Meal (a gruff voice said it this way on TV); and Maypo (a maple-flavored cereal that the TV convinced us to like, sort of).

Get out the Revereware pan with the lid, pour some milk from that half-gallon glass bottle into a reasonably pretty pitcher, put the sugar bowl on the table ... and follow the directions on the box.

Post-Communion School Breakfast

At St. Mary's Grade School, we went to Mass every day before school. You had to fast if you went to Communion, so you couldn't eat breakfast at home. After church, we went to Gerdes's grocery store (an old store that smelled like celery) kitty-corner from the church and bought our breakfast. —*Susan*

Don't forget to take 12 cents with you to school. Walk over to Gerdes's. (Be careful crossing the street.) Select your breakfast from the following:

Twinkies

Hostess Cupcakes with the surprise inside

Sno-balls

Pink Sno-balls

Susy-Q's

Pay the man or lady 12 cents. Walk back to school and enjoy your breakfast with a little glass bottle of GDC milk. Maybe you'll get a delicious goiter pill for dessert!

Gerdes's also had white lemon Alaska Pops in waxy paper bags for 4 cents.—*Julie*

Nichols's Candy Store

A good part of our fifty-cent allowances went into the Nichols's (*that's Nickel-suhs*) cash register. Conveniently located just across from the St. Mary's School bus stop, this store had carved wood paneling and beveled mirrors over elegant display cases of fancy chocolates on one side of the store and a variety of ice creams (for cones and sundaes) on the other. We walked on past this part of the store to the unfinished, dark back section, which was lit only by the bright fluorescent light of a large, curved-glass display case of penny candy.

Here are some of the things our pennies would buy:

"I want red wax lips, a candy necklace, and a Double Bubble."
—Diane

Red Licorice Shoelaces: Play with them first. Make a bracelet. Tie a bow. Make a bunch of knots. Throw them over your shoulders and nibble the ends.

Candy Buttons in Rows on Long Strips of Paper: (How long the strip was depended on how many pennies you spent.) We wore this candy, too. It looked like a belt of "ammo." Bite off a few at a time. If some of the paper comes with it, eat that too.

Chum Gum: Three sticks for a penny. The flavor didn't last too long, but what a deal!

Wax "Buck Teeth": Not quite as popular (or attractive) as the red wax lips. Wear them. Bite into them and gradually chew every trace of flavor from the wax.

Candy Cigarettes: The box looked like a real pack of cigarettes, but these "cigarettes" were white candy with a bright pink tip. "Smoke" them, and when the end dissolves to a point, pull them into your mouth and finish them off.

Little Wax Pop Bottles: There was a little colored syrup in each one. Bite off the top and slurp down the sweet liquid. Chew on the unflavored wax until your jaws hurt.

Candy Lipstick: A tube of chalky, cherry red candy wrapped in shiny gold paper, with a little red candy sticking out the top. Oh, look! Our lips (and fingers and teeth) are all red!

. . . The bus is coming!!—*Susan*

"If you spend your bus money at Nichols's Candy Store, you will have to walk home."

—Diane

Yummy Muffins

These are the first muffins my sisters and I ever made. We learned to make them in our 4-H cooking classes. The recipe below is a streamlined version of the one in the 4-H cookbook *It's Fun to Cook*, which even included a list of the utensils you would need.—*Susan*

MAKES 12 MUFFINS (OR UP TO 18 MUFFINS IF ADDING OPTIONAL INGREDIENTS)

2 cups flour

¼ cup sugar

3 teaspoons baking powder

½ teaspoon salt

1 egg, beaten

1 cup whole or 2% milk (Skim milk will not work in this recipe.)

¼ cup (4 tablespoons) butter, melted

Optional ingredients (choose one):

½ cup nuts

¾ cup fresh blueberries

½ cup chopped cranberries

¾ cup cut-up dates

Preheat oven to 400° and grease 12 muffin cups (you'll need up to 18 with optional ingredients). In a large bowl, sift together the flour, sugar, baking powder, and salt.

Beat the egg until foamy. Stir in the milk and melted butter.

Make a "well" in the middle of the flour mixture and pour in the egg/milk/melted butter—all at once. And here is the muffin rule that will help you with every muffin you will ever make: Stir only until all ingredients are moistened, but the batter is still lumpy. The 4-H cookbook even specified 17 to 25 strokes! (Gently fold in optional ingredients if using them.)

Fill each muffin cup two-thirds full. Bake until the muffins are pulling away from the side of the pan and tops are just turning golden, 15 to 20 minutes. (These are relatively pale muffins.) Muffins always taste best when served warm from the oven.

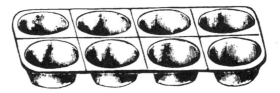

Mother's Day Breakfast

I do have a memory of a Mother's Day surprise breakfast that got, should we say, "soured" when one of us, probably me, dropped a half-gallon glass bottle of Fahrnwald milk. It broke, spewing glass shards and milk all over the kitchen floor! I don't imagine that was one of Mom's favorite Mother's Days. Mom told me recently that once our milkman (To the younger generation: Milk was actually delivered to our door.) dropped several bottles—which broke—down our basement stairs. He felt awful but didn't stick around to clean it up.—*Jean*

"I'm sorry, Mom. I picked you a flower."

"Aaah-choo!"

Cinnamon Breakfast Puffs

These are delicate, light, and delicious muffins.—*Susan*

MAKES 12 MUFFINS

Muffins:

½ cup sugar

⅓ cup shortening (Crisco)

1 egg

1½ cups flour

1½ teaspoons baking powder

½ teaspoon salt

¼ teaspoon nutmeg

½ cup whole or 2% milk (Skim milk will not work in this recipe.)

Topping:

6 tablespoons butter

½ cup sugar

1 teaspoon cinnamon

Preheat oven to 350° and grease 12 muffin cups. In a large bowl, beat sugar, shortening, and egg with a mixer. In another bowl, sift together flour, baking powder, salt, and nutmeg. Alternately add dry ingredients and milk to shortening mixture. Fill muffin cups a generous half full. Bake until golden and pulling slightly away from the edges of the muffin cups, 20 to 25 minutes.

Toward the end of the baking time, make the topping. Melt the butter and pour it into a shallow bowl. (The butter can harden if you do this too early, and it's too late if you wait until the muffins are out.) In a separate, shallow bowl, mix the cinnamon and sugar. When the muffins are done, remove them from the pan and roll each whole muffin immediately in the melted butter and then in the cinnamon/sugar mixture.

Coffee Talk

I think Mom introduced her very first grandchild to "coffee" when she was about six! She was the only one willing to get up at 5 a.m. to enjoy this treat . . . as well as a special time with her grandma. I do remember it was more sugar and milk than coffee. They would sit at the kitchen table, enjoying their coffee, and talk. Years later, they had their coffee in the RV!—*Diane*

Six-Week Bran Muffins

This is a big batch of muffin batter you keep in the refrigerator. There's enough batter here to make hot muffins for six breakfasts.—*Susan*

MAKES ABOUT 5 DOZEN MUFFINS, depending on how many of the optional ingredients you use. (You can bake as much as you want right away and store the rest of the muffin mix in a sealed container in the refrigerator for up to 6 weeks—but don't add dates or other optional ingredients until just before baking.)

2 cups boiling water

2 cups 100% Nabisco or Post Bran Flakes or Kellogg's Bran Buds

3 cups sugar

1 cup shortening (Crisco)

4 eggs, beaten

1 quart buttermilk

5 cups flour

5 teaspoons baking soda

1 teaspoon salt

4 cups Kellogg's All-Bran

optional ingredients: dates, raisins, or chopped apples

Pour boiling water over bran flakes and let stand while you assemble other ingredients.

In a very large bowl, cream sugar and shortening. Add beaten eggs, buttermilk, and water-soaked bran flakes.

In another large bowl, sift together dry ingredients: flour, baking soda, and salt. Stir in (dry) Kellogg's All-Bran. Pour dry ingredients into wet ingredients and stir only until all ingredients are moist. Cover the batter and let it sit in the refrigerator for one day before making the first batch.

To Bake One Dozen Muffins:

Preheat oven to 375° and grease 12 muffin cups. Scoop out about 3 cups of the muffin batter. (Use only 2½ cups if adding optional ingredients.) Place the remaining batter in the refrigerator. Stir dates, raisins, or apples (optional) into the batter and fill muffin cups two-thirds full. Bake until a muffin springs back when touched in the center, 20 to 25 minutes.

Quick Coffee Cake (Grandma Noffke)

Grandma made this classic coffee cake often. The buttery brown sugar and cinnamon topping sinks into the batter here and there as it bakes, making delicious trails of the topping throughout the cake. If you've never made a cake from scratch, this is a good one to start with. It would be perfect for your next kaffee klatsch. (This means "coffee gossip.") While the original recipe calls for an 8-inch square pan, I use a 9-inch round pan, 1¾ inches deep. The cake rises out of the pan a little, so I put something under it in the oven.—*Susan*

Cake:

½ cup sugar

¼ cup (4 tablespoons) butter, softened

2 eggs, well-beaten (a little froth starting to form)

1½ cups flour

2 teaspoons baking powder

½ teaspoon salt

1 cup whole or 2% milk (Skim milk will not work in this recipe.)

Topping:

½ cup brown sugar

2 tablespoons butter, melted

1 teaspoon cinnamon

Preheat oven to 350° and grease and flour an 8 x 8-inch pan. Cream sugar and butter with a mixer until totally combined. Add beaten eggs. In another bowl, sift together flour, baking powder, and salt. Alternately add dry ingredients and milk to butter mixture. Mix until smooth. Pour into pan.

Mix together topping ingredients and sprinkle onto batter. Bake until a toothpick inserted in the center comes out clean, 30 to 45 minutes.

Our mother made a coffee cake from a recipe on the Bisquick package that was very similar to Grandma's, but apparently even quicker. (The last time I bought Bisquick, it wasn't on the package.)—Susan

Dutch Apple Cake (Grandma Noffke)

Grandma Noffke noted on her recipe card: "Not an old recipe." (But she wrote this in the '50s.)—*Susan*

Cake:

¼ cup sugar

¼ cup (4 tablespoons) oleo (margarine) or butter

1 egg

1½ cups flour

3 teaspoons baking powder

¼ teaspoon salt

½ cup whole or 2% milk (Skim milk will not work in this recipe.)

Topping:

2 cups peeled, sliced baking apples (The wrong kind of apple will get
   leathery.*)

½ cup brown sugar

2 tablespoons butter, melted

1 teaspoon cinnamon

Preheat oven to 350° and grease a 9-inch square baking pan (with 2-inch sides). In a large bowl, cream sugar and shortening well. Beat in egg. In another bowl, sift together flour, baking powder, and salt. Alternately add the dry ingredients and the milk to the shortening mixture, mixing only until the flour is absorbed. The batter will be thick. Spread batter in pan.

Mix topping ingredients and spread on top of batter. Bake until a toothpick inserted in the center comes out clean, 25 to 30 minutes.

Grocery stores often have charts in the produce section showing the varieties of apples and what they can be used for. (I used Liberty apples.)—Jean

Lunch

"Soup and sandwich . . ."

11:30 a.m.: "Girls! Time to come in. Lunch is ready!" Lunch was usually a "let's get this over with and get back to what we were doing" meal. Anything remaining from supper the night before was transformed into lunch by our thrifty mother: roast beef, pork, ham, and chicken sandwiches; mashed potato pancakes. Dad liked to make a big kettle of soup on wintry Sunday afternoons, and early the following week Dad's soup would appear at lunch. In the cupboard, a box of Kraft Macaroni and Cheese or cans of tuna, Spam, canned fruit, or Campbell's soup provided a quick meal, and there was always summer sausage in the fridge.

Our grade school, St. Mary's, was more than a mile away so we couldn't come home for lunch. I was the first to go to school, and in first grade, all alone in a new school (taught by a nun who regularly turned yellow and passed out on the floor), opening my red plaid lunch box meant comfort from home. As my sisters started school and the number of lunches to pack mounted, the "hot lunch program" was the best option (but Julie certainly didn't think so).—*Susan*

Chicken Soup (Dad)

Dad throws away all the broth the real chicken makes. He doesn't like how cloudy it is!—*Diane*

Put a whole chicken in a big kettle or soup pot and cover it with water. Cook over medium heat until tender. Remove the chicken from the pot. Take out the bones and cut up the chicken, disposing of the fat and the skin (and the chicken broth, too!).

Put 2 quarts of water in the kettle and add 2 rounded tablespoons of chicken soup base. (This is a yellow paste you will find in the soup aisle at the grocery store.) Add the chicken and vegetables including: celery, carrots, onion, green beans, and sometimes corn. Bring to a boil and then simmer about 10 minutes or until vegetables are tender. Salt and pepper to taste.

Beef Vegetable Soup (Dad)

This soup is always made in a heavy kettle with a handle. It has been around as long as we can remember.—*Diane*

Brown a chuck roast and cover with water that has two beef bouillon cubes dissolved in it. Cook until the beef is tender and falling off the bone. Take the beef out, leaving the juice in the pot. Cut the meat up and dispose of fat and bone. Put the meat back into pot.

Add one 46-ounce can of V8 Vegetable Juice, a sprinkle of dried sweet basil (to taste), a 28-ounce can of diced tomatoes, some green beans, sliced carrots, celery, and onion. Cover and bring to a boil. Turn heat down and simmer until vegetables are tender.

Potato Soup (Mom)

I grew up thinking you actually had to have leftover mashed potatoes to make potato soup! Don't bring me the chunky or cheesy potato soup—this is the kind I like.—*Julie*

In a large saucepan, melt a couple tablespoons of butter. Toss in about ½ cup each of diced onions and minced carrot (optional). Sauté until softened. Add about 3 cups whole or 2% milk and gently heat through. Add about 3 cups of mashed potatoes (about 3 large potatoes) to make a moderately thick soup. Salt and pepper to taste.

I made this when our Aunt Emma was at our house, and she said: "Lucky the man who marries you!" (And right she was!) —Diane

Tomato Soup (Campbell's)

Follow instructions on can. Ladle soup into bowls and put a pat of butter into each one.

Serve with a grilled cheese sandwich made with Wonder Bread—cut in half on an angle.

Alphabet Soup (Campbell's)

Buy some. Follow instructions on can. Lunch will last longer than usual because eaters will try to find their names in the soup.

Chicken Noodle Soup (Campbell's)

Buy some. Follow instructions on can. Slurping alert.

Cream of Chicken Soup (Campbell's)

This is a sauce, not a soup. See One Dish Meals section.

Newly Married Mom's Chili

This is the way Grandma Noffke made her chili. Mom made it this way early in their marriage, but Dad decided he didn't care for that recipe, so he took over the chili-making after that.—*Jean*

Brown 1 pound hamburger with a small onion, diced. Drain off the grease. Add 1 quart home-canned tomatoes and a 16-ounce can of pork and beans. Salt and pepper to taste. (No chili powder in *this* chili!) Heat and serve.

Some Mom Food Facts

Did you know that:

- Mom rarely eats bread with her meals? She credits this with helping control her weight over the years.

- Mom was never served any kind of pasta as a child?

- Mom hates to can?

- Other than trout, Mom's not really crazy about making fish at home? She'd rather make reservations.

- Mom rarely deep-fries anything? Why not? It's not really the fat that's the problem; it's the waste.

- Mom volunteered in the St. Mary School cafeteria on Wednesdays because it was Spudnut Day? Nobody complained about the food on Spudnut Day! (What's a Spudnut, you say? It's a tender, delicious raised donut made with potato flour—hence, "spud"—completely covered in granulated sugar.)

- Mom's KitchenAid dishwasher on Bowen Street helped Dad sell lots of them to building customers? Not many people had dishwashers then.

- Mom would wake up her lazy kids by turning on the intercom and, in a sing-song voice, chant, "The birds are singing. The bees are humming. Wake up, wake up, wake up"? (*Susan remembers: "The sun is shining, the birds are singing . . . "*) This did not last long. (*Susan, who is the oldest daughter, remembers hearing this for a long time.*)

▣ Mom didn't serve us dessert on a regular basis? She didn't want us getting in the habit of eating sweets every day. This didn't work.

▣ Mom would sometimes rename dishes to make them sound more appetizing? This practice of "selling the sizzle, not the steak" did not extend to ice cream. "Hey, Mom, what's for dessert?" we'd ask. "Ice cream," replied Mom. "What kind?" (Can you hear the balloon burst?) "Just plain old vanilla." —*Julie*

"I wonder what a noodle is?" (This is our mother as a little girl.)

Dad's Chili

Chili is a great cold weather/big crowd/not-sure-when-they-are-showing-up meal.—*Jean*

Dad's Chili is more like soup than chili, so don't expect it to be thick.—*Diane*

Brown 1 pound hamburger with ½ cup chopped onion. Drain off the grease. Cook ½ cup sliced celery with water to cover in a small, lidded saucepan until tender. In a large kettle, put browned hamburger, onions, celery with its cooking liquid, and a bay leaf. Add a 46-ounce can of V8 or tomato juice, 1 quart home-canned tomatoes, and a small can of kidney beans. Bring to a boil, then turn down to simmer. Season with 2 tablespoons of chili powder and add sugar and salt to taste. Toss in a good handful of broken-up spaghetti noodles. Cook until noodles are done. Remove and discard bay leaf. Serve with soda crackers.

Hide those kidney beans under the edges of your soup bowl. (Make sure you help to clear the table.)—Susie the Picky Eater

Some Dad Food Facts

Did you know that:

- Dad doesn't like rhubarb and isn't crazy about rice?

- Dad sometimes puts butter on frosted chocolate cake?

- When Dad isn't feeling well, he makes creamed peas on toast?

- Dad ate a lot of mutton in the South Pacific during WWII?

- When Mom's out of town, Dad uses a stack of folded newspapers as a placemat?

- A teenaged Dad ate five tomato sandwiches at a sitting?

- Dad usually requests Pineapple Upside-Down Cake for his birthday?

- One of the few baby pictures we have of Dad shows him with a Shredded Wheat box on his head? (Yes, that's our dad in the photo.)

⊞ As newlyweds, Dad taught Mom a lot about cooking? His mother had taught him how to cook, but Mom was rarely in the kitchen.

⊞ Dad would eat anything I ever made, even when I was nine years old?

⊞ Dad needs some bread with his dinner and likes to use it as a tool to push his food onto his fork?

⊞ Dad blames the beginning of his weight gain on having to finish off our ice cream cones?

⊞ Dad likes to drink milk? When we had all four kids in the house, Dad always drank ice water with his supper. When "the girls" moved out and we moved up north, Dad started drinking milk with his supper. I asked him why he all of a sudden liked milk. He said that he had always liked it, but he drank water to save money and make sure there was always enough milk for all four kids. Thanks, Dad. —*Julie*

"Van's Hot Dogs" (A Re-creation by Our Cousin, Tom Noffke)

There's a little tavern in Oshkosh that has been serving one of Dad's favorite things to eat for years and years. Van is long gone, and the tavern is now called Bob's Trails End, but they still serve Van's Hot Dogs. Inside this legendary treat, you will find a skinny little finger-sized hot dog (Where do they get those?) that is smothered in a very spicy "sloppy joe" and strewn with raw onions. It seems that these are a hit with Mom's side of the family too. Tommy came up with a recipe for making them at home. You won't be able to find Van's skinny little hot dogs, but this will save you a trip to Oshkosh, for now.—*Susan*

I went to the Trails End to taste the real thing (again), and Tommy's version tastes very much like it to me. I only found two differences: original Van's Hot Dogs start with a line of mustard down the crease of the bun, and the texture of the hamburger/chili mixture is smoother than Tommy's—so I put it in the blender for a bit.—*Jean*

> "Good eating. Light sweat. Bad breath."
> —Tom Noffke

½ pound lean hamburger

1 can (15 ounces) Hormel chili (the kind with no beans)

¼ teaspoon red cayenne pepper

¼ teaspoon Colman's English mustard (or any powdered mustard)

hot dogs, cooked

hot dog buns, steamed

⅔ cup diced raw onion (to put on top)

Brown hamburger lightly and drain off grease. Combine with chili, cayenne pepper, and mustard and heat well.

Now, as Tommy puts it: "Build the dog." Put the hot dog in the bun. Pile on the hamburger mixture and put a good amount of onions on top.

Grilled Cheese Sandwich

Mom had a waffle iron that had plates you could insert for grilling flat things, too. If you make this with homemade White Bread (see page 212) and good Wisconsin Cheddar cheese, you will feel like a happy ten-year-old.—*Susan*

> white bread, 2 slices
>
> butter or margarine
>
> American or Cheddar cheese, 2 slices
>
> vegetable oil (or Crisco) for greasing a griddle or frying pan if you don't have a waffle iron (which Diane and Jean tell me does not need to be greased when the outsides of the bread are buttered)

Spread each slice of bread with butter or margarine. The buttered side will be on the outside. Lay cheese slices on one unbuttered side of each sandwich. Cover with the other piece, buttered side out. Heat up your waffle iron (or, put your griddle or frying pan on the stove over medium-high heat and grease it). When hot, put the sandwich in (or on), and grill it until the cheese just starts oozing out.

If using griddle or frying pan, you'll need to flip the sandwich. It's tricky! You might need to put a dome-shaped lid over the top to help the cheese melt.

D id you know that . . .

. . . if you can figure out how to make a Mr. Cinders' steak sandwich, you will be Dad's favorite?

Baloney Sandwich Spread (Mom)

"That's a lot of baloney."
—Mom

"Rosy meat by any other name should smell so sweet (and pickle-y)." I say "Baloney!"—*Susie, the Picky Eater*

Buy a fat, flesh-pink ring of bologna (the kind that looks like a replacement for a body part). Remove the skin and cut into chunks. Get out the meat grinder (medium disk) and run the pink bologna insides through it into a bowl. (Don't look.) Grind up some sweet pickles to add contrast and "tang." Add a little Miracle Whip to hold it together. (Authentic Mom Style: "It might need just a drop or two of pickle juice.") Spread thickly on white bread.

It's also good on crackers.—Julie

Big Baloney Sandwich (also known as
Pack Your Own [Blank!] Lunch Sandwich)

The cafeteria food at St. Mary's was not kid-friendly. Who would serve pea soup to second-graders? Those fake mashed potatoes with gluey gravy, all on a compartmented Melmac tray? Mystery meat loaf? I rebelled and wanted to bring a lunch instead. Mom said I could, but I'd have to pack my own lunch. This is the sandwich I ate 95 percent of those days:

Miracle Whip
2 slices LaFontaine's white bread
1 slice Oscar Mayer big bologna
iceberg lettuce leaves

Spread a "just right" amount of Miracle Whip on both pieces of bread. Too little is too little and too much will just about choke you. Place one slice big bologna on the bread (never two) and close sandwich. Put it in a Waxtex bag and complain that other kids get plastic bags and their bread doesn't dry out. Continue preparing lunch while Mom turns a deaf ear. In a second (*hmpf!*) Waxtex bag, place the lettuce and a damp paper napkin to keep the lettuce fresh. Finish lunch with an apple that you NEVER eat, any cookies you can find (graham crackers will do if no cookies are available), and some carrot and celery sticks or chips. Remember to ask Mom for 10 cents because you need a milk ticket for this week—milk in little bottles is 2 cents a day. When eating the sandwich, remember to eat the doughy little bump on the side of the crust first—it's the best!—*Julie*

Hot Lunch

Mrs. Boehm ran the hot lunch program at St. Mary's. She was heavyset, with thick glasses and a really nice disposition (especially when you consider she had four hours to make food for about eight hundred kids). We could see the steam rising from cookers and the big metal trays that held our lunch as Mrs. Miller punched our lunch tickets at the door. We picked up pastel Melmac trays and held them out over what we wanted. Volunteer mothers helped with dishing up and cleaning up. (Our mom helped on Wednesdays.)

We always had chicken noodle soup on Mondays. The soup was yellow with wide flat noodles and a sprinkling of parsley. Jean fondly remembers the day she found a piece of chicken in her soup. Sometimes we had mashed potatoes with turkey chunks and gravy or tomato noodle casserole with tiny flecks of hamburger. Mrs. Boehm made really good homemade donuts. Friday at a Catholic school meant no meat for lunch (which wasn't too much of a problem!). Pale macaroni and cheese with big flattened noodles, tomato soup with grilled cheese sandwiches, and fish sticks with tiny French fries were what we had on Fridays.

The last lunch lady offered peanut butter, or just butter, sandwiches, always cut into triangles. The peanut butter was grainy and dark (Mom says it was "government issue"), but it tasted good if you didn't like the other food and were hungry enough. At the end of the line was a little room with stacks of metal carriers holding little glass bottles of milk, chocolate and white. Chocolate milk was a big treat, even if it tasted terrible with most of the food.

Don't forget to pick up one of those little straws before you enter the "hot lunch only" room. (The "cold lunch" room, which had a smell of oranges and bananas, was only for kids who brought their lunches.) Eat your lunch fast so that you can get a swing on the playground.—*Diane*

"Faux" Summer Sausage Sandwich

Deer sausage was a "hard-sell." —*Diane*

When nobody is looking, slice up the rest of the deer sausage, butter up some bread, and make a sandwich. (If you have any Oscar Mayer wrappings, scatter them around the kitchen so it will look like you used "real meat.") Serve the sandwich to the next person who walks into the kitchen and says she is hungry. Tell that person she can't have dessert until she has finished her lunch. *Voila!*

We had real summer sausage sandwiches, too.—*Jean*

A Good Chicken Sandwich

One more reason to roast a chicken. —*Susan*

Lay two slices of homemade white bread on the counter. Spread lavishly with mayonnaise (or I suppose you *could* use Miracle Whip). Put some pieces of iceberg lettuce on one slice. Bring out the delicious roast chicken you had *last night or one night before that*—*not a week ago,* cut off some breast meat (if there is any), and put it on the lettuce. Salt and pepper the chicken. Close the sandwich and cut it in half. Pour yourself a nice cold glass of milk and enjoy!

Mom-Seal-of-Approval Chicken Salad

This is a really good way to make chicken salad. The grapes provide little bursts of sweet tartness, and the almonds add crunch, especially if you toast them. (Diane and I, the two oldest sisters, remember when Mom's chicken salad only had mayonnaise and celery.)—*Susan*

4 cups cubed cooked chicken (no more than two days old, or no Mom-Seal-of-Approval for you)

1 cup halved green grapes

1 cup chopped celery

1 package (3½ ounces) sliced almonds with skins (toasting* them is optional)

¾ cup mayonnaise

¼ cup sour cream

1 teaspoon salt

¼ teaspoon pepper

"Never order chicken salad in a restaurant or buy it at the store. It's made with old chicken and will probably make you sick."—Mom

Combine chicken, grapes, celery, and almonds in a large bowl. In a small bowl, combine mayonnaise, sour cream, salt, and pepper. Stir dressing into the chicken mixture. Chill well before serving.

To toast sliced almonds: Place almonds in a heavy, ungreased frying pan over medium heat. Stir often until almonds are golden brown. Watch them. Golden brown turns into burnt in a few seconds.

Meat Loaf Sandwich

Some people (like me) put ketchup on the inside of the bread.—*Jean*

Onion haters alert: Don't forget to pick out the onions before you make the sandwich.—*Susan*

Cut ⅓-inch slices of leftover meat loaf and place between two slices of substantial bread. (No Wonder Bread here!) Butter the outside of each piece of bread. Heat up a cast-iron griddle or frying pan over medium heat, add a little Crisco or vegetable oil, and fry sandwich as you would a grilled cheese sandwich. If the outside is browning faster than the inside is warming, put a dome-shaped lid over the sandwich to hold the heat in. (If you fry the meat loaf slices for a few minutes before putting them on the bread, you won't have this problem.)

Tuna Salad Sandwich

Under the influence of her Homemakers Club (The Busy Badgers), our mother sometimes rolled the edges of a Tuna Salad Sandwich in chopped pecans. —*Diane*

Drain a can of tuna and put the tuna in a bowl. Add sliced celery and enough Miracle Whip to hold it together. Find yourself some decent bread and make a sandwich.

Ham Sandwich

An obvious lunch in the week after many holidays.—*Susan*

The components are:

ham, hacked off a leftover baked ham in good, thick hunks

butter, lots of it

buns*

Also great with a little mustard and brown sugar.—Jean

*Ideally these would be homemade, soft, and a little on the sweet side. See Good Fast Bread, page 216.

Egg Salad Sandwich

We seem to like our egg salad squishy, so . . . —*Susan*

Dice up some boiled eggs (see recipe on page 53) pretty fine, and add celery, sliced or diced, and mayonnaise or Miracle Whip—enough for this to be as squishy as *you* want it. Make a sandwich, and, as you take the first bite, put one hand under your sandwich to catch that falling blob of egg salad.

"Hey! Who ate all the potato chips?"

Open the Sanvidge cupboard and you will find:

- Kix—More fun checking out the box than eating it.

- Rice Krispies—Don't get your ear wet listening for the "Snap, crackle and pop."

- Cream of Wheat—Good to warm you up on a cold morning with lots of sugar and Fahrnwald milk to disguise the gritty texture.

- Oatmeal—Use this for *cookies*, Mom!

- Kraft Macaroni and Cheese—For quick meals and no-meat Fridays (and Christmas Eve).

- Angel food cake mix—For the birthday of the next little angel in the house.

- Popcorn—Be sure you have *permission* to make this!

- Egg noodles—For tuna casserole.

- Graham crackers—Slather with soft butter and top with another cracker.

- Soda crackers—Slather with soft butter and eat with raisins. You can eat soda crackers when you don't like the soup.

- Onions—Susie says, "Toss them!"

- Potatoes—*Should* be in the cupboard (if Mom didn't put them in the freezer!)

- Butter cookies (the kind with the hole in the middle and the scallops all around)—it's food and a toy wrapped up in one. Put on finger and eat around until you have a "ring."

- Flour—No weevils in Mom's flour! She uses it too fast.

- Pepper seed spice—Where did *that* come from? Throw it away before Jean ruins another pizza!

- Oreos—A favorite cookie jar filler. Remove the first side and let pieces of it melt slowly in your mouth . . .

- Windmill cookies—A not-so-favorite cookie jar filler.

P.S.: Close that cupboard door!—*Jean*

Cold Hard-Boiled Eggs with Butter

Most people think putting a little slab of butter on a boiled egg is gross, so this is "one of ours." —*Susan*

Put eggs in an enameled or stainless steel pan. Cover with cold water to 1 inch above the eggs. Bring to a boil. Immediately turn off the heat, cover the pan, and set a timer for 15 minutes.

Pour the hot water out and set the pan of eggs under cold running water to cool. (Mom often adds ice cubes to the water to speed this along.) Remove the eggs from the water after they have cooled. (Put them in the refrigerator if you'll be eating them later.)

To eat a Cold Boiled Egg à la Sanvidge: Peel it. Cut it in half as shown and put an ample amount of butter on each side. (Keep the butter nearby for re-buttering after each bite.) Add salt. (Pepper is optional.) You may want to slice off, and discard, the egg equivalent of the chip-less cookie, the extra white "point." (Also optional.)

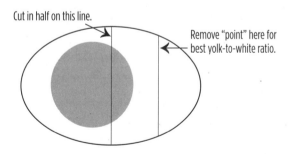

Cut in half on this line.

Remove "point" here for best yolk-to-white ratio.

X-ray view of boiled egg, showing Sanvidge cut.

Hot Hard-Boiled Eggs with Butter

A solitary, one-course lunch.—*Susan*

Make the eggs according to the instructions for Cold Hard-Boiled Eggs, but leave them in the cold water for only a minute or two (they will be easier to peel). Peel and chop up the eggs while still warm. Add butter (which will melt on the warm eggs), salt, and pepper.

Salmon Patties (Mom)

Frying the patties in butter gives a tasty little "crust." Little Susie the Picky Eater didn't like these, but big Susie does.—*Susan*

MAKES 6 SMALLISH PATTIES (SERVES THREE, MAYBE FOUR THIN LADIES)

1 can (14.75 ounces) pink salmon

1 egg, beaten

½ cup soda cracker crumbs

1 tablespoon finely chopped onion

pepper (optional), but no salt (The crackers will provide enough salt.)

¼ cup (4 tablespoons) butter, for frying

Drain the salmon and remove skin and bones. (*This will take some time and is not a job for the squeamish.—Susan*) Break it into flakes.

In a bowl, mix the beaten egg, cracker crumbs, and onion together well. Mix in the flaked salmon and shape into 6 patties, 3 inches in diameter. (They won't be very thick so they can cook through.)

Melt the butter in a frying pan over medium to medium-high heat. Fry patties until they are lightly browned to golden.

Mom says that Grandma Noffke served Salmon Patties with cream sauce (which Grandma Sanvidge called "milk gravy.") See recipe for Cream Sauce on page 90.

Smoked Chubs

Buy some smashed-flat, whole smoked chubs (which look like they have been gilded) at the grocery store. They're good!—*Susan*

Carrot and Celery Sticks

The most common "side dish" on our lunch table. You don't really need a recipe for this, do you?

Appetizers

"Something to tide you over..."

Authentic *Sanvidge appetizers* are sometimes as simple as Mom putting out some summer sausage and a chunk of Wisconsin Cheddar on one of Dad's cutting boards (or the pig-shaped cutting board Grandpa Sanvidge made), with a basket of crackers on the side. Those crackers are likely to be Waverly Wafers, Ritz Crackers, or Wheat Thins. There might be a crock of Kaukauna Club cheese or the infamous, gelatinous head cheese (*sülze*). You might see little pimiento-stuffed green olives or the big, black pitted ones, Milwaukee brand dill pickles or those crinkly-sliced sweet pickles, and muenster, brick, or Mossholder's cheese (a kind of brick cheese that Dad bought from a cheese factory on a farm in Appleton). During fishing season, Dad makes smoked trout. In hunting season, the deer goes to the butcher to make deer sausage (after years of trying to get us to eat venison). Back when Dad went ice fishing, we had smoked sturgeon.—*Susan*

> **"God, kid, I LOVE that stinky cheese!"**
> —Aunt Emma

This is a sturgeon.

On special occasions, smoked oysters are served with . . .
"How about a Manhattan?"*

Manhattan

Dad's favorite drink.—*Julie*

Fill a short glass with ice. Add 2 ounces brandy and a generous half-ounce of sweet vermouth. Pour in a good ounce of maraschino cherry juice. (Dad uses less cherry juice for people who don't like their Manhattans sweet.) Garnish liberally with cherries, pickled mushrooms, or pimiento-stuffed olives on a long toothpick.

"No one ever comes to my house without being offered a drink of some kind! Jeeze!"
—Dad

Please note: A Manhattan does not require a special occasion.

Shirley Temples

For the "under-21" crowd.—*Susan*

Fill a short glass with ice. Add 2 ounces Pepsi and a generous 2 ounces of 7UP. Pour in some maraschino cherry juice. Pop in one cherry. Have a lot more cherries ready.

"No thanks, I usually limit myself to two Shirley Temples before noon."—Diane

Julie's Oshkosh Saturday Night Cocktail Party

I really don't know where everyone was when I did this—out? In bed? I really didn't care! On Saturday nights at 8, "Saturday Night at the Movies" was on. I watched the movie 'til 10, then the local news, and the Late Show at 10:30. Here's what I ate, because I wasn't allowed to use the stove by myself to make popcorn.—*Julie*

big bottles of sour mix, cold or warm
whole box of Food Club soda crackers (5-inch squares)
maraschino cherries, if available
giant pretzel sticks
Dad's Zippo lighter

Make yourself a kiddie cocktail with sour mix and cherries. If there's no ice because someone forgot to refill the trays or because you've pinched your fingers on the aluminum ice trays and have given up on the thought of cold pop, drink it warm right out of the big bottle. Serve with whole squares of soda crackers. Savor the parts that are well-browned. Practice "Communion host" consumption with little squares of it, by dissolving on tongue without touching teeth. Try to break off whole long shards and use to simulate the cigarettes the pretty lady in the movie is smoking. Get a great idea from the bad guy who's smoking a cigar and get a giant pretzel stick. Try lighting it with Dad's lighter. Where are those grown-ups, anyway? When you're full, suck your thumb. Go to bed when the late, late show comes on, 'cause it usually stinks!

Green Pepper Jelly (Dad)

Mom says: "Serve Green Pepper Jelly with Ritz crackers and cream cheese. Spread the cracker with cream cheese and top with a dab of jelly."

MAKES FOUR 16-OUNCE JARS

3 large green bell peppers

1½ cups vinegar

6½ cups sugar

3 teaspoons crushed dried red pepper (Dad often uses only 1½ teaspoons)

6 ounces Certo fruit pectin

8 drops green food coloring

You will also need: four 16-ounce glass jars with lids, all sterilized, and a large stainless steel or enamel kettle

Remove stems and cores from peppers and chop. Put the cut-up peppers and vinegar in a blender and puree until smooth.* Pour into a large stainless steel or enamel pot and bring to a boil. Boil for 1 minute. Add remaining ingredients. Boil for 2 minutes. Skim off foam. Ladle hot jelly into sterilized jars, leaving ¼-inch headroom. Adjust two-piece lids. Process 10 minutes in boiling-water canner.

There should be only very tiny flecks of dark green pepper in the lighter green of the finished jelly.

Dillweed Dip (Mom)

Everybody likes this!—*Jean*

1 cup sour cream
⅔ cup mayonnaise (Hellman's)
1 teaspoon dried dillweed
1 teaspoon Beau Monde seasoning (Spice Island brand)

Mix all ingredients well. Serve with cut-up raw vegetables.

Half Dillweed Dip and half Mom's French Dressing (see page 76) combined makes a delicious creamy salad dressing.—Jean
. . . if you like onions.—Susan

Dorothy's Vegetable Dip

Our mother says this dip is *delicious* and we have to put the recipe in. Dorothy's husband, Tony Bevers, was an Army buddy of our Dad's, and our families got together often. Dorothy looked like a model. If her dip had anything to do with that, we should all eat a lot of it.—*Susan*

⅓ cup French dressing, bottled or homemade (See Mom's French Dressing, page 76.)
⅓ cup ketchup
1 large package (8 ounces) cream cheese, softened

Beat cream cheese with a mixer, and then add French dressing and ketchup. Blend well. Serve with carrot and celery sticks.

This is also good (according to our mother) as a spread on crackers.

Deviled Eggs

I'm pretty sure that Mom adds sweet pickle juice to her deviled eggs and potato salad. I do neither. One time when Mom and Dad were visiting, I made potato salad and Mom doctored it up with pickle juice while I wasn't looking! The same thing happened to my friend Mary Ann with her mom.—*Julie*

Cook the eggs (see page 53), cool thoroughly under cold running water, and peel. Cut each peeled egg in half lengthwise and pop the yolk out into a mixing bowl. Save the whites.

In the mixing bowl, mash the egg yolks with a fork and add a little dry mustard. Add Miracle Whip (to moisten yolks and hold them together). Season with a squirt of sweet pickle juice (*This will guarantee plenty left for the grown-ups.—Susan*) and a little salt. Mix well. Using a teaspoon, fill the empty whites with this mixture. Sprinkle paprika on top of the yolk mixture to make them pretty.

If you are out of sweet pickles, just a little sweet pickle relish will do.—Jean

Radishes with Salt

So simple!—*Susan*

Clean and pare radishes and put them into cold water. Serve them with a little saucer of salt to dip them in.

Green Onions with Salt

Some people call them scallions. Either way, these were the only onions I would eat.—*Susan*

Wash the green onions, dry them, cut off the roots, and trim off about half of the green part. Serve with a little saucer of salt for dipping. (You will be eating the white part and a little way into the green. Most of the green part is too tough to eat this way.)

Open the Sanvidge refrigerator and you will find:

- ⊞ Milk—Those half-gallon glass bottles can be tricky . . .

- ⊞ Butter—A stick of this should be out of the fridge (if it's the salted kind we use), so Jean won't whine about hard butter tearing her bread.

- ⊞ Ketchup—The name of one of our dyed Easter chicks—the *dark pink* one. (*Dyed baby chickens were sold at Easter in those less enlightened times.*)

- ⊞ Mustard—The name of the *yellow* Easter chick.

- ⊞ Horseradish—The name of the *purple* Easter chick.

- ⊞ Beer—Schlitz or Blatz was Dad's choice of brew.

- ⊞ Leftovers—If it's dessert, eat it now or kiss it good-bye.

Open the Sanvidge freezer and you will find:

- ⊞ T-bone steaks—For those special meals, or fly-swatting. (Not recommended for use on windows, especially when still frozen.)

- ⊞ Fish sticks—Good for young children who won't realize these were once real fish.

- Venison—Be sure not to tell anyone what it is until *after* they've eaten it.

- Hamburger—You can do a lot with hamburger.

- Popsicles—Store-bought or the homemade kind made in ice cube trays with flimsy toothpicks to hold onto.

- Frozen vegetables—Just make sure you don't serve them "al dente" to Dad!

- Vanilla ice cream—Last resort dessert.

- Chicken—Good, big roasting chickens from Roy Carpenter. "Mom, what's a capon?"

- Turkey—Make sure to remove that little bag first . . .

- Duck—"Dad, are you sure this isn't Duck Duck?" *(our pet mallard)*

- Pheasant—The feathers made great hats. *(Mom and Grandma Noffke covered hat forms with patterns of overlapping pheasant feathers.)* Wear it. Don't eat it.

- Elephant—Just kidding. But this is the answer if our neighbor asks what Dad's cooking on the grill.—*Jean*

Grasshoppers (Dad)

Sometime in the late '60s we acquired a blender. My sisters and I used it to make "Cocoa Whip," a super-thick shake made with vanilla ice cream, milk, cocoa powder, and sugar. Mom used it to make orange juice in the morning, with so much froth, you'd miss the bus by the time you got to the juice. Dad made great use of the blender by making Grasshoppers, just like those at supper clubs. (Sometimes he gave us a little slurp!)—*Julie*

For each drink:

2 scoops vanilla ice cream
1 ounce crème de menthe
a little milk for thinning the mixture

Place vanilla ice cream and crème de menthe in a blender. Blend to make a very thick mixture. Add enough milk to make the drink pourable (and drinkable) and blend to make a great after dinner drink.

The Card Party

Here's all we knew about card parties: When the card party was going to be at our house, we had to go to bed early. Mom and Dad's card parties took place in the kitchen, and even though we were on the other end of the house, we could always hear them talking and laughing. One time they made popcorn—we could smell it. We went to the kitchen in our pajamas, blinking in the bright light, and asked for some.

I had to ask Mom what the card parties were really like. The first card parties involved their good friends, Ed and Del, and a pie. When the party was at Ed and Del's, Mom brought a pie; for the next party, at our house, Del brought back the pie tin—with a pie in it. Whoever gave the party got the rest of it. (Is this why Mom likes pie for breakfast?) Pretty soon, the neighbors from across the street, Roy and Doris, joined the group. (This was a fun group of people—even we thought so. We knew them all.) After the original card party couples moved away, Romie and Donna and Clair and Helen took their places.

Mom would put out bowls of salted peanuts or mixed nuts, and many times she would buy Brach's Bridge Mix for the card parties. (Candy in the house, and we didn't know about it?) Beer and mixed drinks—brandy, whiskey, or gin with 7UP or sour mix—would be served during the party. (*The Brandy Slush recipe that follows this story was a later addition.*)

The party usually started around 7 and went on until midnight, and the card game they played was always poker, 50-cent limit, dealer's choice. Often it was "five-card stud." (Don't ask me what this means.) Del, definitely a fun grown-up, had her own version of the game that she called "putsy and takesy." One time Dad stacked the cards so two of the women would have really good cards. Everybody kept their "poker faces" until one of the women said, "Don't you think we could up our limit *just a little?*"

Near the end of the evening, Mom would make coffee and bring out a dessert. When the smell of coffee wafted down the hall, we could tell the card party was almost over.

—*Susan*

Dad took this photo at a card party held in the Kelleys' apartment above their bakery in Oshkosh. (Left to right: Donna Sawicki, Mom, Romie Sawicki, and Del and Ed Kelley.)

Brandy Slush

I can almost hear the Sawickis and the Martins coming up the walk for the card party.—*Susan*

    1 can (6 ounces) frozen lemonade concentrate
    1 can (6 ounces) frozen orange juice concentrate
    1 can brandy *(use the empty can from above)*
    2 cans water *(ditto)*
    ½ cup sugar

Put all ingredients in a blender and mix.

Freeze in a wide-mouth jar or Tupperware container.

To serve:
crushed ice
"50/50" or sour mix

Take out 2 heaping tablespoons of Brandy Slush mix and put into a glass over crushed ice. Add "50/50" or sour mix and stir.

> **"I forget now (tee-hee) . . .**
> **Whose turn is it to deal?"**
> —One of the female card players

Fizz-Niks

We all remember Fizz-Niks. They were two-piece plastic balls with short tubes on the bottom and top. (One tube went into a bottle of pop and one went into your mouth.) They looked like *Sputnik*, the famous (at the time) Russian satellite, and came in different color combinations. With the help of a Fizz-Nik, you could have an instant ice cream float: Put the tube part of the bottom piece into a bottle of pop, fill the "dish" part with ice cream, put on the top piece, and tip up the bottle. It tastes like an ice cream float! (It also dribbles down on your clothes.)—*Diane*

"Pleeeeeeeeze buy me a Fizz-Nik." —Diane

"You kids drink too much pop already. Have some plain vanilla ice cream." —Mom

(Mom bought them for us anyway.)

The Relish Tray

A Relish Tray was always part of dinners for company. The contents varied, but the serving dish was often similar to the one below. Sometimes the dish had little dividers inside. —*Susan*

Choose several of the following for your relish tray:

carrot sticks

celery sticks

radishes

pimiento-stuffed green olives

black olives

cucumber sticks

sweet pickles

green pepper strips (Mom)

pickled beets

pickled crabapples (Grandma Sanvidge)

sweet gherkins

Pickled Crabapples (like Grandma Sanvidge served on her relish tray)

In later years, I'm pretty sure Grandma Sanvidge's pickled crabapples were store-bought. She was a working girl, after all.—*Julie*

We could not find her recipe for pickled crabapples, but we did find Grandma Noffke's. (Mom remembers sucking the syrup off before eating the apple.) Grandma Noffke apparently did not consider pickled crabapples a relish tray item, because they never appeared on her relish trays. Grandma Sanvidge would probably be a little miffed, but here is Grandma Noffke's recipe just as she wrote it. (Crabapple season passed us by, and we have not been able to try this recipe yet. The syrup sounds so enticing.) —*Susan*

"8 # [*pounds*] crab apples

2 qts. vinegar [*Mom says: "Grandma always used cider vinegar."*]

9 cups sugar

4 long sticks cinnamon

1 tbsp. whole cloves

Select firm, ripe crab apples. Wash and remove blemishes. Combine vinegar, sugar, spices and boil together five minutes. Add apples and cook gently until tender, but not broken. Stand in syrup overnight. The next morning, drain the syrup from the fruit and boil it until almost as thick as honey. Pack the apples in hot, clean jars, covering with the hot syrup and seal immediately."

Sliced Cucumber Pickles (Grandma Noffke)

These are sweet-sour, almost like bread-and-butter pickles, but the thinness of Grandma's slicing made them distinctive and delicious. (Disclaimer: There are no pickle-makers among us, so we haven't attempted to make these pickles. You might want to consult some experts, or books, about canning.) Grandma's recipe below is exactly as she wrote it.—*Susan*

MAKES ABOUT 7 QUARTS OR 14 PINTS (BASED ON EQUIVALENT RECIPES IN THE BALL BLUE BOOK**).**

"20 medium cucumbers

12 onions sliced

5 tablespoons salt [*Consult your canning book for the kind of salt to use.*]

5 cups cider vinegar

4 cups sugar

1 teaspoon celery seed

4 1-inch pieces cinnamon bark

1½ teaspoons turmeric

1 tablespoon mustard seed

1 teaspoon peppercorns

6 cloves

> "The host with the most always lets his guests use his beer bottle* binoculars . . . look at the plane!"
> —Diane

> *You might want to make sure the bottles are empty.

Sprinkle sliced cucumbers & onions with salt & let stand 1½ hrs. Drain well. Combine remaining ingredients & bring to a boil. Add cucumbers & onions & simmer 10 min. Spoon into hot sterilized jars & seal."

Dandelion Wine (Grandma Noffke)

Mom says: "My brother Hank and I picked the dandelions for this wine in Erb Park across the street from our house in Appleton. We each had a cardboard box and felt quite important to be doing this. We were instructed to pinch the blossoms off without including any of the stem. (I got stung by bees twice.) This wine was served to company, and as children we drank it, too, diluted with water."

I remember hearing about Grandma's Dandelion Wine, but I never have tasted it (watered down or not). The recipe is here word for word, but we have not tested it. I haven't seen that many dandelions for a long time.—*Susan*

3 peach baskets of *[dandelion]* flowers *[the equivalent of about 5 gallons, based on a similar recipe in the 1938 Settlement Cook Book. No stems at all!]*
6 gallons of water

Boil water. Add flowers.
Let stand for ½ hour. Strain.

Add:

15 lbs. granulated sugar

6 oranges

3 lemons

1 lb. raisins (or more)

1 yeast foam [*The 1938* Settlement Cook Book *to the rescue again (we hope): 5 ounces of yeast would be the amount needed here, scaling up from their recipe. "Yeast Foam" was a trade name for a yeast product made by the Northwestern Yeast Company in Chicago. An unspecified number of cakes (of unspecified size) came in a wooden box.*]

After five days, skim oranges and lemons and raisins out. Let work until clear."

Salads

Yes, Jell-O is a salad.

There weren't many salad vegetables in those dusty little corner grocery stores—iceberg lettuce, waxy cucumbers, carrots, radishes, and tomatoes in season. (In winter you could buy four small pink tomatoes lined up in a flimsy little cardboard box, but they were expensive.) No wonder marshmallows and pineapples were considered salad ingredients.

The salads we ate when we were growing up fit roughly into three categories: the Tossed Salad, which didn't vary much and was usually served with bright orange French dressing, homemade or from a bottle; the Jell-O Mold (your "salad" is floating around in there); and Vegetables from the Garden that tasted so good that you just ate them as is.—*Susan*

Basic Mom Salad

This salad was served in little wooden bowls.—*Susan*

> iceberg lettuce, cut into chunks and broken apart
> tomatoes, cut into wedges
> cucumbers, peeled and sliced

You could add one or two of the following:
sliced radishes, green pepper chunks, grated or sliced carrots

French Dressing (Mom)

The classic dressing for the Basic Mom Salad. It is definitely "the orange kind."—*Susan*

If you use the dreaded blender, the dressing will not separate.—*Jean*

MAKES ABOUT 1 QUART

> 1½ cups vegetable oil
> 1 cup sugar
> 1 cup ketchup
> ¼ cup vinegar
> juice of 1 lemon (about 2 tablespoons)
> ½ cup finely chopped onion

Combine all ingredients and blend well. Pour into a jar and refrigerate.

Grandma had Mom's recipe in her files, too. She noted: "Make ½ recipe."—Susan

French Salad Dressing (Grandma Noffke)

Grandma's French dressing is thinner and spicier than Mom's.—*Diane*

½ cup vinegar

½ cup ketchup

½ cup sugar

½ teaspoon salt

½ teaspoon paprika

½ teaspoon dry mustard

1 small onion, chopped finely

½ cup vegetable oil

Mix all ingredients, except the vegetable oil, together. Drizzle in oil slowly, stirring constantly. Pour into a jar and refrigerate.

Cucumber Salad (Mom)

A cool and refreshing salad for a hot day.—*Diane*

4 medium cucumbers
1 small onion
⅓ cup white vinegar
⅓ cup sugar
⅓ cup half-and-half or whole milk
salt and pepper to taste

Peel cucumbers, cut into slices about ⅛-inch thick, and put in a bowl. (Many people salt and then rinse the cucumbers to keep them from making the sauce watery, but our mother does not.) Grate the onion and combine with the cucumbers.

Make the dressing by stirring together the vinegar, sugar, and half-and-half or whole milk. Pour over cucumber and onions. Add salt and pepper to taste. Chill.

Carrot Pineapple Jell-O Salad (Grandma Noffke)

This particular Jell-O mold was often part of a big meal "for company" at our house, at Grandma Noffke's, and sometimes at Grandma Sanvidge's.—*Susan*

1 cup canned crushed pineapple (Save the juice. You can use all of the juice from the can, but you'll just have to eat any extra pineapple.)

1 small package (3 ounces) lemon Jell-O

½ cup finely diced celery

½ cup shredded carrot

You will also need: a ring mold

"Eat your vegetables!"

Add enough water to the canned pineapple juice to make 1½ cups. Put this liquid in a small saucepan and bring it to a boil.

Put the Jell-O powder in a bowl and pour the boiling liquid over the gelatin. Stir the Jell-O until it dissolves. Let the mixture cool until it's somewhat thick.

Stir the vegetables and 1 cup pineapple into the cooled Jell-O. Pour into a ring mold. Place mold in the refrigerator to chill until firm.

To unmold, place the bottom of the ring mold in warm water for a few seconds. Lay a serving plate upside-down on top of the mold and flip it over.

A Jell-O Unmolding Tip from Jean: Put the filled Jell-O mold upside-down on the serving platter. Drape the mold with a hot, damp dish towel for a few minutes. Gently lift the mold and remove it when the molded Jell-O plops down.

Aloha! Hey!

Did we grow up in Wisconsin . . . or Hawaii? Can you believe how many of these "salads" have pineapple in them? (And there's more pineapple in the Desserts section.)—*Susan*

Lime Cottage Cheese Salad (Mom)

This "salad" was also served at company dinners. It is a pale, milky green Jell-O mold with interesting little things in it to chew on. Susie the Picky Eater likes it.—*Susan*

1 small package (3 ounces) lime Jell-O

1 cup boiling water

2 cups miniature marshmallows

1 can (9 ounces) crushed pineapple (do not drain)

dash of salt

1 cup small curd cottage cheese

1 cup cream, whipped

½ cup chopped pecans

You will also need: a Jell-O mold*

Dissolve Jell-O in boiling water. Add marshmallows and let melt. Stir in pineapple with juice and add salt. Chill until slightly thickened. Fold in cottage cheese, whipped cream, and nuts. Turn into a Jell-O mold. Chill.

When ready to serve, put a plate on top of the Jell-O mold and flip. (See tips for doing this on page 79.)

You could just chill this in a bowl and scoop it out to serve.—Jean

Dinners for Company

Often when Mom was busy preparing a big company meal, she would give us the job of setting the table and putting together a centerpiece. Clever Mom! She got us distracted with our task so she could concentrate. I do believe it fostered a lot of creativity in all of us girls. I still enjoy setting the table for company, making sure all the silverware matches. (I'm not sure where that pet peeve came from!)—*Jean*

Mom drew the line at potted plants: "No dirt on the table!"

Cream Cheese Salad (Grandma Noffke)

You might not have to go to the store if you make this Jell-O salad Grandma's way . . . —*Susan*

This is really delicious. (I love whipped cream.)—*Jean*

> 1 cup hot water
> 1 small package (3 ounces) lemon or lime Jell-O
> 1 cup cold water
> 1 package (8 ounces) cream cheese
> 1 can (20 ounces) crushed pineapple, drained
> 1 cup cream, whipped
> You will also need: a Jell-O mold

Combine hot water and Jell-O. Stir until Jell-O is dissolved and then stir in cold water. Refrigerate until firm.

Beat Jell-O mixture with an eggbeater or electric mixer. In a separate bowl, beat cream cheese and (drained) pineapple together. Pour mixture into Jell-O and mix well. Fold in whipped cream. Pour into Jell-O mold or pan. Refrigerate. (Can be made the day before.)

Cranberry Relish Mold (Grandma Noffke)

Grandma was a frugal woman who often wrote her recipes on paper from advertising pads that came to Grandpa's business (Noffke Fuel, later Noffke Lumber). This was written on "Mule-Hide Products" stationery. This recipe makes a jewel-like, dark red Jell-O mold that will taste a little bitter to people who do not like the taste of cranberry relish. Be sure to use a thin-skinned orange (or just use the orange part of the peel and the fruit when you grind it up).—*Susan*

"1 (9-oz.) can crushed pineapple (save juice) [*Note that it says* syrup *below.*]

1 (3-oz. pkg.) cherry-flavored gelatin

½ cup sugar

1 cup hot water

1 tablespoon lemon juice

1 cup ground fresh cranberries

1 cup chopped celery

1 small orange (peel on, seeds removed) ground ½ cup

½ cup chopped walnuts

Drain pineapple, reserving syrup. Add enough water to pineapple syrup to make ½ cup. Dissolve gelatin & sugar in the hot water. Add reserved syrup and lemon juice. Chill until partially set. Add pineapple and remaining ingredients. Pour into a 5-cup ring mold. Chill overnight. 8 to 10 servings."

Crushed pineapple comes in 8-ounce cans now. I used an 8-ounce can, and the mold set up like Jell-O should. I don't have a grinder, so I used my food processor for the orange, walnuts, cranberries, and celery. (An interesting note: cranberry Jell-O is available now. That could help this multiple-personality Jell-O mold reduce its identities by at least one— the cherry flavor.)—Julie

Three Bean Salad

Both of our grandmas had this recipe in their files. One-half cup of chopped green pepper was in the original recipe, but our grandmas never put it in.—*Jean*

1 can (16 ounces) cut green beans, drained
1 can (16 ounces) cut yellow wax beans, drained
1 can (16 ounces) red kidney beans, drained
⅔ cup white wine vinegar
⅓ cup vegetable oil
¼ cup sugar
2 tablespoons finely chopped onion
1½ teaspoons salt
½ teaspoon black pepper
You will also need: a 1-quart jar with lid

"You can hardly taste the _____ in it."

In a large bowl, combine all of the beans. In a quart jar, combine the remaining ingredients. Put the cover on the jar and shake together thoroughly. Pour over beans. Mix together gently. Chill overnight or for several hours. (*Or, in my opinion, until the end of time. The grown-ups really seem to like it, though. —Susan*)

Raggedy Ann Salad

We made this salad for Julie's sixth birthday party. There was supposed to be a raisin for a nose. Julie said that Raggedy Ann's nose was an equilateral triangle, so we had to change it.—*Diane*

Make a Raggedy Ann on each plate:

Head: half of a boiled egg, cut through the middle (Use the rounded half.)

Body: canned peach half

Skirt: ruffly piece of lettuce (Put it under the bottom half of the peach.)

Arms and legs: celery sticks

Shoes: raisins

Buttons: raisins (Put three in a row down the middle of the peach.)

Hair: grated yellow cheese or sticks cut from sliced American cheese

Eyes: raisins

Mouth: piece of maraschino cherry

Nose: piece of maraschino cherry (Cut into an equilateral triangle.)

Julie had just started kindergarten when Jean made this Halloween costume for her. She told Jean to make an equilateral triangle on her nose (with lipstick), and a few months later she made the same request for her birthday party salad (but we used a cherry).

Tomatoes from the Garden

Take a good long sniff of that garden tomato fragrance.—*Susan*

Slice the tomatoes fairly thick. Lay the slices on a plate. Put a salt shaker next to the plate.

Lettuce from the Garden

Well, it *seemed* like a good idea to grow our own lettuce . . . —*Susan*

Carefully gather your fragile, home-grown lettuce and put it in the sink. Wash under cold, running water for a very long time to remove grit, slugs, and insects. Take a bite of a leaf. It will be bitter. Throw it out.

Mom says: "Tsk. Tsk. The first lettuce that comes up is the best (and it's all downhill from there). My mother always served first-growth garden lettuce with this dressing: ½ cup cream, 1 tablespoon white vinegar, and 1 tablespoon sugar."

Did you know that . . .

We used to eat fish food wafers and pretend they were Communion hosts when we "played church"? (The chalice was one of Mom's dark green goblets with the fancy clear glass stems.)
—*Diane*

Vegetables and Fruits

"They're good for you!"

Some of the vegetables we ate as kids were canned: creamed corn, French-cut green beans, yellow wax beans, and peas. Later we had more frozen vegetables: bright green peas and beans and whole-kernel corn. Carrots were always made from "real carrots." The backyard garden Dad tended provided homegrown versions of most of those vegetables in the summer and introduced us to beets and kohlrabi.

Mom's standard answer to "I'm hungry" was "Have a banana." There was almost always a bunch of bananas draped across a wooden platter somewhere in the kitchen. We also ate a lot of apples. The apples we bought by the bushel every fall were kept in the basement, and they made it smell so good. Grandma Noffke's cellar and Grandma Sanvidge's closed-in porch smelled like apples, too. One of the first things I did when I had a house of my own was to buy a bushel of apples for the basement.—*Susan*

Weird Raw Vegetables for Starving Kids Who Wouldn't Eat Them Cooked

Like most kids, we weren't that big on vegetables, except carrots, so when Mom was making dinner she pulled a little trick on us. I used this. It still works.—*Susan*

This is kohlrabi. It looks like this at the grocery store. You eat the peeled, pale green root part (not the leaves). It's really pretty good—a light, sweet cabbage taste and a crisp texture.

> rutabaga
>
> kohlrabi
>
> cabbage
>
> cauliflower
>
> or, less odd, green beans, potatoes . . .

In the hour before dinner is ready, cut up raw pieces of whatever vegetables you will be cooking. Present them nicely.

I call them "hors d'oeuvres," but Mom just handed them out and we scarfed them down. I still like raw potatoes, with a little salt.—Susan

This is rutabaga au naturel. To recognize it at the grocery store, you should look for a hard, round vegetable that is the color of a second-day bruise, thickly covered with wax, about 6 inches around, with the leaves and whiskery roots lopped off. "Yum!" It's good for you.

Cooked Carrots

Carrots were always in the Acceptable Vegetable category, even when they were cooked.—*Susan*

Peel and slice as many carrots as you want to eat. Put them in a saucepan (with a lid). Cover the carrots with water, add a little salt and a tiny bit of sugar, and bring to a boil. Cover and cook over medium heat for about 35 minutes or until you can pierce them with a fork. Drain the liquid and stir in butter while carrots are still in the pan.

Try a little dillweed (and butter) on plain cooked carrots. Mom made them this way for a Homemakers Club lesson.—Jean

Mom sometimes made carrots with cream sauce when we were kids. Now that I think about it, cream sauce might have been another one of Mom's Ways to Get Us to Eat Vegetables. She used it on peas, green beans, and yellow beans. We ate them. Be sure to drain the vegetables first.—Susan

Cream Sauce:

2 tablespoons butter

2 tablespoons flour

1 cup warm whole or 2% milk (Skim milk will not work for this recipe.)

salt and white pepper to taste

Melt butter in a pan over low heat. Whisk in flour until no lumps remain and it starts sizzling a bit. Add milk slowly, stirring as it thickens. Season to taste with salt and white pepper.

Yellow wax beans in cream sauce was one of Grandma Sanvidge's favorite vegetable dishes.—Jean

Cile

Cile (Lucille Degner) was both cook and housekeeper for Grandma and Grandpa Noffke her entire adult life, starting in 1935, when she was twenty-five. (Grandma worked all day as the bookkeeper for Grandpa's business. He must have realized Grandma shouldn't

Cile at the sink in Grandma Noffke's kitchen.

have to do both jobs—or maybe our grandpa, who *really, really* loved his food, was worried about getting his meals on time!) Cile called Grandpa "H.A." and Grandma "Kid," which was amazing to us. She was thirteen years younger than Grandma Noffke, but they got along like sisters. (We always thought Cile was eighteen; she seemed more like a kid than a grown-up.) She rode her bicycle everywhere in all kinds of weather and could stop Grandpa's teasing, better than anyone, with a withering look. Cile could be very prim and businesslike, until something would strike her as funny. She would play Old Maid and Uncle Wiggly with us and get to laughing so hard, almost squeaking, that tears would be running down her cheeks.

When I was very little I used to go with Cile to her mother's house. "Grandma Degner" always had toys and a little set of dishes for me to play with. (I used to tell people I had four Grandmas. Grandma Great was the other one.) Cile brought us clothes from her nieces: a T-shirt with "Nancy" on it in red and white striped letters had me wanting my name to be Nancy throughout fourth grade. She bought us Christmas presents, and she sent me birthday cards long after I moved away from home. Cile is not only responsible for some of the most memorable food in this cookbook, she is part of our family.—*Susan*

Cile's Baked Beans?

Cile was famous for her baked beans, but nobody could ever find her recipe. So you can imagine why I was so excited to run across this recipe among Grandma Sanvidge's recipes (surprisingly) in a cookbook compiled by members of Cile's church! Mrs. Carl Schloesser had submitted it, but it was subtitled "Lucille's favorite"!

I decided to give it a try. My first attempt was a failure. I didn't boil the beans long enough, used black strap molasses, which was too strong, and got them way too done trying to get the beans tender. I ended up throwing the whole big batch away! I gave it another try, this time with mild-flavored molasses and simmering the beans longer. I'm including the original recipe here (with my comments in brackets); try making them and see what you think. (Mom thinks they taste like Cile's!)—*Jean*

"2 lbs. Great Northern beans

1 lb. salt pork or side pork

8 tbsp. brown sugar

1 tsp. salt [*If you use side pork, this is not enough salt. We just salted the beans I made when they were on our plates.*]*

Dash of pepper

2 tsp. dry mustard

1 c. molasses [*I recommend mild-flavored molasses.*]

Boiling water

"Remember Cile's Baked Beans?"—Everybody

Wash and soak the beans overnight. In the morning cook the beans until the skins break when you blow lightly over them. Cut pork into chunks and place 3 or 4 pieces in bottom of crock [*or roasting pan*]. Pour beans into crock [*or roasting pan*] (saving water they were cooked in). Place rest of pork on top. Mix sugar, salt, pepper, and mustard and finally add the molasses and some of the boiling water the beans were cooked in. Pour over beans with just enough cooking water to cover beans.

Cover and bake until beans are tender and brown. The temperature of the bean crock should be 300°, and the beans should take about 5 to 6 hours. If using a roasting pan, set the oven to the same temperature and bake for the same amount of time. (The secret of baked beans is to keep them covered with liquid except during the last half hour of baking when you allow the water to bake away.) A half hour or so before the beans are done, take off the cover. Best baked the day before you want to serve them."

To help estimate salt amount: Baked Beans for Easter (see page 322) calls for 1 tablespoon of salt for the same amount of beans (with ½ pound of bacon).—Susan

A Baked Bean Tip:

If you forget to soak the beans, don't fret. Pick through the beans, looking for any bad ones or stones. Rinse the beans well. Put them in a pan and cover with water and bring to a boil. Boil for 2 minutes, uncovered. Remove from heat. Cover and let stand for 1 hour. Put the pan back on the stove, uncovered, and bring to a simmer. Simmer for 50 minutes to 1 hour. Just follow the rest of the recipe for baking the beans.—*Jean*

Mashed Rutabaga

I tried this, once.—*Susan*

Wash rutabaga and peel off that wax-coated skin.
Cut this very hard vegetable into uniform-size pieces
with a substantial knife. Cover and cook in a small
amount of boiling, salted water, about 30 minutes or
until "fork-tender." Drain, mash, and add butter, salt,
pepper, and a little sugar.

"You'll never know until you try it."—Mom or Dad

Sweet Potatoes

How many should you make? Count the number of adults
who will be at your table. You won't need more.—*Susan*

Scrub sweet potatoes. Pierce them here and there with a
fork. Bake them in a 350° oven for 1 hour or until tender.
Serve with butter, salt, and pepper.

Mashed Squash (or more elegantly, **Butternut Squash Puree**)

The pureed squash is a beautiful yellow orange. It looks good, and tastes good, with roast pork.—*Susan*

1 large butternut squash
1 tablespoon butter
¼ cup hot whole or 2% milk
salt and pepper to taste

Cut and peel* the squash into roughly 2-inch cubes. Put a small amount of water (as if you were making frozen vegetables—this squash has a lot of water in it) at the bottom of a lidded pot large enough to hold the cubes. Bring water to a boil and put in the squash. Cover and cook until squash is soft enough to mash.

Take pan off the stove and use an electric mixer to puree the squash while still in the pan. Beat in the butter and add hot milk. (This process is very similar to making mashed potatoes, but the squash is soupier. The milk gives it a better texture.) Put pot back on stove over low heat to evaporate any excess liquid. Season to taste with salt and pepper. Put the squash into a serving dish and top with a pat of butter.

If you cut the unpeeled squash into 2-inch slices, there will be less chance of cutting yourself. Lay the thick slices on a cutting board to chop off the peeling. Scrape out the seeds with a spoon and cut into 2-inch cubes.—Susan

Scalloped Corn (or **Baked Corn**, Grandma Sanvidge)

This is a good dish for a buffet. Just bake it and keep it warm. This is so easy to make you can worry about the rest of the meal instead.—*Diane*

1 can (16 ounces) cream-style corn
1 can (16 ounces) whole-kernel corn, drained
1 egg, beaten
½ cup soda cracker crumbs
½ cup sour cream
½ teaspoon salt (or more, to taste)
dash of pepper (If you have white pepper, use that.)

Preheat oven to 350° and butter a shallow 2-quart casserole dish. In a large bowl, combine all ingredients and mix well. Pour into casserole dish. Bake until firm, about 40 minutes.

Blue Willow Like Grandma Sanvidge's

Every one of "The Girls" has exactly the same
Blue Willow mugs. We bought them without
knowing that we each had them. We were at Diane's
getting ready for Mom and Dad's Oshkosh anniversary party when
Diane brought out her Blue Willow mugs to a three-sister chorus
of "I have mugs just like that!" Then we found out that *all of us* have
nearly a full set of the dishes, too!—*Julie*

Corn on the Cob

We love corn on the cob. Does it really belong in the Vegetable section? (Yes, Jean, I know it's actually a grain.)—*Susan*

> Buy fresh corn at a roadside stand. Put a big kettle of water on to boil. Shuck the corn. When the water is boiling, put in the corn, and sprinkle in a little salt. Cover and turn heat down to simmer for about 5 minutes or until it looks a bit yellower. Put the corn on a platter and get out those little yellow plastic corn holders. Serve with butter and salt.

"Pass me a toothpick."
—Dad and Jean

Beet Greens (Dad)

Beet greens make a beautiful dish, with their red stems and dark green leaves. This is Dad's favorite way to eat his homegrown beets. Beet greens from the garden don't come in pounds: "a good-sized gob of butter" and "sprinkle of vinegar" are the seasoning proportions for any amount of greens. —*Susan and Julie*

> beet greens
> butter
> white vinegar
> salt

If you are thinning the beets in your garden, it's time to make beet greens. You can leave those baby beets on.

Set some salted water on to boil. Wash the greens carefully to remove all grit. (Dad leaves his beet greens whole and cuts them up on his plate when he eats them, but you can cut the greens before cooking them.) When the water is boiling, toss in the greens, turn the heat to medium-low, cover, and cook to taste. It won't take long, so check them often.

Take out the cooked greens with tongs (easier if you left them uncut like Dad does) and put them in a shallow dish. Add a good-sized gob of butter and sprinkle with white vinegar and salt. Toss to distribute the seasonings. Eat while still hot.

Mom says: "Some people aren't that crazy about vinegar. You could put the vinegar in a little cruet and serve it on the side."

I'm not that crazy about vinegar, but I like it on this—it cuts the richness of the butter. Beet greens are often hard to come by if you don't have a garden. Red Swiss chard is very similar to beet greens and makes a perfect substitute—if you can find red Swiss chard.—Susan

Stewed Tomatoes (Dad)

This is another one of Dad's favorites. It tastes best with tomatoes from the garden.—*Diane*

Scald red, ripe, good tomatoes by putting them in boiling water until the skins crack. Remove the tomatoes from the water and let cool for about 5 minutes. Peel off skins and cut tomatoes into roughly ¾-inch pieces. Put tomatoes in an uncovered pan on low heat and cook very slowly for about 20 minutes, stirring occasionally. The tomatoes are done when they are very soft and velvety-looking, cooked through, but still somewhat lumpy. Season to taste with sugar, salt, pepper, and butter. Don't skip the sugar—it makes the tomatoes taste even more tomato-y. Eat right away. (These tomatoes are not meant for canning.)

Dad likes a big slice of homemade bread (with lots of butter on it) with his stewed tomatoes.—Susan

Canned Vegetables: Creamed Corn, Wax Beans, French-Cut Green Beans, Beets . . .

Open can. Pour contents in pan. Heat and serve.

Frozen Vegetables: Peas, Corn . . .

Follow directions on package.

Asparagus (circa 1959)

I have to say that I'm not fond of cooked asparagus to this day, after having to sit at the table until I ate it (which I think was about 8 p.m.) It was a lot too slimy for me, and when I put it in my mouth it wanted to come right out again.—*Jean*

> **"Offer it up for the poor souls in Purgatory."**—Mom

Buy one can of asparagus at the store. Open the can and let the limp stalks slither out into a saucepan. Heat them up. Let them slither into a dish. Serving suggestion: lots of milk to help this vegetable slither down your kid's throat.

Canned asparagus, tied up, so it won't slither off the page

I Dare You!

One night, before we did the dishes, a ghastly concoction of leftovers was mixed up by one of us (probably me). Diane offered me a generous amount of money if I would eat it, figuring there was no way I would actually eat it. As usual, I was in need of money, so I took her up on the bet. As I got more serious, she started dropping the price until Susie made her hold it at five dollars. Diane did consent to giving me warm water to choke it down—which I did.—*Jean ("Now, girls . . . ")*

Do-It-Yourself Vegetables

As we roamed the empty lots and sidewalks of the neighborhood in Oshkosh or the woods up north, we occasionally nibbled a wild "vegetable" or two, between bites of Oreos.—*Susan*

Green cheese

Green cheese—A nutty-tasting, future seedpod of the common mallow, also called cheeses, that grew all over Grandma and Grandpa Sanvidge's lawn. Our cousin Bert introduced us to this. It looks like a tiny round cheese.

Sour clover

Columbine blossom tips—The rounded tips taste sweet. *(Now we find out that parts of Columbines are poisonous.)*
Sour clover (wood sorrel)—The leaves are tart and lemony-tangy.
Abandoned garden potatoes—An empty lot treasure.

Dad's Applesauce (also known as Grandpa's Applesauce)

There is no applesauce you can buy that is as good as home-made. I like to spoon homemade applesauce onto a piece of buttered bread or toast. Dad freezes this in jars and gives it to lucky people.—*Susan*

MAKES ABOUT 2 QUARTS

About 20 decent apples (preferably Cortlands, but McIntosh are good, too)
very little water
½ cup sugar, depending on the sweetness of the apples
cinnamon to taste
You will also need: a large stainless steel pot with a tight-fitting lid

Peel apples and slice about ³⁄₁₆-inch thick.

Put a very small amount of water in the pan—just enough so the apples do not burn before melting into their own juice. Put the lid on the pan and cook on medium heat for ½ hour. Turn heat down to low. Cook with lid on for 2 to 2½ hours, stirring from time to time, until the apple pieces have broken down. Dad cooks his until there are few to zero lumps. (*I think Dad sometimes uses a mixer to smooth out the lumps towards the end of the cooking time.—Jean*)

When done, turn off heat and stir in *about* ½ cup of sugar* while the apples are still hot. Add cinnamon until it tastes and smells like you want it to. Dad uses enough to darken the color of the applesauce.

If you are a Sanvidge blood relative, you will have been eating apple slices while paring and will have some idea of how much sugar you need to sweeten the apples you are using. Dad makes his applesauce pretty sweet, with lots of cinnamon.—Susan

24-Hour Salad (Grandma Noffke)

This is a classic fruit salad. The colors of the fruit show up here and there in all that fluffy whiteness. The marshmallows are saturated with the fruit juice . . .
—*Susan*

> 1 can (13.5 ounces) pineapple chunks (save juice)
> 3 egg yolks, beaten
> 2 tablespoons sugar
> 2 tablespoons vinegar
> 2 tablespoons pineapple juice (from can of pineapple)
> 2 tablespoons butter
> dash of salt
> 1 cup heavy cream, whipped
> 1 can (1 pound) white cherries, drained and pitted*
> ½ cup miniature marshmallows

Drain the pineapple chunks and reserve 2 tablespoons of the juice. Set pineapple aside.

Combine beaten egg yolks, sugar, vinegar, 2 tablespoons pineapple juice, butter, and salt in a pan. Cook until thickened slightly, stirring all the time (mixture scorches easily).

Let mixture cool and then fold in whipped cream. Gently stir in pineapple, cherries, and marshmallows. Chill for 24 hours before serving.

I am sorry to say that canned white cherries (Rainier cherries are one of the varieties) will be difficult to find now. Fresh Rainier cherries (their coloring is like nectarines) are sometimes available from very late June through early August. Dark cherries would stain the white dressing in this salad. Mandarin oranges could replace the cherries.—Susan

Green seedless grapes cut in half lengthwise are a good substitute for the hard-to-find white cherries.—Jean

The Grandchildren Remember . . .

Decorating Easter eggs, homemade applesauce on toast, little boxes of cereal, granola bars, the Captain Kangaroo cups with the moving eyes, pot pies, the basement refrigerator, the Wild Wolf Inn, and Schwann's peach ice cream.—*Diane*

Fruit Salad with Fluffy Fruit Dressing

I entered the 4-H Food Revue at the end of the second year of cooking class. I had to demonstrate how to make the dressing and arrange the fruit plate. I brought a place setting of Mom's brown dishes with the drippy-looking edge and a tan placemat and napkin with fringed edges. I got a red ribbon (second place).
—*Diane*

Fluffy Fruit Dressing:

1 egg yolk

¼ cup honey

¾ cup cream, whipped

2 tablespoons lemon juice

Fruit:

whole strawberries

oranges, sectioned and cut in half (Remove any seeds you see.)

watermelon, cut into bite-sized pieces (Remove any seeds you see.)

You will also need: a double boiler

Beat egg yolk and honey in the top of a double boiler. Cook 1 minute until thick. Cool. Fold in whipped cream. Add lemon juice and stir in gently.

Arrange fruit on a platter. Serve fruit dressing in a bowl for dipping.

Ambrosia

Oranges and bananas are available year-round, so when you are craving a fruit salad in the middle of winter, Ambrosia, "food of the gods," may well live up to its reputation. This is based on a very simple beginner's recipe in our old 4-H cookbook, *It's Fun to Cook.*—*Susan*

4 oranges
3 ripe bananas
½ cup flaked coconut

Squeeze the juice from 1 orange into a bowl big enough to hold all the ingredients and let you stir them. Peel the 3 remaining oranges. (Now that you're old enough to use a knife, it's easier to cut off the orange peel.) Break the sections apart and cut each one into three or four pieces. Put them in with the juice.

Peel and slice the bananas right into the bowl with the oranges and juice. (The orange juice will help keep them from getting brown.) Mix together and eat right away (best), or chill if you will be eating it later. To serve, spoon mixture into 6 serving bowls and sprinkle with the coconut.

Waldorf Salad

This recipe goes back to at least the late '30s, but Mom made this, frequently enough for me to remember it, in the '50s. It's an interesting (and healthy) combination of tastes and textures, and every now and then I just crave it. —*Susan*

6 ribs celery, cut into chunks (about 2 cups)
3 Delicious apples, unpeeled, cut into chunks (about 2 cups)
about ½ to ⅔ cup mayonnaise
1 cup walnut halves, broken in large pieces

Combine the celery and apples and mix with enough mayonnaise to cover. Stir in the walnuts. Add a little more mayonnaise, if necessary, to hold everything together (like a chicken salad). Chill before serving.

 Remember when . . .

. . . we ate bread and homemade apple jelly in Aunt Emma's kitchen? When we opened the jar there was a geranium leaf on top of the jelly. (We couldn't find Aunt Emma's apple jelly recipe, but every one of us remembered that she always put a geranium leaf on top before sealing the jar.)—*Susan*

The Whole Fruit and Nothing But the Fruit

We ate a lot of this fast food.— *Susan*

Serve these fruits whole and unadorned, washing or peeling as needed.

The standbys—

Apples: This fruit tastes best (and *keeps* best) when it's cold. (After our old refrigerator was banished to the basement, the apples we bought by the bushel were kept in there.) Following our Dad's example, most of us like salt on tart or green apples.

Bananas: Few families are lucky enough to have somebody who likes to eat each of the banana's stages: green-tipped, all yellow, brown-flecked, or all-brown. We were no exception, and at our house we had an incentive to leave those last two overripe bananas on the platter: banana bread.

Oranges: It's a good thing oranges last so long. They are so much trouble to peel that the only time we greeted the offer of an orange with much enthusiasm was when our grandparents brought mesh bags of Temple oranges back from Florida and gave us little plastic gizmos to pierce the orange and suck out the juice. After those little gizmos disappeared* we had to wait for Grandpa Noffke to come over and demonstrate his fancy orange-peeling methods. The one I remember most was the "basketball": Cut off the ends, make cuts through the peeling like the seams of a basketball, and pull off the pieces of peel. Jean remembers Grandpa cutting the unpeeled orange in half across the "equator," laying each half face down, and cutting it into six wedges. The orange was zipped off the skin by your teeth starting at a point. No sticky hands!

*I found mine! It's called an O. J. Squeater.—Jean

Seasonal and much loved—

Tangerines: Easy to peel and delicious to eat. Squeeze the peels to make the air smell like Christmas.

Grapes: Seedless green grapes were our favorite kind. They were often served still in the colander, on a plate. The dusty red grapes (with the bitter seeds) were less popular at our house.

Strawberries and raspberries: Wash them and watch them disappear.

Bing cherries: Dad's and Jean's favorite. Dad bought them by the lug at the peak of the season. Wash them, pop them in your mouth, and spit out the pit. (Make sure to hide the pits so no one can tell how many you ate.)

Whole Coconut

It's a project. It's a snack.—*Susan*

Get a hammer out of the garage and find a really big nail. Take the coconut outside on the cement. Bring a glass with you. See where the three little spots are? Hammer a nail through two (or all three) of them and pour the coconut "milk" out into the glass. It will smell good (if it's not spoiled! If it is, toss the whole thing.), but no one will want to drink it. (It has a science class look about it.)

Shut your eyes really tight and give the coconut a good whack with the hammer. (Remember where it is.) Squint, and whack the coconut into smallish pieces. The part you want to eat is white, and the very thin brown rind on the edge is okay, too. Your teeth are the tool. It takes a lot of time to eat fresh coconut, but it's really good.

Found Fruit

We gathered tiny wild strawberries on sunny banks and found them in the woods by our cottage. Abandoned orchards provided the only apples our mother could eat after she developed an allergy to pesticides. We picked pails full of blackberries by the side of the road in August and hickory nuts in the fall out by Bob Carpenter's farm.—*Julie*

Potatoes

Everybody likes potatoes.

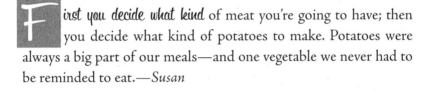

First you decide what kind of meat you're going to have; then you decide what kind of potatoes to make. Potatoes were always a big part of our meals—and one vegetable we never had to be reminded to eat.—*Susan*

Mashed Potatoes

It amazes me how many family recipes we found for leftover mashed potatoes. I thought we ate every last bit—we all love mashed potatoes. Multiply the quantities below, because it doesn't sound like enough, and you might want leftovers.—*Susan*

6 medium red-skinned or all-purpose potatoes
3 tablespoons butter plus more to put on top
⅓ cup hot whole or 2% milk (See how much of
    this the potatoes need.)
salt to taste

"I just love mashed tertaters and gravy!"—Diane, age 4 to ?

Put a pot of water on to boil. Peel and cut up the potatoes and keep them in cold water until the pot is ready. When water is boiling, put in potatoes, add a little salt, bring to a boil, then turn heat down to a simmer. Cook potatoes until you can pierce them with a fork.

Drain the potatoes and use an electric mixer* to mash them while still in the pan (so they stay hot). Beat in the 3 tablespoons butter. Pour in hot milk a little at a time, beating until potatoes are the consistency you like. (You may not need all the milk.) Add salt to taste. Beat with mixer until all lumps are gone. Serve in a heated dish and top with a good-sized piece of butter.

If you want to do this "by hand" the old way, you'll need a potato masher.

Leftover Mashed Potatoes Au Gratin (Mom)

I do love this, but for some reason it is unnaturally HOT when it comes out of the oven—think lava! I used to burn my tongue every time I ate it. Come to think of it—I still do. I can't seem to wait for it to cool off to eat it!—*Julie*

Using a little black frying pan like Mom's, sauté ½ cup of onions in 2 tablespoons of butter. Use a fork to mix the onions into 2 to 4 cups of leftover mashed potatoes. Add a little milk or half-and-half to the potatoes to loosen them up a bit. Put in ovenproof casserole dish. Top with sliced or shredded Cheddar cheese. Bake at 350° for about 20 minutes until hot as lava.

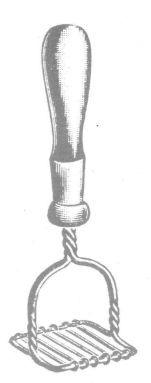

"Egg and Potato" (Grandma Noffke)

The original "Egg and Potato" was a tiny, yellowed newspaper clipping in Grandma's recipe file suggesting a way to use leftover mashed potatoes. I tried this, and it is a very good suggestion. (The recipe below is based on what I have learned by making this many times.) It will make light, airy potatoes out of the cold leftover mashed potatoes in your refrigerator, and . . . not look like leftovers.—*Susan*

Grandma Noffke

4 cups leftover mashed potatoes

1 egg

butter

paprika

Preheat oven to 400° and butter a 1-quart baking pan or soufflé dish. Put leftover mashed potatoes (which I am presuming are already seasoned) into a mixing bowl, break the egg into them, and use an electric mixer to blend the ingredients. Put mixture into the baking dish, dot with butter, and sprinkle with paprika. Bake until the top has browned a little and the tines of a fork inserted in the center are hot, 30 to 45 minutes.*

*The timing will depend on how cold the potatoes are. Up to 6 cups of leftover mashed potatoes will work fine with only one egg, but less than 4 cups of potatoes will taste too eggy.

Grandma Sanvidge's Creamed Potatoes

These were so good that I asked Grandma how she made them. She wrote me a letter, and here are her directions exactly as she wrote them. Don't skimp on the pepper!—*Julie*

Grandma Sanvidge

"You asked about creamed potatoes & I think you mean the way I fix them when I used left over ones the way all my boys and Grandpa like them. You have to have potatoes that won't get mushy. So I'll start a new page and try to explain. Use leftover boiled potatoes or even baked—no matter, just so they are firm. Cut and slice as for frying. Pour milk in fry pan & add butter or margarine. I use margarine these days. It's hard to say the amount because I have never done that—just experiment but be sure they aren't too soupy. When it comes to a boil, add potatoes. Season with salt & pepper & simmer down until they look glossy. You've eaten them so you know how they should look. Sometimes, if you like a little onion, you can add a little diced to milk or you can sauté the onions in the butter before adding the milk. I hope you can make sense out of all that. The other creamed potatoes would be just thickened milk with some butter or oleo added like I use for any creamed vegetable like peas or beans.

Asking me for receipts like that is hard for me to give as I just pour things out according to the size of the family ... Hope the potatoes didn't spoil while waiting for this receipt ... Well, let me know how you came out with the potatoes. Love you, Gran S."

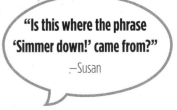

"Is this where the phrase 'Simmer down!' came from?"

—Susan

Grandma's Salt and Pepper Shakers

While we waited for dinner, we loved to look at Grandma Sanvidge's salt and pepper shaker collection and count the pennies in the big Mogen David bottle. Our favorite shakers were the before-and-after bride and groom—lovely and handsome on one side and pregnant and unshaven with beer belly on the other. We also loved the little chrome toaster with the white and brown slices of toast (the shakers) and the black frying pan (pepper) with the slice of ham (salt) inside.—*Julie*

This is what Grandma's toaster salt and pepper shaker looked like.

Baked Potatoes

What could be easier? You don't even have to peel them.—*Susan*

Scrub russet potatoes (these are the brown ones). Prick all over with a fork. (It will be a science experiment if you don't do this.) Bake for 1 hour at 400°. Serve with sour cream or butter, and salt and pepper.

Twice-Baked Potatoes

Twice-Baked Potatoes are a good choice for a company meal. You can make them ahead of time and it will look like you "fussed," but this recipe isn't fussy at all. —*Susan*

If you aren't covering the potatoes with Cheddar cheese, use a cookie press (the nozzle that looks like a dunce cap with the end blown out) to fill the potato shells. They will look pretty fancy.—*Diane*

2½ pounds Idaho potatoes (7 to 8 potatoes about 4 to 4½ inches long)
¼ cup (4 tablespoons) butter
½ cup sour cream
salt and pepper to taste
1 cup grated Cheddar cheese (optional, but our mom always used it)
2 tablespoons butter, melted
paprika

Preheat oven to 400° and scrub and pierce potatoes with a fork. Bake for 1 hour. Turn oven down to 350°.

Cut the potatoes in half lengthwise while they are still warm, and carefully scoop out the contents into a mixing bowl (you will be using the potato skin shells). Add the 4 tablespoons butter and the sour cream. Using a mixer, combine well. Season with salt and pepper to taste. Fill the potato shells with this mixture. (If you make your potatoes really full, you won't fill all the shells.)

Sprinkle each stuffed potato with Cheddar cheese, if you are using it. Dribble each with melted butter and sprinkle with paprika. Bake until heated through and cheese is melted, about 25 minutes.

When Mom's Away . . .

I remember the time that Mom went to Washington, D.C., for a 4-H conference (I think). Susie took on the job of fixing supper. Since she was a bit of a novice at it, the dishes of food hit the table at intervals of about 30 minutes. Maybe that's where the expression "timing is everything" came from. I hope that we didn't complain too much, because at least she was willing to cook for us.—*Jean*

Jean was being really nice to me and had written "10-minute intervals," but I made her correct it to 30. It was probably longer! They just left the table and came back when the next dish was ready. (It was a very long meal.) I don't remember complaints, but you can bet I was teased.—Susan

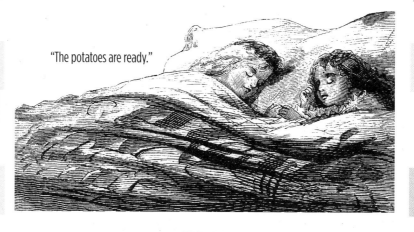

"The potatoes are ready."

Boiled Potatoes

There are plain boiled potatoes and then there are "new potatoes," the tiny red ones, which are a favorite with us. (Leave the peels on new potatoes and cook them whole.)—*Jean*

Put water on to boil. Peel and cut up big potatoes (the red kind are best for boiling), or just scrub and remove the "eyes" of small new potatoes, and put them in cold water until the pot is boiling. Put potatoes in boiling water, add a little salt, and return to a boil. Turn down to a simmer immediately, cover, and cook until potatoes are tender enough that a fork pierces them easily. Drain and serve with butter. (You could still make mashed potatoes . . .)

Fried Potatoes

. . . but you wanted leftovers so you could make these.—*Susan*

Slice up leftover boiled potatoes. Melt Crisco* in a cast-iron frying pan and brown some finely chopped onion. Put in the potatoes and fry until crisp. Salt and pepper lavishly.

*About 2 tablespoons of Crisco for 4 medium-sized potatoes. When I made these recently I remembered that I always ate them with ketchup.—Diane

Raw Fries

These are really good. The outside potatoes have a brown crust the color of dark French fries. Most of the inner potatoes stay white and are like creamed potatoes. When you put in a spatula to dish them out, you get a nice cross-section of textures. The salt and pepper seems evenly distributed even though you put it on only one side.—*Diane*

This way of making fried potatoes came from our Dad's family. Ever protective of our health, our mother would not make these if the meat would be fried, too. —*Susan*

4 medium-sized potatoes (the everyday brown kind)
2 to 3 tablespoons Crisco
salt and pepper to taste

Peel potatoes and slice them thin, about ⅛ inch thick. Don't blot them dry after slicing them. Melt shortening in an 8-inch frying pan on medium-high. The potatoes should be about 1¼ inches high in the pan. When the shortening is hot, put in the sliced potatoes, pat down, and cover. Fry until the potatoes on the bottom are browned, 8 to 10 minutes.

Turn the potatoes over. You will have to do this in pieces. Pat down firmly, cover, and fry until potatoes can be easily pierced with a fork, another 8 to 10 minutes. Salt and pepper to taste. You would think the potatoes would come out as a big "cake," but the pieces remain separate.

Potato Salad (Mom)

If you don't mind a slightly pink potato salad, our mother has been known to add a little ketchup from time to time.—*Julie*

1 quart (4 cups) boiling potatoes, peeled and cut in chunks
1 small onion, chopped
1 cup chopped celery
2 hard-boiled eggs, cut up
½ teaspoon salt
1 cup Miracle Whip
dash of sweet pickle juice
paprika

Put water on to boil. Peel and cut up potatoes and put them in cold water until the pot is boiling. (Mom of the Asbestos Hands peels and cuts up the hot potatoes *after* they are cooked.) Put potatoes in boiling water, add a little salt, and return to a boil. Turn down to a simmer immediately, cover, and cook until potatoes are tender enough that a fork pierces them easily. Drain, and put the potatoes in a bowl with the chopped onion, chopped celery, and cut-up boiled eggs. Sprinkle with salt. Add Miracle Whip and toss. Add a spritz of sweet pickle juice. Taste and adjust seasonings. Sprinkle paprika on top. Chill.

German Potato Salad (from Mickie Zaddack)

Phone message: "Susan, it's Diane. If you do find the recipe for German Potato Salad . . . that same recipe (minus the potatoes) wrapped in a dish towel around your neck is the cure for a sore throat."—*Susan*

½ pound bacon (uncooked), diced

½ cup finely chopped onion

2 cups water

½ cup sugar

⅓ cup white vinegar

1 tablespoon salt

pepper to taste

3 tablespoons cornstarch

½ cup water

4 pounds of red potatoes (about 8 to 10 potatoes, depending on size)

Put bacon pieces in a large frying pan with onions and "fry out" until the bacon fat is transparent (not browned). Leave in pan and set aside.

In a saucepan, combine the 2 cups water, sugar, vinegar, salt, and pepper. In a small bowl, mix the cornstarch with the ½ cup water and add to saucepan. Bring to a boil. Cook until sauce is slightly thickened.

Set water on to boil. Wash, peel, and cut the potatoes into thick slices (cut large slices in half) or bite-size chunks. When water is boiling, put potatoes in, and bring back to a boil. Turn down heat to a simmer immediately and cook until potatoes can be pierced with a fork. (Sliced potatoes won't take long at all.) Drain the potatoes and put them in the frying pan with the cooked bacon and onions. Pour the thickened sauce over them, stir, and cook for a little while to meld the flavors. Serve warm.

Mickie and Marv Zaddack are long-time "up north" friends of our parents. While Dad and Marv are splitting logs in the driveway, Mom and Mickie are drinking coffee and trading recipes in the kitchen.—Susan

French Fries

Mom made these from scratch several times with her French fry cutter and they were really, really good but a total mess to make (and "such a waste of good oil!"). So you can either go to a restaurant or . . .

Buy frozen crinkle-cut French fries and follow directions on package.

Tater Tots

Fun to say "Tater Tots," and fun to eat them.—*Susan*

Buy Tater Tots. Follow directions on package.

Meat

"What are we having for supper?"

Mom and Dad would often buy meat in bulk from farmers they actually knew. There were butcher shops all over Oshkosh, and even the small corner groceries had their own butchers. We would often make a little detour on the way to the cottage to buy sausage in Black Creek, and Grandpa Noffke made sausage in his basement. Our dad loved to go fishing so we could have had fresh fish really often . . . if we had wanted to eat it. (We made an exception for trout.)—*Susan*

Roast Chicken (Mom)

We were into free-range chicken before we knew what it was. Every year, Mom and Dad would ask Roy Carpenter to raise about a dozen chickens for us. Dad says they were White Rocks.* They were big chickens, like small turkeys, and made the best gravy ever.—*Julie*

Thaw one of Carpenter's chickens and use a match to singe off any stray feathers. Check the tail for any bits of feather. Wash out well and blot dry. Set aside the gizzard, heart, neck, and whatever the heck else is in there. You'll simmer those up later to include in your dressing. Rub the outside with some butter. Salt and pepper it well inside and out. Put it in a large, covered, enamel roasting pan with the vent open.

Roast at 325° until done, using a meat thermometer for accuracy. To get the chicken nice and brown, take the cover off about halfway through the process, but don't let the pan completely dry out. When done, take the chicken out to rest a moment while you make the gravy. Take a little jar and put in a bit of flour and cold water. Shake until well mixed. Pour the pan juices into a large saucepan, taking time to skim off the fat. Bring to a boil. While stirring, add the flour mixture. Cook until thickened and season with lots of pepper.

> **"What lovely brown gravy!"**
> —Dad (in a falsetto voice), imitating one of his elderly female relatives

In later years, when we couldn't get these wonderful chickens, the pan juices just weren't as chicken-y. We stopped using the flour and water mixture and started adding a can of Campbell's cream of chicken soup to the pan juices instead—and the gravy was delicious every time.—Julie

*Every time I make one of those big Perdue roasting chickens, it reminds me of the chickens we had at home. I found this out recently: They are a cross between Cornish chickens and . . . White Plymouth Rocks.—Susan

Poultry Stuffing (Dad)

Dad has never been a "measuring cook," so I kept track of the numbers when I made his memorable stuffing (which I ate with gusto, and gravy, and I didn't even pick out the onions and giblets!) —*Susan*

MAKES ENOUGH TO FILL A 2 1/2-QUART SHALLOW CASSEROLE DISH

10 cups bread (cut or torn in smallish pieces, ¼- to ⅜-inch pieces of bread, not granules)

about 1 cup milk to moisten bread (amount will depend on type of bread)

4 tablespoons shortening (Crisco), for frying onions and celery, then giblets

½ cup finely chopped onions

1 cup diced celery

giblets from the bird you are roasting (gizzard and heart only, no liver), chopped fine

2 medium-sized, red-skinned tart apples, unpeeled, but cored and cut up

¼ cup raisins (cut up a bit, or they will puff up)

2 eggs, lightly beaten

¾ teaspoon sage

1 teaspoon poultry seasoning

salt and pepper

Moisten the bread pieces with milk. Put shortening in frying pan and sauté the onions with the celery until limp. Put in the chopped giblets and sauté until brown.

Put the frying pan mixture in a bowl. Add the moistened bread pieces, tossing and stirring. Mix in the chopped apples, raisins, and beaten eggs. Add the sage and poultry seasoning. (You want to *smell* this dressing. Dad might add more than I did! Unlike Mom, he has a heavy hand with the seasonings.) Season with salt and pepper.

(Using this stuffing to actually stuff the bird is optional.) Grease a casserole dish, fill with stuffing, and cover with tinfoil. Bake in the oven with your turkey or chicken(s) at either 325° or 350° (whichever temperature you are using to roast your bird) until fluffy and cooked through, 1 to 1½ hours.

Use a lot!

Dad made so much that there was always a whole cake pan of this fragrant stuffing next to the stuffing-stuffed turkey, but I don't recall any leftovers sitting in the fridge.—Susan

Pork Roast, Potato Dumplings, and Sweet and Sour Cabbage (Dad)

This is a Bohemian dish that Dad's grandma and mother used to make. When I went to Prague for my honeymoon, I learned that Dad's great-grandparents had lived there. To my great surprise, I was served this exact dish in a little Prague restaurant. The only difference was that they sliced their dumplings, and Dad doesn't.—*Julie*

Uncle Clifford often asked Dad to make this when Mom and Dad were in Georgia for a visit.—*Susan*

3 to 4 pound pork roast (Buy a shoulder or butt roast so there will be enough fat for it to be tender.)
salt and pepper

Cabbage:
one-half cabbage, cut up a little coarser than cole slaw
1 teaspoon caraway seeds

Sweet and Sour Sauce for the Cabbage:
2 tablespoons butter
2 tablespoons flour
1 cup water
vinegar
sugar
¼ teaspoon salt
⅛ teaspoon white pepper

Potato Dumplings:*

2 medium potatoes, grated

½ teaspoon baking powder

½ teaspoon salt

flour (quite a bit—enough to make this all hold together so you can form the
   dumplings)

Preheat oven to 325°. Rub the pork roast with salt and pepper and put in a
roasting pan fat side up. Cook roast for 50 minutes per pound (a little longer
is fine). (Save the pan juices to make gravy.)

While roast is in the oven, put cabbage and caraway seeds in a pan with
enough water so the cabbage floats a little. Cover and cook over medium heat
until limp. Drain. (Some of the caraway seeds will stay with the cabbage.
This is good.)

To make the Sweet and Sour Sauce: Melt the butter in a saucepan over
medium-low heat. Stir in the flour and heat until starting to bubble. Gradually
add water, stirring all the time, until sauce is smooth and starts to thicken.
Flavor the sauce (and make it sweet-sour) by adding vinegar and sugar:
1 teaspoon of each at a time, but you must use equal amounts of vinegar and
sugar. (2½ teaspoons of each will make it mildly sweet-sour.) Season with
salt and white pepper. Cook over low heat for 10 minutes. (Mom and Dad
describe this as "glossy" and "a pretty sauce.") When both cabbage and sauce
are done, combine them. (You can reheat this when the rest of the meal is
ready.)

Make the dumplings (working fast, so the potatoes don't discolor): Put a large kettle of salted water on to boil. In a bowl, combine potatoes, baking powder, salt, and flour. Keep stirring in more flour until you are able to form dumplings that will hold together. Dad makes his dumplings almost tennis-ball-size. (The dumplings might have a better chance of cooking through if they are a little smaller. See note below.) Put the dumplings into boiling water for 20 minutes. They will float to the top very soon (which usually means a dumpling is done), but you will need the full 20 minutes to cook the raw potatoes.

Make gravy from the pork roast juices and pan scrapings to put on the dumplings. (See Beef and Pork Gravy, page 136.)

Please Note: Dad says these dumplings are "off-white to gray and will look like you found them on the floor." You've been warned. If you happen to have a recipe for Bohemian raw potato dumplings around, you might want to use that. The second time I made the dumplings for Dad's "Bohemian Rhapsody," I added 1 beaten egg, used a rounded ¾ cup of flour, ⅛ teaspoon of white pepper, and made the dumplings only 2 inches in diameter. This made them a little better. The rest of this dish is very good, but the dumplings have always been a bit on the gluey side. (Now I'm in trouble!)—Susan

Pot Roast (Mom)

This is the dish I requested on my birthday. A few years back, Mom and Dad came to visit me in Ohio. I had to work one day and Mom said, "How would you like me to make your favorite Pot Roast tonight?" I was so excited about the prospect of enjoying her Pot Roast that evening that I raved about it all day to my co-workers . . . "Oh, the carrots and onions get caramelized . . . the celery melts in your mouth . . . the outsides of the potatoes are tinged with brown and the insides are snowy white . . . the gravy is so rich and brown . . . and the beef is juicy, falls apart when you touch your fork to it—a complete melt-in-your-mouth experience." They made me promise to bring them leftovers. I hummed all the way home from work and floated in anticipation into my little house. Hmmm, I thought . . . it doesn't smell like Pot Roast . . . Mom walked into the room and said, "Dad and I got busy sightseeing and didn't have time to make the Pot Roast, so I warmed up last night's leftovers in foil for dinner tonight." I have nothing more to say.—*Julie*

Take a well-marbled chuck roast and brown well in a Dutch oven on the top of the stove. Add water (about a half inch deep in the pan), some quartered onions, several whole carrots, cut in two, and several sticks of celery about 4 inches long. Cover and simmer on a very low setting for 2 to 3 hours. Check it once in a while to see if it needs more water. If it boils dry, you will smell it and it just won't turn out the same. If you have reason to believe the water doesn't seem beefy enough after a while, you could add a bouillon cube or two. In the last hour or so, add peeled, halved potatoes and get them down into the broth so they soak up some "brown." When it's done and you've removed everything from the pan, you can turn the juice into gravy, but I seem to think Mom just skims off the fat and serves the juice.

This works great in a slow cooker . . . just put all the vegetables on the bottom, the roast (browned or not) on top, and sprinkle with an envelope of Lipton's Onion Soup Mix. Cook on low all day. Can't run out of time this way.—Julie

Beef and Pork Roasted Together (Mom)

This makes the world's greatest gravy!—*Julie*

Choose a chuck or blade-cut beef roast and a shoulder-cut pork roast of approximately the same size. (If one is a little larger, it should be the beef roast.) Salt and pepper the roasts and brown them in the same pan. The roasts should have a decent amount of space between them when you put them in the oven. Roast uncovered at 325° for about 60 minutes per pound. When the pork is done (no pink inside, 185° on the meat thermometer), you're all set.

I made this with 2 pounds of beef and 1¼ pounds of pork, and both meats were fork-tender at 3 hours.—Diane

Beef and Pork Gravy:

Use the juices and brown bits in the pan, taking time first to skim off the fat. Add a little water or beef broth if necessary for volume. Pour into a medium saucepan and heat until it simmers. Meanwhile, shake up a little cold water and flour in a jar and add gradually to the simmering juices, stirring constantly. Continue simmering until it thickens to your liking. Season to taste with a generous amount of salt and pepper.

Pork Roast by Itself

Pork roast, mashed potatoes, and gravy with green beans or carrots was one of my favorite meals growing up. The pork roast was always tender and succulent, with chewy browned edges, and I loved to smush it in with the potatoes. The secret to making a good old-fashioned pork roast is to buy the cheap shoulder blade or butt roast and roast it slowly.—*Susan*

pork roast, shoulder blade or butt

salt and pepper

Preheat oven to 325°. Wipe the meat with a paper towel and rub with salt and pepper. Tie with string if it is falling apart. Put the roast in a shallow roasting pan, fat side up, uncovered, and pop it in the oven. Allow 50 minutes per pound (a little extra time won't hurt it at all, but pork roast should never be underdone—a meat thermometer should read 185°).

Remember when . . .

. . . we might have a rare Friday night family supper out at Pucci's on Rugby Street in Oshkosh . . . if Dad could just find the place? *"No, I don't want to stop and ask. It's got to be around here somewhere!"*—*Jean*

The Ham Glaze with 7UP in It

This is enough for a 5-pound ham. According to Mom, this glaze was used on the hams baked to make sandwiches for Grandpa's coal yard workers. Dad, who used to work for Grandpa, got this recipe from Ray Siewert, who used to work at Schubert's Meat Market (where the ham always came from). I was surprised to hear that 7UP was around in those days.—*Susan*

whole bone-in ham, up to 5 pounds
jellied juice from the ham package
½ cup brown sugar (or less if you don't like your ham to be very sweet)
1 or 2 teaspoons prepared mustard
7 ounces* of 7UP (It came in a 7-ounce bottle back then.)

In a saucepan, melt the ham juice. Stir the brown sugar and mustard together and add to ham juice with the 7UP. Cook until ingredients are dissolved and glaze has thickened. Pour over ham and bake according to the directions on the ham you bought.

*Some glass measuring cups have ounce measurements.—*Jean*

Canned Ham Glaze (Grandma Noffke)

This glaze will give the anemic-looking ham a bronzing.—*Jean*

If you like beer and onions on your ham, you might like this . . . —*Diane*

½ cup beer

¼ cup brown sugar

2 tablespoons ketchup

1 teaspoon finely grated onion

¼ teaspoon dry mustard

canned ham, up to 3 pounds

Preheat oven to 350°. Combine all ingredients and stir until brown sugar is dissolved.

Place ham in a baking pan. Cover with glaze. Bake until ham is well heated and glaze has a deep, rich sheen, about 30 minutes.

At Grandma Noffke's House

At Grandma Noffke's, we ate off multicolored Melmac dishes in her kitchen and yellow and brown plaid dishes in the dining room. In the cookie jar (which was inside a cabinet) you'd find snickerdoodles, Peanut Butter Cookies, or Ginger Krinkles. Meat was always cooked until it fell off the bone: roasted chicken, pork roast, beef roast. Watching Grandpa eat chicken was a wonderment, with those big jowls of his jiggling and the bare bones emerging from his mouth. Grandma had a big garden and froze green beans, raspberries, and strawberries in leftover milk cartons. She stored never-washed carrots in gunny sacks in the basement next to the jars and jars of rainwater to water her African violets. We ate every kind of cream pie—lemon meringue and coconut cream were our favorites. Cile's Baked Beans were the best ever. We can't forget Ambrosia, sweet Liver Sausage, or the distinctive smell of Cile's coffee. For Grandpa's birthday, it was Blitz Torte or apple cake. When it was time to do the dishes, out came the dishpan and a box of Dreft.—*Julie*

Doing the dishes in Grandma Noffke's kitchen. Grandma Noffke is washing the meat platter. Our Aunt Dorie (the mother of our across-the-street Noffke cousins) and Mom are ready with dish towels.

At Grandma Sanvidge's House

At Grandma Sanvidge's house, we ate in her big country kitchen off a vast collection of Blue Willow dishes. While we waited for dinner, we would pass the time examining Grandma's fascinating salt and pepper shaker collection. Grandchildren received special treatment and drank out of jelly jar glasses with nursery rhymes printed on them. We loved the black olives, Spiced Apple Slices, and sweet gherkins on the relish trays, pies made from the Wealthy apples in their yard, and the circus animal cookies dipped in frosting and covered with multicolored sugar beads. Grandpa liked a crisp cookie, we were always told, and so Grandma always had rectangular, brown "Icebox Cookies" for him. Grandma was a very good cook and shared her cooking knowledge with her sons. One year we were invited for Thanksgiving dinner, and we showed up expecting a big spread. Instead, we saw Grandma putting on her mink scarf (with the heads biting the tails). "We've got to hurry," she said. "Our reservations at Hesser's Supper Club are in fifteen minutes!"—*Julie*

Dinner in Grandma Sanvidge's kitchen. That's Grandma Great on the right, Mom and Grandma Sanvidge (behind Helen Nancy, Dad's cousin-who-was-raised-as-his-sister, in plaid), and Jean in the foreground.

"Fake-Baked-Ham" Spam

It *is* very cute.—*Susan*

> 1 can (12 ounces) Spam
> whole cloves
> ⅓ cup brown sugar
> ½ teaspoon white vinegar
> 1 teaspoon prepared yellow mustard
> 1 teaspoon water

Preheat oven to 375°. Place the Spam in a small greased* casserole dish. Cut criss-cross lines on top just as if you were doing a real ham. In the center of each diamond, neatly insert a clove.

Mix remaining ingredients and brush mixture over the little Spam. Bake 20 minutes, basting several times.

*. . . *because that sugary sauce really bakes on. As Mom used to say: "This one's a soaker."*—*Jean*

Apricot Nectar Chicken (also known as Luau Chicken)

Once a year, Mom's Busy Badgers Homemakers Club would have a ladies-only dinner. The one we remember best was Luau Night. It was held at our house and featured things we considered exotic at the time: a grass skirt left over from Dad's WWII tour of duty in the Pacific, blender drinks made with rum, whole pineapples, coconuts, and . . . girdle-less women. At that point in our social history, nice ladies always wore a girdle. My mom doubted that Hawaiian ladies wore them, so she had a box at the back door marked "All Girdles Here Please" and reserved the den as a temporary changing room. No wonder the ladies all had such a good time—they were finally comfortable! They sat right down on the living room floor and had their luau. This delectable chicken was the main course.—*Julie*

1 frying chicken, cut up into serving pieces
1 envelope Lipton's Onion Soup Mix
1½ cups apricot nectar
1 or 2 tablespoons soy sauce

Put the chicken pieces in a 9 x 13-inch glass baking pan. Combine the onion soup mix, apricot nectar, and soy sauce and pour over chicken, turning pieces to make sure all are coated. Marinate in the refrigerator for several hours or more.

Preheat oven to 325°. Bake chicken uncovered in the marinade 1½ hours, basting frequently. The sauce will thicken considerably. Great served with fluffy white rice.

Something I remembered today:
"Cinderella, dressed in yella, went downtown, to see her fella,
"On the way, her girdle busted, all the people were disgusted."—
Julie

Diane in the grass skirt.

Kitchen Time

Sometime in the '60s, our kitchen on Bowen Street was graced with new "cuisine-themed" wallpaper. Mom thought it would be a great idea to use that wallpaper for the background of the old kitchen wall clock.

Not too long afterwards, we had rearranged our bedroom, and I was excited about sleeping in the newly redone room. I guess I was too "wound-up" to sleep well. This was before the advent of the lighted alarm clock (at least in our house). I got up, not sure what time it was, and stumbled into the kitchen. I glanced up at the newly wallpapered clock and was upset to discover that we had overslept! (It was funny that our usually very observant neighbor didn't call us when she didn't see the lights on . . .) I quickly got everyone up and going, and then somebody took a better look at the clock and realized it was the middle of the night. The little basket on the wallpaper had camouflaged the hour hand, and it was 3:30, not 6:30! Oops! Sorry!—*Jean*

. . . then Mom tried a black construction paper background, and the red nail polish she had put on the clock hands didn't work too well with that either. (The invisible long hand is on the six!)

Beef Stroganoff (Grandma Noffke)

Both Grandma Noffke and Mom made this stroganoff, but Mom came up with a "budget" version. (See next page.) We are much more familiar with the budget version.—*Susan*

1 cup diced onions (Grandma cut her onions in half and then sliced them.)
½ cup (8 tablespoons, or 1 stick) butter
1 pound beef tenderloin, cut into ½-inch strips and then chunks
1 jar or can (4 ounces) mushrooms
1 tablespoon Worcestershire sauce
½ cup sour cream
salt and pepper to taste
hot cooked egg noodles

Cook onions in butter until golden brown. Add beef and cook over medium heat, stirring often, until meat is tender and cooked through. Stir in mushrooms and Worcestershire sauce. Season to taste. Stir in sour cream and cook through. Serve over hot egg noodles.

Beef Stroganoff (Mom's Budget Version)

Sour cream was not widely available when we were growing up. "Why would I want to buy sour cream?" was the general consumer reaction, so it was marketed as "cultured cream" for a while. The lemon juice at the end of Mom's recipe turns evaporated milk into a version of sour cream.—*Susan*

scant tablespoon of butter for the frying pan

½ cup finely chopped onion

1½ pounds round steak, cut into ¾-inch cubes

1 beef bouillon cube dissolved in 1 cup boiling water

1 can (4 ounces) chopped mushrooms and their juice

1 can (5 ounces) evaporated milk

1 teaspoon Worcestershire sauce

2 tablespoons flour mixed with ½ cup water, to thicken sauce

½ teaspoon lemon juice

salt and pepper to taste

hot cooked egg noodles

Melt butter in a frying pan and sauté the onions until transparent. Add cubed round steak to brown it a little. Add dissolved beef bouillon and mushrooms. Cover and simmer over low heat until meat is cooked through, about 1½ hours. Stir in evaporated milk and Worcestershire sauce. Stir in flour and water mixture. Cook uncovered, stirring occasionally, until sauce thickens. (This process could take 20 to 30 minutes.) Five minutes before serving, stir in the lemon juice. Salt and pepper to taste. Serve over hot egg noodles.

Barbecued Spareribs

Mom uses the "country-style" ribs for her spareribs.—*Diane*

4 pounds spareribs
2 tablespoons butter
3 tablespoons minced onion
1 cup ketchup
5 tablespoons brown sugar (or white sugar)
¼ cup lemon juice
2 tablespoons vinegar
1 tablespoon Worcestershire sauce, optional
1 teaspoon dry mustard
salt and pepper, to taste

Preheat oven to 375°. Wipe spareribs and place them in an ungreased 2- to 2½-quart shallow casserole dish in one layer and bake for 45 minutes.

While the meat is cooking, make the sauce. Melt butter in a saucepan. Sauté onions until tender. Add remaining ingredients and cook 15 to 20 minutes over medium-low heat so flavors blend. (This makes 1½ cups of sauce.)

After the ribs have been in the oven for 45 minutes, cover with barbecue sauce and bake until very tender and falling off the bone, about 30 minutes more.

Buckshot Buffet

Not all the meat we ate came from the Piggly Wiggly. Some came from a creel, the deep pocket of a hunting coat, or the bed of a pickup truck. Trout is our favorite wild game of all, and we were sad to see "catch and release" become necessary. We ate venison, an occasional goose, duck, pheasant, partridge, and various kinds of fish. (When Diane was first married, she and her husband were very ambitious and thrifty and ate wild game to save money. It worked—they paid off their first house in just a few years.)—*Julie*

Bear and elk (stringy, dark, dry) each made one appearance on our table. (You will find recipes for trout and venison in our Up North section.) —Susan

"Pounded" Round Steak (Dad)

Since Dad was famous, or should we say infamous, among the neighbor kids for threatening to "pound them into the ground" if they didn't behave, I guess his method for making round steak was a natural. I really enjoyed round steak prepared Dad's way and would eat as much of it as I could get away with. (You can buy this already "pounded" now.)—*Jean*

Cut the steak into portion-size pieces, remove all fat and gristle, and pound the "heck" out of them with a meat tenderizer. (Sometimes Dad just used the back edge of a meat cleaver.) Then dredge the pieces in flour that has been seasoned with salt and pepper. Melt a good-sized glob of Crisco in a cast-iron frying pan on a fairly high heat and fry the steaks quickly. Dad usually had more than one frying pan going, because if the pan got too encrusted, it would have to be scraped out and "re-Criscoed."

Needless to say, this is a great meal to eat (especially if it is served with mashed potatoes and corn) but a pain to clean up after!—Jean

Meat Loaf (Mom)

Meat Loaf was usually served with mashed potatoes (with butter, not gravy) and green beans. The leftovers make a good sandwich. It's in the Lunch section. —Diane

⅔ cup soda cracker crumbs
1 cup whole or 2% milk
1½ pounds ground beef
1 egg
¼ cup chopped onion
1 teaspoon salt
⅛ teaspoon pepper
ketchup for the top

Preheat oven to 350°. Soak cracker crumbs in milk. Add rest of ingredients. Mix well. Press into 4¾ x 8¾-inch loaf pan. Bake for about 1 hour (until a meat thermometer reads 160°—but Mom never used a meat thermometer back then). Top with ketchup in a swirly pattern. Bake 10 minutes more (until meat thermometer reads 165°).

Stuffed Meat Loaf (Grandma Sanvidge)

There were several years during the Great Depression that Grandpa Sanvidge went without work and Grandma had to pinch every penny. She came up with this "receipt" as a way to stretch the meat. It is delicious.—*Julie*

Make a small quantity of stuffing using stale bread, onions, butter, celery, and seasonings. Set aside. How much meat do you use for your regular meat loaf? Well, just take half to a third of that amount and mix it with a few bread crumbs, an egg, and some salt and pepper. Press the meat mixture into a loaf pan like you're making a crust with it. Save enough of the mixture to cover the top. In the meat "crust" you've formed, put the stuffing. Cover the loaf with the reserved meat mixture, pressing it down with your fingers to smooth the top. Don't put any ketchup on it, but if you have a slice of bacon or two, you could put that on top. Bake at about 375° 'til done. Let stand for about 10 minutes, take out of the pan, slice it, and enjoy Grandma's creativity and thrift!

"I ate quite freely of it."
—Grandpa Sanvidge

Ice Fishing

When we went along ice fishing with Dad, we took our ice skates and a big thermos of cocoa.

Ice fishing was a strange process. I remember being in a dark ice shanty, looking into a big rectangular hole in the ice (about 6 feet by 3 feet), while Uncle Keith and my dad watched for a shockingly huge, prehistoric-looking sturgeon to swim by so they could spear it. They sprinkled corn kernels into the hole to make the lake bottom lighter so the dark sturgeon would show up better. When Dad caught a sturgeon, he always had it smoked. The pinkish meat with the black skin was a big treat at our house, offered to people dropping by.

For smaller fish, circular holes were cut into the ice and short wooden fishing poles were set up next to them. There was a little gizmo connected to each pole called a tip-up, and a red flag would pop up when there was a fish on the line. The "fun part" of ice fishing was using the skimmer (a disk with holes cut into it attached to a handle—the one Dad used was hand-made by his dad) to strain out ice particles and keep the hole from freezing up again.

We went along ice fishing only a few times. It was very, very cold out there in the middle of the frozen lake, and we were drinking all that cocoa . . .

It is a mystery what happened to the smaller fish Dad caught. He must have given them away, because Mom didn't like to cook those fish, and we didn't like to eat them. In our opinion, all fish (except trout, which our Dad had convinced us was the "cleanest fish") had to be boneless, skinless, and geometric in shape. Fish sticks were fine with us. Broiled haddock (shaped like Nevada) was borderline. We made another exception for the deep-fried perch served at Friday night fish fries (with tartar sauce, rye bread, and French fries) at the Knights of Columbus and at taverns all over Oshkosh. Crunchy is always good—even if there's fish inside.

—*Susan*

This photo was taken on a frozen Pearl Lake near Oshkosh. Jean is in the foreground next to Jean Grose (famous for her Apple Slices; see page 187). Jean's husband, Lester (Dad's mason, famous for always giving us DoubleMint gum and being called The Old Goat by our dad), is tending his hole in the ice, with his minnow bucket nearby. That's Dad at the far left, making another hole in the ice, with Diane and Susan looking on.

Salmon Steak with Sweet-Sour Pea Juice Sauce

We'll let our Mom tell you about this recipe from the late '40s:

"Years ago, when I was a newlywed, a very favorite company dinner was salmon steak. I bought them fresh in the meat case. I would broil the steaks with melted butter (poured over them) and salt and pepper. I served them with this sauce."

4 salmon steaks

Sweet-Sour Pea Juice Sauce for Broiled Salmon:

2 tablespoons butter

2 tablespoons flour

½ teaspoon salt

¼ teaspoon pepper

1 cup hot canned pea juice (or other vegetable liquid or soup stock)*

2 tablespoons sugar

2 tablespoons vinegar

Brown butter well over low heat. Stir in flour and let brown slightly and add salt and pepper. Stir in ⅔ cup of the hot liquid, let thicken, then stir in the rest. Add sugar and vinegar and cook over medium heat until sauce has thickened and you can't detect the vinegar fumes. You may want to add the sugar and vinegar in smaller (but equal) quantities and adjust this to your taste. (*I made this sauce and thought it was lovely as is.*—Susan)

The sauce was served on the side, so it was optional whether you put it on the salmon or not.

*A can of peas has a scant ⅔ cup of liquid. You can freeze the juice until you have enough, or add stock (or water) to make 1 cup.—Susan

Lobster Tails

We used to eat lobster on a fairly regular basis. Remember the melted butter in little shot glasses?—*Julie*

There was a time, during the building boom of the late '50s and early '60s (our Dad built houses) when this little treat was no stranger to the Sanvidge table. We loved it and still do.—*Susan*

We would go up to Grandma and Grandpa Noffke's cottage at Three Lakes every August to buy our school clothes in Rhinelander. I remember almost always having lobster for one of the meals.—*Jean*

Mom bought the lobster tails frozen, put them in boiling water, reduced the heat to a simmer, drained, and served the lobster tails with melted butter in little shot glasses.

T-Bone Steak

We had T-bone steaks pretty often in the Lobster Years. Mom thinks a good steak is a well-done steak. Dad thinks a good steak is a rare steak, so . . . —*Susan*

> **"Please pass the salt."**
> —Dad and Jean

Broil the steaks under the watchful eyes of all the other members of the household who do not like them the way you do. Serve with baked potatoes and French-cut green beans or a Basic Mom Salad (see page 76).

Mister Pester

One of the drawbacks of Dad being in business for himself is that he spent most of his evenings seeing customers. One of these customers would always come just before supper and talk and talk and talk. We would make as much noise as we could when we set the table, so he might get the hint. I'm sure that Mom cringed at our antics. We dubbed him "Mister Pester."—*Jean*

"Maybe if we rattle the silverware again . . ."

Spamwiches

This recipe is one of Mom's "latter-day" concoctions (after moving up north). She got the recipe from Lumina Brazeau, the organist at St. Stanislaus Church up north. This recipe makes enough for four sandwiches, but you can get twelve sandwiches out of one can of Spam.—*Jean*

I was in the church choir (yes, me) when Lumina was the organist, and one time I must not have been singing loud enough for her. She turned slightly on her stool and shouted, "Sing it, Sammich!"—*Julie*

> 2 half-inch-thick slices of Spam, cubed
> 2 quarter-inch-thick slices of Cheddar cheese, cubed
> 1 hard-boiled egg, chopped (Mom often leaves this out.)
> a little diced onion
> 2 to 3 tablespoons mayonnaise (will need 3 if using the egg)
> 1 tablespoon ketchup
> ½ teaspoon prepared yellow mustard
> 4 hamburger buns

Preheat oven to 350°. Combine Spam and Cheddar cheese in a bowl. Add the boiled egg (unless you're Mom) and onion (unless you're Susie). In a small bowl, stir mayonnaise, ketchup (unless you're Jean), and mustard together. Add to rest of ingredients. Put filling in buns and wrap each bun individually in foil. Bake for 15 minutes.

Sloppy Joes (also known as "Joosburgers")

Mom made a batch of these for our cousin Carol's wedding shower. I hope the guests weren't too dressed up. This will make a *lot* of Sloppy Joes.—*Susan*

1 cup finely chopped onion

2 tablespoons butter

4 pounds ground beef

1 bottle (14 ounces) ketchup

1 cup water

½ cup finely chopped celery

¼ cup lemon juice

2 tablespoons brown sugar

1 tablespoon Worcestershire sauce

1 tablespoon salt

2 teaspoons vinegar

½ teaspoon dry mustard

hamburger buns

In a small frying pan, sauté onions in butter until transparent. Brown the ground beef gently in a large stainless steel frying pan until no pink is left, breaking down the chunks as you are moving the meat around. Drain off excess fat. Add the sautéed onions (do not drain off the butter). Combine the rest of the ingredients and stir into browned meat. Cover and simmer on medium heat, stirring frequently, for 30 minutes. Serve on store-bought hamburger buns. This recipe can be made ahead and reheated. It's one of those recipes that tastes better on the second day.

Get out a big pile of napkins. Can't you just feel the "joos" dripping down your chin?
—Susan

Glorified Hamburgers

How is it possible that adding liquid to ground beef patties could actually make them drier? Find out for yourself . . . —*Julie*

Preheat oven to 350°. Form 1½ pounds of ground beef into patties. Brown on both sides in a frying pan. Place in an 8 x 8-inch baking dish. Pour 1 cup of beef bouillon broth over patties. Add a few thinly sliced onions and one 4-ounce can of mushrooms, drained. Bake for 20 minutes.

To serve: Put a ground beef patty on each person's plate. Spoon the thin sauce and mushrooms over the hamburgers.

"The mushrooms are the 'glorifying' part," Susan added dryly.

Fried Pork Chops

I could eat three of these when I was very little and skinny. I even ate the fat.
—*Susan*

Sprinkle pork chops with salt and pepper to taste. Brown in a little Crisco in a hot skillet. Turn heat down to the lowest setting. Cover and cook very slowly until chops are well done and browned on each side.

Pizza Burgers

Was Mom trying to avoid having the messy ketchup bottle on the table when she came up with this?—*Jean*

Combine ground chuck (not as much fat as hamburger), diced onions, cubed Cheddar cheese, and ketchup. Spread on the open face of a split hamburger bun. Broil until meat is done, cheese is melted, and the pizza burgers are sizzling.

I like to put chopped green pepper in Pizza Burgers, and I turn the oven to 350° and give them about 5 more minutes to make sure the meat is done.—Jean

Jean *likes her meat more well-done than* Mom?—*Susan*

Liver Sausage (Grandma Noffke)

I called Aunt Marion for this recipe, because Uncle Hank makes it for his kids. Marion mailed a photocopy of Grandma's original recipe, which we are presenting here exactly as written. Grandma's recipe credits Lena Noffke (our great-aunt) as the person she got it from.—*Jean*

At our house, Mom would often fry up a piece of the Liver Sausage Grandma sent over for herself. (Dad was the only other person in our family who would eat it.) When Mom was growing up, Liver Sausage was fried and served with bread and butter for a simple supper, most often on Sunday when the main meal of the day was always at noon.

NOTE: There were no quantities for the seasonings on Grandma's recipe, but Marion sent Hank's amounts for making this with 20 pounds of liver, which I, Susan (an "Art Person"), converted to teaspoons and divided by five (and rounded off a little). You have been warned. I put Hank's quantities in **bold letters** after the 4-pound version. Combine all the spices (**not the amounts in boldface!**). Uncle Hank advises seasoning a small portion of the liver sausage first, frying it up and tasting it, before seasoning the whole batch.—*Susan*

"4# Pork Liver (**20 pounds**)
2# fat side pork (**10 pounds**)

Grind liver raw thru food chopper. Boil pork until done and add the juice it was boiled in. Grind also.

Add:
salt [scant 2½ teaspoons (**4 tbsp.**)
sugar [¾ cup (**4 cups**)]
black pepper [1¼ teaspoons (**2 tbsp.**)]
allspice [1½ tablespoons (**8 tbsp.**)]
cloves [½ teaspoon (**1 tbsp.**)]
cinnamon [6½ tablespoons (**33 tbsp.**)]

This is what Grandma is talking about when she says "food chopper."

Heat a few bay leaves and crush them fine. Put them in a cloth bag. About 4 slices of dry bread may be ground thru food chopper with liver. Mix all together thoroughly and add flour until like stiff cake batter. Put in casserole or any granite [enameled] cake pan and bake at 335 degrees until done. Slice and fry brown. Serve hot.

"I have some extra for you girls…"
—Kate Noffke Erick (our cousin who makes Liver Sausage, with the tongue! And **likes** it!)

It is done when liver is not red when tried with a fork."

This will look kind of like devil's food cake . . . and be quite a surprise for the unwary eater. Grandma had several different versions of the Liver Sausage recipe. One involved a hog head, two pork hearts, and two pork tongues. Mom's comment on that version: "I tell you! I hated to see those tongues cooking!" Apparently Grandma did, too.—Susan

Visiting Fritz and Lena on the Farm

One hot summer day, our parents took us to visit Fritz and Lena (brother and sister, our great-uncle and great-aunt) on their farm in Bonduel where our Grandpa Noffke grew up.

As we came out of the bright sunlight into the dim farmhouse kitchen, it was as if we had entered the past. There was a huge black cast-iron stove in the middle of the kitchen, with a stovepipe going up to the ceiling. The stove had those little circles you lift out to put in more wood. (I had seen stoves like this on TV westerns.) A wood ironing board stood next to it, and two all-black metal irons (no cords) were sitting on the big black stove. The irons had to be heated up on the stove, and there were two so one would always be heating. Lena must have had to use a potholder to iron without burning her hands. The sink was on a back wall, but instead of faucets, there was a red pump. That meant there was no hot water, so she had to heat that up on the stove, too.

Fritz and Lena led us into "the parlor" and offered us lemonade. Uncle Fritz was a gentle and likable man of average size with a nice smile. Aunt Lena was a big-boned, heavy woman with a surprisingly high voice. As we looked around the parlor we saw tall mahogany cabinets crowded with ornate china and a bay window filled with ferns and hanging plants. We sat down on the heavy horsehair sofa and jumped right back up again. (It was really scratchy, and we were wearing shorts.) We found smoother chairs, sipped our lemonade, listened to the murmur of the grown-ups talking, the buzzing of occasional flies, and looked around. This old farmhouse was probably very much the same as it was when our Grandpa was growing up.

After the visit we walked out the door into the bright sunlight and headed toward Oshkosh, electricity, plumbing, hot water, TV . . . —*Susan*

Great Aunt Lena at her old wood-burning stove. (There is a refrigerator in the pantry behind her, so Fritz and Lena must have put in electricity by the time this photo was taken. Mom says Lena still kept using the old stove.)

Blood Sausage (Mrs. Carrie Becker, Grandma Noffke's cousin who was called "Aunt Carrie" because she was so much older)

Like liver sausage, blood sausage was served as part of a simple supper. I am copying this as it was on the recipe card. After Mom found out it was actually made from blood, she never ate it again. She spared us, too.—*Susan*

"That'll put hair on your chest!"

"2 qts. hog blood. Strained. Pork from head or other fat meat. Boiled. Ground through food chopper. Mix blood, ground meat, crisps after frying out lard juice where meat was cooked in. Add stale bread when grinding meat. Salt, pepper, nutmeg, bay leaves dried in oven and crushed, sugar and flour. Try a sample [*Taking a sniff might be better—the blood is not cooked.*] and when ready, put in pans. Bake in oven till done. Fry."

Maybe you can find a volunteer to try this recipe. We couldn't.
—*Susan*

One Dish Meals

"Waste not, want not!"

"Don't waste food!" was the motto of our parents, who had gone through the Depression and World War II. Scraps of ham were used to make scalloped potatoes, leftover chicken was transformed into a savory chicken pie, and some casseroles were made from scratch. Sometimes vegetables and meat were cooked together in one pot (or frying pan) so the ingredients would flavor each other (and so there weren't so many pans to wash).—*Susan*

Chicken Pie (Mom)

This is not like frozen chicken pot pie with the dented, kelly-green peas, three peas per pie, for "color." (We had that when Dad went hunting.) This is a big, chilly-day meal, steaming hot under a crusty top. The amounts for the chicken stew part are pretty flexible, but I had to call "Mom-1-1" to find out why my crust was always uncooked on the bottom. (You will find the answer below.)—*Susan*

Chicken Stew:

about 6 carrots, peeled and sliced

about 6 smallish (or 3 medium-sized) boiling potatoes, cut up

about half of a cooked chicken, cut up, shredded (3½ cups, more or less)

leftover gravy, if you have it

pan scrapings, if it was a roast chicken

cream of chicken soup, to add if you need more gravy (Better too much gravy than not enough. There should be enough gravy that there is plenty to use on the biscuits, too.)

about 1 cup of whole-kernel corn (optional)

Baking Powder Biscuit Top:*

2 cups flour

4 teaspoons baking powder

1 teaspoon salt

2½ tablespoons Crisco

¾ cup milk

paprika

You will also need: a deep 2½- to 3-quart casserole dish

Cook the carrots and the potatoes. (Mom cooks them together and uses the cooking water as part of the gravy.) In a large pot, combine the gravy and pan scrapings. (If necessary to make more gravy: Stir in the cream of chicken soup over heat to combine.) When the gravy is hot, add chicken, cooked carrots and potatoes, and corn. Simmer to heat everything and season to taste. (Secret: The stew has to be HOT when you bake the crust, because you are baking ONLY the crust.) Have casserole dish ready.

Preheat oven to 450°. Sift flour, baking powder, and salt together into a mixing bowl. Cut the shortening into the flour with a fork. Make a well in the center. Pour in the milk all at once and stir only until moistened. Roll out on floured surface to diameter of casserole dish. (*I use the casserole dish lid to help make it the right size.—Susan*)

Pour hot stew into casserole dish. Lay biscuit carefully on top. Cut vents. Shake on a little paprika. Bake until top is golden and cooked through, 10 to 15 minutes. (Put something under it if you don't love to clean your oven.)

You could use Bisquick to make this (following the directions on the package).

Beef or Pork Pie

"When in doubt, throw it out!"

Leftover beef or pork roast can be transformed into a savory pie, too.—*Susan*

Follow the chicken pie recipe above, substituting cream of mushroom soup to supplement the leftover meat gravy. Peas can be substituted for the corn in the chicken pie recipe.

Chicken and Broccoli

We ate a lot of casseroles! I love this recipe so much that I made it for brunch the day after my wedding. It can be assembled ahead of time and baked at the last minute. The inclusion of curry powder is an exotic surprise in the Sanvidge kitchen!*—*Julie*

We didn't have casseroles very often because Dad didn't like them.—*Jean*

Cooking for six, then three, may account for this difference! —*Susan*

2 packages (16 ounces total) frozen broccoli
1½ to 2 cups leftover cooked chicken, cut up

1 can cream of chicken soup

1 cup sour cream

2 cups grated sharp Cheddar cheese (divided: 1½ cups for sauce, ½ cup for topping)

1 teaspoon curry powder

3 cups cubed bread tossed with 3 tablespoons melted butter or margarine

Preheat oven to 350°. Cook frozen broccoli as directed and drain. Put broccoli in the bottom of a 9 x 13-inch cake pan or casserole dish. Cover with a layer of chicken.

In a medium bowl, stir together cream of chicken soup, sour cream, 1½ cups of the Cheddar cheese, and curry powder. Spread over the chicken and broccoli.

Sprinkle remaining ½ cup Cheddar cheese over the top. Add buttered bread cubes on top. Bake uncovered for 30 minutes. (Can be assembled a day ahead.)

If you want to use fresh broccoli: Cut one bunch of broccoli into florets. Put into a saucepan with a small amount of water, cover, and cook until tender.—Julie

**Mom was looking over this recipe and guess what she said?
"I eliminated the curry powder."*

Old Spices

I think it's time for this little story. In our Bowen Street kitchen, the spices were in a very high cabinet *above* the refrigerator. (You had to climb on a chair to reach them.) After Mom, Dad, and Julie moved up north, the spices were put in a cabinet *above* the stove hood, barely reachable. I think Mom's placement of the spices is symbolic of her attitude towards them: They are just too much trouble.

Mom will buy spices and herbs to try a new recipe (and later leave them out), so there really are lots of little boxes and jars up in that cupboard, but . . . you may want to check the expiration dates. Some of those quaint little containers would be welcomed with open arms at the antique mall.—*Susan*

Ground Beef and Mashed Potato Casserole
(Ginny Lux)

Dad didn't like this one at first (but later he did), so Mom would make it only when he went hunting.—*Julie*

This small-size casserole was made after some of us had left home. Ginny Lux was our neighbor and the mother of our playmates and longtime friends Patsy and Mary Lou.—*Susan*

1 can (14.5 ounces) green beans, drained

1 pound ground beef, well-browned and drained

1 can Campbell's tomato soup

mashed potatoes (enough for an inch-thick layer)*

2 tablespoons butter

paprika

Preheat oven to 350°. Put green beans in bottom of a shallow 9 x 9-inch baking dish. Top with a layer of ground beef, layer of tomato soup, and a layer of mashed potatoes. Dot top with butter and sprinkle with paprika. Cover with foil. Bake until heated through, about 30 minutes. (Remove foil for the last 5 minutes to lightly brown the top.)

Originally the recipe called for "box potatoes," but Mom makes the mashed potatoes fresh.

Scalloped Potatoes and Ham

If you have some leftover ham, this is a way you can use it. This is a satisfying meal for a cold day.—*Jean*

¼ cup (4 tablespoons) butter

¼ cup flour

2 cups hot whole or 2% milk

¼ teaspoon white pepper

salt to taste

4 cups peeled and sliced (about ⅛ inch thick) raw potatoes (the brown kind),
   blotted dry (3 large or 4 medium)

leftover ham, cut into pieces (about ¾ pound)

Melt the butter in a saucepan over low heat. Whisk in the flour until mixed well and cook until it starts to bubble a little. Stir in the hot milk gradually and cook over low heat, stirring constantly, until the mixture thickens. Add the white pepper and salt to taste. (Remember that the ham is salty.) Set aside.

Preheat oven to 350° and butter a shallow 2-quart casserole dish. Place one-third of the potatoes at the bottom and cover with half of the ham. Cover with one-third of white sauce. Make the second layer with another third of the potatoes, the remaining ham, and another third of the sauce. Top with the rest of the potatoes and cover with the remaining sauce. Bake until potatoes can be pierced with a fork and top is slightly browned, about 1 to 1½ hours.

Lasagna (Mom)

Please note: There is not one drop of Italian blood in our family.—*Susan*

1 pound (or a little more) ground beef
1 can (28 ounces) diced tomatoes
1 can (14.5 ounces) seasoned tomato sauce
salt to taste
9 lasagna noodles
6 to 8 ounces thin-sliced mozzarella cheese
1 cup cream-style cottage cheese
½ cup grated Parmesan cheese

Brown meat slowly. Spoon off fat. Add tomatoes and tomato sauce and simmer for 40 minutes, stirring occasionally. Salt to taste.

Cook noodles in boiling, salted water. Drain well.

Preheat oven to 350°. Butter an 11½ x 13-inch pan. Spread a little sauce in the bottom of the pan and lay in 3 noodles. Cover with one-third of the sauce, one-third of the mozzarella, and half of the cottage cheese. Put on 3 more noodles and repeat the layers. Add the last 3 noodles. Cover with the remaining sauce and mozzarella. Top with Parmesan cheese. Bake until cheese is melted and sauce is bubbling, about 30 minutes.

What's been in the Sanvidge cupboard since the 1970s?

The Money Jar—*"Six dollars. Do I really have to split it seven ways?" "Let's see . . . crackers . . . cake mix . . . There It Is!" "I'm over thirty and I still look for the Money Jar."—Diane (quoting the oldest grandchild)*

Baked Pork Chops with Creamed Corn

This "down-home" style, simple casserole was liked by all of us, except Julie. She wrote, "This is awful. Do not make this!" on the recipe card. (Mom and Jean made this again recently, and *they* both still like it.)—*Susan*

pork chops (as many as you need, but they should fit the frying pan in one layer)
salt and pepper
1 cup cubed soft bread
⅓ cup whole or 2% milk

1 egg

1 can (15 ounces) creamed corn

You will also need: a large cast-iron frying pan

Preheat oven to 325°. Salt and pepper the uncooked pork chops and put them into the frying pan in one layer. Mix the rest of the ingredients to make a dressing. Spread over the pork chops. Bake until the top is golden brown and pork chops are cooked through, 1 to 1½ hours.

"Use your judgment."

—Mom

Pork Chops and Rice

I make this a lot. It's easy and it's good. Even Susie likes it.—*Jean*

8 pork chops

2 cans cream of chicken soup

2 cups uncooked white rice

4 cups water

small can of mushroom stems and pieces, drained (optional)

Preheat oven to 325°. Place the pork chops in a 9 x 13-inch pan or casserole dish. (Make sure this is deep enough, because rice will double in volume.) Spread soup on top of the pork chops. Bake, covered, for 1 hour.

Turn oven up to 350°. Remove pork chops from pan and set aside. Add rice and water to pan. (If using mushrooms, add them now.) Stir. Lay pork chops on top and bake until rice is cooked, about 30 minutes.

Did you know that . . .

. . . Mom doesn't like to see the milk carton or bottle on the table? It was a rule when she was growing up.

Green Beans with Pork (Mom)

You can have your barely cooked, crisp, and lightly dressed green beans. This is home-cooking!—*Julie*

Brown some pork chops in a Dutch oven over medium-high heat. When they've given off a little fat to grease the pan, add a sliced onion or two and finish browning. Add water to about ¾ inch in the pan and put in one chicken bouillon cube. Top with a big mess of fresh green beans that have had the stems and tails removed. You can crowd the pan to the top with the beans because they really cook down. Bring to a boil, cover, and turn heat down to a low simmer. Cook for about 3 hours, adding peeled, halved all-purpose potatoes in the last half hour.

Take care to purchase stringless beans—I didn't once, and it was like eating a plate of shoelaces! In recent years, I have been substituting little red potatoes and, in the last 15 minutes or so of cooking, sprinkling the top with one ripe tomato, diced. It makes this very tasty dish a little brighter, to the eye and to the palate.—Julie

New England Boiled Dinner (Mom)

If we find out that the cast aluminum Dutch oven that Mom has been using for all these recipes for fifty-plus years is actually leaching harmful molecules into our food, we are all in big trouble. My sisters may disagree, but I don't remember this meal showing up until we moved up north.—*Julie*

In a Dutch oven, place the following: the last meaty remnants of a big bone-in ham; one green cabbage, quartered; some peeled, all-purpose potatoes; a few stalks of celery cut in half; a few carrots pared and cut in half; two sliced onions; and water to about 3 inches in the pot. Bring to a boil, cover tightly, and reduce heat to a simmer. Cook on very low heat for 3 hours on top of the stove and serve in a deep serving dish. You're going to want to put some of that "pot likker" on your smashed-up potatoes. Just an observation. Mom always mashes her cabbage into the potatoes on her plate and puts a little of the juice and some butter on top.

I've always loved the name of this recipe. I even liked the colors, the pink ham, orange carrots, and pale green celery and cabbage, but I didn't like to eat it. We definitely had it in Oshkosh, or I wouldn't remember not liking it. (I never lived up north.) —Susie, the Picky Eater

"Don't you want to belong to the Clean Plate Club?"

Sauerkraut with Pork (Mom)

If you don't want to stink up the house, make this in a slow cooker out in the garage.—*Julie*

Get a package of the leanest, meatiest country-style pork ribs you can find. Brown them well in a Dutch oven and pour off any excess grease. Pepper the meat, but don't use salt. Pour a 1-quart jar or can of sauerkraut on top of the pork and spread it over the meat. Cover with water and put in 2 tablespoons brown sugar. Simmer on low heat for 2 hours. Add peeled, cut-up, all-purpose potatoes and cook until potatoes can be pierced with a fork, 25 to 30 minutes.

If you want everything to look richer, stir in a few drops of Kitchen Bouquet when it's all done. It works wonders.

To make this less fattening, I use a 2-pound pork loin roast. Place in a slow cooker (no browning necessary), add sliced onions, ½ cup water, and top with drained sauerkraut and little red potatoes. Sprinkle with a good bit of black pepper. Cook all day on low—you'll think Mom is right there in your kitchen.—Julie

Old sauerkraut cutter

Let's Have a Sauerkraut Party!!

Mom and Dad acquired an antique sauerkraut cutter from Dad's cousin, Marvin "Plunk" Safford, and several large crocks from Grandma Noffke. Mom and Dad moved the picnic table into the garage, invited their friends over to take turns cutting the cabbage, packing it into the crocks, and to have a little liquid refreshment, too! Some people brought their own cabbage cutters, and Marv Zaddack's great garden supplied the cabbages. When the kraut had cured, it was time to divide it up among the *krautmeisters*, package it, eat a potluck supper, and have another drink!

The dates and proportions are still written on the garage wall:

"October 9th: cut the cabbage.

Heaping 5 qt. ice cream bucket shredded cabbage to scant ¼ c. salt.

December 14th: Bag to freeze."—*Julie*

When Mom was little, her family made sauerkraut in the attic of the coal yard office so it wouldn't smell up the house. Mom says: "Grandpa shredded; Grandma seasoned; the kids 'smacked it down.'"—Susan

A sauerkraut party in the garage up north. People have brought large stoneware crocks inherited from their parents, and sometimes really old cutters, but the lady here is slaving away with a knife on our picnic table. The men leaning over the crock in the background are packing the cabbage tightly. (Getting the stinky cabbage ready was not the fun part of the party, even with an accordian playing.) When the cutting and packing are done, there are Sloppy Joes, potato salad, and cold beer waiting on the workbench. There'll be another party when the kraut has "worked" and is ready to package up and take home.

Our "Saturday-Night-In" Dinner

We had this on Mom and Dad's occasional Saturday night out (often to The Roxy). Frozen dinners were a fairly novel thing in the '50s. They were tasty and reasonably priced, and the aluminum tins could be discarded, which meant no dishes to wash!—*Jean*

Buy as many Swanson's Chicken Pot Pies* or Chicken Dinners as you have children. (Get the kind with the mashed potatoes, corn, and little section with the cinnamon apple dessert that always burns your tongue.) Follow directions on package. Tell the babysitter to listen for the timer.

And save the little round tins for me to make pies in the sandbox!—Julie

On those evenings, Aunt Emma often babysat for us, which we enjoyed—unless she wanted to watch boxing on TV. I can still hear that Gillette theme song when I think of it. Aunt Emma would let us stay up until we heard the car come in the driveway. We'd tear off to our beds, sure to turn our faces to the wall so we wouldn't give ourselves away.—Jean

I'm sorry to say that I don't remember being quite that savvy when the headlights streaked across the darkened (Aunt Emma–style) living room. I'm pretty sure we all thought fake snoring (literally "honk-phew") would be very convincing.—Susan

I remember "All Star Wrestling"! Mad Dog Vichon and the Crusher, etc. I'm sure if a boxing match had been on, she would have watched that, too! She used to ask me what time I planned to go to bed. "Midnight!" "OK, that's your bedtime, kid!"—Julie

Up North

"Hurry up! Dad's getting antsy."

Time to get away, slow down, relax the rules. Whether it was camping in our old bus, weekends at our cottage, or trips up to Grandma and Grandpa Noffke's cottage, the atmosphere was relaxed, and so were the meals. For all of us, except Dad who hated eating outside because of the bugs, food tasted soooo much better in the fresh air! *Girls, set the picnic table.*—Jean

Tuna Noodle Casserole

This was a frequent Friday dish. When we traveled in our bus, Mom would put a Tuna Noodle Casserole in the old icebox; after the cottage was built, a newspaper-wrapped Tuna Noodle Casserole would be put in the car to eat when we stopped at a halfway point, so Dad could go fishing the moment we got there.—*Jean*

1 can (6 ounces) tuna, drained

1 can (10¾ ounces) cream of mushroom soup

¾ cup whole or 2% milk

3 cups uncooked egg noodles (8-ounce package)

1 can (15 ounces) peas, drained (*Mom used early June peas.—Jean*)

1 cup crushed potato chips

Picture this in a can.

Put a kettle of water on to boil for the noodles. Combine tuna, cream of mushroom soup, and milk in a saucepan. Stir and heat. Cook noodles according to directions on package. Preheat oven to 350°. Rinse noodles with hot water and drain well.

Grease a 2-quart baking dish. In the bottom of the dish, put half of the cooked noodles, half of the peas, and half of the liquid mixture. Put in the rest of the noodles, peas, and liquid mixture. Stir a little to make sure the sauce is distributed. Cover with potato chips. Bake uncovered for 30 minutes.

"Red Rover"

In the mid '50s, before we had the cottage, we traveled from trout stream to trout stream in an elderly city bus that Dad had converted into an early form of an RV. (This was so unusual at the time that there was an article about us in the *Oshkosh Daily Northwestern,* with a photograph of our family in the bus.)

Our bus, Red Rover (which seems to have been originally named The Rover), in our Oshkosh driveway. (Left to right: Diane, Susan, Jean; our little neighbor Howie Jones is in front.) After Julie was born, our family didn't fit in the bus anymore, and Dad built the cottage up north.

Dad took all of the seats out except for the two that face each other in the front (so we would have a place to sit while traveling) and the long one across the back (which became a bed for Jean, who was still in the toddler stage). He installed a double bed right next to Jean's for Mom and himself and another double bed above it (like a bunk bed) for Diane and me. We would stand on Mom and Dad's bed, grab the hold-on bars (from the original bus), and swing ourselves up like monkeys.

In the middle part of the bus, Dad built plywood storage cupboards above the windows (like on an airplane), and on one side he made a linoleum countertop with cupboards below. The stove and icebox were on the other side. Mom made it feel homey with little print curtains.

It was like traveling in a time warp. A big old-fashioned milk can held our water supply and provided a much-fought-over seat next to Dad, our "bus driver." The icebox was exactly that, and we had to scout out obscure places in the countryside with deep pits of sawdust where they stored blocks of ice. (Diane has an ice tongs scar she'll show you.) The stove was a tiny gas model (the tank was on the outside of the bus) and the toaster was the on-the-stove kind you see at the antique mall. The dishwasher was Mom, using water from the big milk can, heated on the tiny stove, and an enameled dishpan. You can see why Mom didn't want to do much cooking on the bus.

Our trips in the bus were always an adventure. We made it through a windstorm with the bus swaying and trees falling down all around us. Another time we had to leave in the middle of the night when a group of drunken men tried to get into the bus. (They insisted on seeing what the bus looked like inside, and Dad had to shoot his pistol in the air to get them to leave.) Once the hook of a trout fly got caught in Diane's head, and another time we had to get back into the bus very carefully when we spotted a big rattlesnake (a pine rattler, we think). We even had a skunk settle in under the bus door.

We went to campsites and parked the bus in pastures (with lots of dried "cow pies") near trout streams when Dad got permission from the farmer. There would be gates to open all the way down the little winding roads. We loved it when we went through a town and someone thought it was a real bus and tried to get on!

We listened to old 78s on a wind-up Victrola (a relic from Mom's childhood), played games, and explored each new campsite. There were trips with Grandma and Grandpa Sanvidge, Lester and Jean Grose, our "John and Jack(ie)" cousins (John had outfitted a Greyhound bus for his family), and the Sawicki family. Once we went to a drive-in movie, *Song of the South*. Dad backed in and we watched the movie out the back window from the bed while Mom made us popcorn on the stove, right there in the bus.—*Susan*

Apple Slices

Jean Grose, the wife of Dad's mason and fly-fishing mentor, Lester Grose, was a very welcome guest at our cottage. She was a really nice lady, and—she always brought a huge pan of her very popular Apple Slices. Later, Dad started making Apple Slices too, but he always waited for me to frost them.

I called Jean's daughter, Marge, to get her mom's recipe, but sadly, she never wrote it down. Marge did remember the list of ingredients; that McIntosh apples were the kind her mother used; and that her mother had always frosted the Apple Slices while they were still hot. I made them to determine the ingredient amounts.
—Jean

YOU CAN CUT THIS INTO 24 SLICES FOR NORMAL APPETITES OR 15 IF YOU LIKE THEM AS BIG AS WE DO.

Crust:

5 cups flour

1 teaspoon salt

1¾ cups shortening (Crisco)

about 12 to 13 tablespoons cold water (Stop adding water when dough forms a ball.)

Filling:

9 to 10 McIntosh apples (a sweet apple)

about ¾ cup sugar (amount will depend on sweetness of the apples)

1 teaspoon cinnamon

3 tablespoons flour

3 tablespoons butter

Frosting:

2 cups sifted powdered sugar

1 teaspoon vanilla

3 tablespoons whole or 2% milk

You will also need: an 11 x 17-inch jelly roll pan

Mix flour and salt in a bowl. Cut in shortening with a pastry blender or fork until it forms small crumbles. Sprinkle water, a tablespoon at a time, mixing until dough forms a ball. Divide dough into two flat rectangular shapes (one a bit bigger than the other—for the bottom). Wrap individually in plastic wrap and chill.

On a floured sheet of waxed paper, roll out the larger piece of pie dough to fit the bottom and sides of the jelly roll pan. (It's easiest to do this if you fold it in half before moving it.) There should be enough dough on the sides to be able to pinch together when you put on the top crust.

Peel and slice the apples. (Taste a piece to see how much sugar you will need.) Stir sugar and cinnamon in with apples. Sprinkle in the flour and stir to distribute. Put apples into dough-lined pan. Dot with butter.

On another floured sheet of waxed paper, roll out the other rectangle of pie dough to fit the jelly roll pan and place on top of the apples. Crimp edges on all sides and cut some slits in the top crust. Chill while preheating oven to 375°.

Bake until crust is lightly browned, 50 to 60 minutes. If the crust is browning too quickly, reduce the heat to 350° for the last 10 minutes.

While Apple Slices are baking, combine the frosting ingredients and stir until smooth. Frost Apple Slices while still hot.

What makes Apple Slices more than just a big pie? The frosting is one thing, and most of the rectangular pieces have no outside crust to deal with, so they're "all pie." —Susan

Save me the crust pieces!—Jean

"It's a Dessert!" Fruit Cocktail

If Jean Grose is not coming with her big tray of gorgeous Apple Slices, this could be the "treat" at the end of a meal in the bus.)—*Susan*

Open the can and dump it into a mixing bowl. (*Sigh.*)

High on the Hog

Diane and I drew a complete blank when we tried to think of the food we had when we went on camping trips in our converted bus, so I decided to ask Donna Sawicki, whose family went camping with us. She couldn't remember anything special, but each family brought their own things to eat, and she thought it was the usual hamburgers-and-hot-dogs type of food. She did say that Mom had shared a lot of dessert recipes over the years and that Mom was a better cook than she was! She called me back a few minutes later to tell me something else she remembered. When Dad went hunting with his buddies, the Sawicki "boys," the food took a whole different turn. The men ate, as Donna said, "high on the hog." They'd buy their food the day before, and it was steak, not hot dogs, that they'd feast on!—*Jean*

Guess who's finally going to have his steak rare?

Toasted Marshmallow on a Stick
(a hamburgers-and-hot-dogs meal dessert)

A good time to use the jackknives our son-less father gave to his daughters.
—*Jean*

> Campfire marshmallows
> twigs, freshly cut
> campfire

Open up the bag of marshmallows* and have a few to get up some energy.
Look for low branches, about ¼-inch diameter, to slice off with your jackknife.
Trim the ends to a point. Push marshmallows onto the points. You can toast
them to a golden brown on the edges or let them catch on fire and turn pitch
black. It's up to you.

Much better when they came in little paper-covered boxes and weren't so squishy.
—*Diane*

Cinnamon Buns (Grandma Sanvidge)

Grandma would bring these along when she and Grandpa came up north, and we'd eat them all weekend. If there were any left by Sunday morning, they'd be a little stale, but the cinnamon sugar and butter had gotten extra soft and "carmelly" by then. Mmmm. Grandma used something called hot roll mix in later years to make these. This is how I make them—Cousin Ken says they're just like Grandma's.—*Julie*

Get as many bags of frozen bread dough balls as you will need. (They usually come 36 to a bag and would turn into dinner rolls if you let them. If you can't find the dough balls, you can use frozen bread dough loaves, figuring that every loaf makes about 12 medium-sized rolls.) Defrost the dough balls in a well-greased 9 x 13-inch pan, keeping them covered with plastic wrap during the process. When they are defrosted and have risen, form each ball into a "snake" about 5 inches long by rolling it between your palms. Dip in a mixture of melted but slightly cooled butter and margarine,* then coat with a cinnamon sugar mixture. (*Putting the cinnamon sugar in a shaker makes this easier.—Jean*) Knot them and place them back in the greased pan. Don't crowd them—about 16 rolls fit in a pan. Let rise and then bake at 375° for about 20 minutes, or until not doughy or burned!

About the butter and margarine: If you use all butter, they burn before they are done. I think Grandma used "olie."—Julie

Getting Away from It All

Dad has always been a man who knows the importance of playtime. (Trout fishing is his favorite playtime activity.)

During the week, Dad was a busy contractor and carpenter. After being on the job all day, he willingly spent his few waking hours at home seeing customers, doing his bookkeeping, drawing house plans, estimating jobs, and (not so willingly) returning and answering phone calls. He hated the phone.

But the weekends were another story. It was time to escape to a place where the phone couldn't ring. After Julie was born, we were cramped for space in "Red Rover," our old bus, and it was time for a safer, more permanent location. Dad found land for sale up north on the Wolf River, near one of our former "bus stops," and bought it. Then Dad and his crew built us a cottage.

Our cottage had dark red shingles and white trim. Inside were two bedrooms (ours was furnished with a Dad invention—a double-bed bunk bed); a bathroom; a long combined kitchen and living room with a fireplace at the end; and *no telephone*. All of the walls were covered in knotty pine. The cottage was built on high ground next to a steep slope, and below it ran the beautiful river. Around the cottage were trees of all shapes and sizes. Dad bought a thousand little Norway pines (the baby trees all fit in the trunk of the car) and hired our neighbor, "Grandpa" August Buettner, to plant them in the woods.

"Getting away" for Mom wasn't quite the relaxing time it was for Dad and us girls. She was taking care of *two* houses. As Friday approached, Mom had to make sure she had planned the meals for the weekend, bought the groceries to take along, and done the laundry to make sure we had clothes to pack. Mom always wanted to "come home to a clean house," so she cleaned the house, too. Then she packed everything up for the trip and had us all ready to leave by 4 o'clock when Dad got home. Once we reached our destination, she served a hasty simple supper (if we hadn't eaten supper on the way), so Dad could head off to fish.

There was plenty to keep us occupied up north: playing with the Peters girls; picking bouquets of wildflowers, looking for four-leafed clovers, or making maple leaf necklaces; swimming, rock-hopping, or playing in the woods; reading comic books or playing cards and games; sitting on a blanket looking for satellites in the pitch black night sky; finding "pictures" in the knotty pine paneling; and eating at the picnic table.—*Jean*

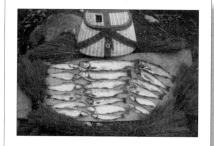

Dad's creel and a catch of trout from the Wolf River.

Pan-Fried Trout

Jean and I gave fishing a try for a while. Dad set us up with our own fishing rods, spinning reels, and little tackle boxes. (I still have my rod and reel, a pink "Princess" model, and the jackknife Dad gave me to put in my tackle box.) When we were very young, we used Dad's little wooden ice fishing poles (just our size) for summer fishing. It was Dad's Rule that you had to bait your own hooks and clean your own fish. (By the time I was eleven or twelve, I was too squeamish to do any of this.)

I remember the first trout I ever caught. I cleaned it, took it up to the cottage right away, fried it, and ate it.—*Susan*

Scrape the little scales from the sides of the cleaned (*headless, please!*) trout. Rinse and dry the trout. Dip it into a mixture of flour and salt and pepper. Heat up a cast-iron frying pan and put in some Crisco. (*I used butter for my trout.—Susan*) Fry the trout on both sides.

"Gosh oh fishhooks!"
—Grandma Noffke

Cold Cuts and Fresh Fruit Platter
(for a Hot Summer Day at the Cottage)

Our mom always taught us to make the best of a situation, so . . . on a hot summer day, when Dad was off fishing, why heat up the house by turning on the stove or oven?—*Jean*

Out from the fridge would come white waxy paper-wrapped packages full of luncheon meat.

The unwrapped parcels revealed:

turkey, thinly sliced

chicken

ham

(Skip the olive loaf—none of us girls liked that.)

Mom would arrange the meat slices on one end of a big platter with:

crispy lettuce (must not have been from the garden)

ripe red tomatoes, sliced (must have been from our garden—not store-
   bought)

Fresh fruit was always a favorite at our house and a great accompaniment to cold-cut sandwiches. The fruit on the platter could include:

watermelon (Mom would thump to check for ripeness.)

cantaloupe (She would look for one with no green and a sweet smell.)

strawberries (her favorite)

green grapes (if they were in season and not too expensive)

Mom cut up the watermelon and cantaloupe in hunks, washed the strawberries (leaving the tops on), and rinsed the grapes. She cut the bunch of grapes in small clusters and arranged the fruit on the other end of the platter.

Then she would get out the:
Miracle Whip (and butter for Susie)
bakery buns (the best Mom could buy)

And . . . tell us to carry the paper plates, cups, and napkins out to the picnic table.—*Jean*

The Cottage Kitchen

A red bandana-print oilcloth on the table; a floor that looks like river pebbles; jadeite cups; an old-time refrigerator with a potato bin in the bottom; Fizzies; grape pop; little boxes of Kellogg's cereal; dinners with the Peters family with kids at one house, parents at the other; Jean Grose's Apple Slices; ice-cold tap water straight from the well.—*Julie*

Broiled Trout

Dad always brought his catch back already cleaned and gutted (or we wouldn't have had trout so often).—*Julie*

Take some cleaned, beheaded, scaled trout and put them in a well-cleaned sink. Cover with cold, salted water. Let them sit there for a half-hour or so—a process that we think makes it all taste less fishy. Line a broiler pan with foil and heat up the broiler. Lay the trout open, skin side down. Brush with ¼ cup melted butter or "olie" mixed with the juice of one lemon (for four to six trout). Salt and pepper the trout well. Broil 'em, but watch 'em like a hawk because they can go from perfect to too-done in a flash. Garnish with lemon slices and serve immediately. A little soy sauce is a nice accompaniment.

Dad's Smoked Trout

This is a mysterious process that involves a shoebox-sized, sheet-metal smoker unit that Dad has had for years. It is the best smoked trout you ever had. You'll have to get the details from Dad.—*Julie*

Put some denatured alcohol in a little thingy. In another little thingy, put some kind of sawdust. You might have to dampen the sawdust. I can't remember—ask Dad. Put a couple of trout in there (not real big ones) on the little grate and slide the cover shut. Put the smoker unit on the sidewalk by the garage. Light the alcohol and warn the little kids that "That damn thing is hot!" and "Don't touch it!" Wait a certain amount of time—ask Dad— and remove the trout. Eat every last bit, cold or hot.

"I Scream, You Scream, We All Scream for . . ."

If we timed our chorus of "Ticka-ticka-ticka" (to sound like a directional signal) just right, we might get Dad to stop at Pierre's store in Leeman for ice cream cones. We always had better luck coming back on Sundays, when there was even time to stop and look for deer, than on Fridays, when "trout fever" ruled.

If we were successful, we'd all enter the quaint country store hoping to see *Mrs. Pierre*, who was much more generous with her scoops than her husband, who probably paid the bills.—*Jean*

Kraft Macaroni and Cheese with Tuna

What's in that knotty pine cupboard? A package of macaroni and cheese and a can of tuna! Did we remember to buy milk and butter on the way up here? Yes! (The color combination is a little odd, but this is better than it sounds.)—*Susan*

"The Indian reservation has seen a lot of Sanvidge recipes… second-hand. (Please pass the Dramamine.)" –Diane

Make the Kraft Macaroni and Cheese (Original Flavor: "The Cheesiest") according to the package directions. After it is all mixed, toss in one can of tuna, drained. (Make sure you have removed any evidence that tuna is a fish.) Stir and heat until warm.

A Week at Three Lakes

Many summers in August, Mom drove us girls up to Grandma and Grandpa Noffke's cottage in Three Lakes. On one of these trips, I brought along a small toad that managed to get loose on the floor in the front seat of the car while Mom was driving—not a good idea! Needless to say, the toad was dropped off before Three Lakes, probably next to one of those Burma Shave signs. Mom would leave us at Three Lakes and head back to be with Dad.

Some of the memories of those times include hot chocolate in cute little mugs; berry-picking with Grandpa; playing Uncle Wiggly; reading *Mrs. Ticklefeather*; giggling with Cile; Grandpa in his rocker, smoking his pipe and listening to a baseball game on the big old radio; the badger pelt above the fireplace; the smell of the hemlock trees; rides on the wood carrier (which I now have); the old sharpening grinder; swimming at Telling's beach; playing on that big swing set; long walks to the mailbox; the white arrow name signs; the cozy bedroom in the unfinished attic; morning light shining off Laurel Lake, dazzling us awake; shopping

for school clothes in Rhinelander; the old-fashioned telephone for direct calls to Grandma's friend "Telling"; hollow glass horsehead bookends filled with colored cottonballs; the metal sailboat on a lake of blue glass; the white log bridge to the "island" with the white Adirondack chairs.—*Jean*

When I was four, I spent four months in Three Lakes with Grandma, Grandpa, and Cile. Grandpa took me with him to taverns and bought me grape pop and Bun bars. If I wanted three pork chops, I got three pork chops. Milk-cooked rice with maple syrup was my favorite dessert, so that's what we had. Grandma and Cile played games with me and read to me. I have those glass horseheads (Thank you, Diane.) and Mrs. Ticklefeather (Thank you, Jean.), and one of the chairs is in my attic. (Thank you, Mom.) The rest of that cottage is in my head forever.—Susan

Campfire Girls Potatoes in Tinfoil Packets

We once made an attempt at "roughing it" by pitching a tent—about 5 feet from the cottage. A Campfire Girls handbook had a recipe for potatoes cooked over an open fire that we wanted to try. There was some talk about the animals that roam the woods at night. After a glance at the teeth and claws of the bear pelt on the cottage wall, we headed out into that black night, in our pajamas. There we were, in the tent, talking and giggling, lantern aglow—when we heard scraping on the canvas walls and rustling noises. We "piped down" right away! Something was scraping at the tent flap . . . (The final episode will air after this recipe.)—*Susan*

Prepare as many squares of tinfoil as you have campers. Peel and dice as many potatoes as you want, and put some on each piece of tinfoil. Dot lavishly with butter and season with salt and pepper. Wrap each package securely and put over an open fire.

After several hours, the potatoes will have the same sharp edges they had when you cut them, be exactly as raw, and have enough "smoke flavoring" to sell as a product all by itself. It's amazing! But it's not good.

. . . Could it be a BEAR*??? The tent flap is opening . . . It's Mom! (She thought this was a real stitch.)—Susan*

Venison Swiss Steak (Dad)

Dad has several tips for making this so good. First, when you bag the buck, get the skin off ASAP and get it to a meat locker as fast as possible to cool it down. This keeps it from tasting too gamy. Have your pan good and HOT and have your serving platter nice and WARM. Eat it right away! In later years, we turned a little gourmet and tried a very peppery version, which we finished off in the pan with a glug of brandy. Watch out—it might flame up!—*Julie*

Get a cast-iron frying pan good and hot with a good amount of Crisco in the bottom. Take some venison steaks—preferably the tenderloin or round steaks—and cut into cutlets. Remove all fat and gristle and pound the hell out of them with a tenderizing hammer. Mix up some flour, salt, and pepper in a shallow dish. Coat the cutlets with a bit of the seasoned flour and fry very quickly until just done. Serve immediately to all who are willing to eat it.

"Think of the starving kids in India (Africa, Biafra, Korea . . .)"

Deer Hunting Season 1972-1976

You've heard of the Million-Man March? It's what Michael Feldman of American Public Radio called deer hunting season in Wisconsin. In White Lake, it's such a big deal that kids are allowed to take the week off from school. Dad's been a hunter all of his life, but once we moved up north, our house became a very fancy hunting shack. Dad would invite his crew of hunting buddies like Marv Zaddack and Kenny Peters to start the season in style with a big breakfast in the wee, wee hours of opening day. Mom soon caught on to this and planned extended visits to see Grandma. I was old enough to do the dishes, and do the dishes I did.

The night before, Dad would get everything ready—skillets ready on the stove with Crisco and spatulas in them, table set, blaze-orange hunting clothes poised for donning the way I imagine firemen arrange their clothes at a firehouse. I'm not sure what time the buddies arrived, but by the time I woke up at 7 or so, all that was left of them was a grease-splattered stove, lots of dirty dishes, and some old coffee. By the time I'd get the mess cleaned up, they were back for a coffee break. Cookies, donuts, coffee. Another mess! Clean it up, Julie. Hey, it's 11:30, and they're back for lunch already! Vegetable soup, sandwiches, beer, a jolt of something a bit stronger perhaps, and a short nap on every

couch in the house. See ya 'round dark—have some cheese and crackers ready, hey? Clean up the lunch dishes . . . it's starting to rain and here they come! Day two? Just replay opening day, and you'll get the idea.—*Julie*

"Don't worry, Bambi, it's almost time for their coffee break."

Hot Cocoa in a Pitcher

For many years our time at the cottage was limited to weekends between May 1 (the beginning of trout season) and Labor Day (the end of trout season), but one year our parents decided that we should go up the week after Christmas. We were upset at the thought of leaving our friends and our Christmas tree. And what would we do up there in winter?

As we opened the cottage door, we found a Christmas tree! Our neighbor (and later Dad's cabinetmaker), Fritz Buettner, had turned on the heat, put up a Christmas tree, decorated it, and put presents under the tree for all of us.

What did we do up there in the winter? The boulder-studded slope down to the frozen river was a thrilling ride on our "flying saucer." There was a big, smooth hill nearby for tobogganing, a frozen lake for skating, and lots and lots of fluffy snow. To add one more thing that would make us like going to the cottage in winter (because we were going to be doing this every year), our mother made us a big pitcher of hot cocoa (the same battered aluminum pitcher that held our Kool-Aid in the summer) to drink out in the snow . . . —*Susan*

½ cup sugar

¼ cup unsweetened cocoa (We used Hershey's in the tin.)

dash of salt

⅓ cup hot water

4 cups whole or 2% milk

Mix the sugar, cocoa, and salt in a saucepan big enough to hold 4 cups of milk. Stir in hot water. Cook this mixture and stir over medium heat. Bring to a boil and then let sit for 2 minutes.

Stir in the milk and heat. Do Not Boil. Remove from heat. Pour into a pitcher and serve. (*Don't burn your tongue!*)

Popcorn à la Dad

... and Dad made us popcorn to have with our cocoa. This is one of our favorite combinations: sweet-creamy, salty-buttery. I tried to make popcorn as good as Dad's for many years, and one day I asked the Master of Popcorn how he did it.—*Susan*

Crisco or vegetable oil

WHITE popcorn kernels* (*You will never go back to the tough yellow kind.*)

butter (*Dad sometimes uses margarine.*)

You will also need: a 1½-quart saucepan with a tight-fitting lid**

Put pan on burner to start heating up (medium-high, closer to high). Melt a fullish tablespoon of Crisco, or put in enough vegetable oil to cover the bottom of the pan, a scant ⅛-inch deep. Put three popcorn kernels in the pan. These will pop when the oil is the right temperature. (*Susan does this; Dad just knows when it's right.*)

After those three kernels have popped to various obscure spots in your kitchen, put in enough popcorn to cover the bottom of the pan or a little more. Put on that tight-fitting lid and shake from time to time. When the popping stops, it's done. (Will burn if you wait too long.) Put the popcorn into a bowl.

Hot cocoa and popcorn in the snow at the cottage. Jean is facing the camera; Susan is pouring cocoa from the beat-up aluminum pitcher into Diane's cup. The popcorn has already been eaten (it was in that black roaster pan insert on the picnic table).

For the next batch, skip the three-kernel thing (you know the pan's hot) and add more shortening or oil. Let it heat a bit and put in more popcorn.

After you have enough popcorn, take the pan off the burner to cool it, turn the burner to low, and put a decent amount of butter (or margarine) into the pan. Rotate the pan to melt the butter without burning it and let it cool just slightly before putting it on the popcorn, or the popcorn will shrivel. (If you stir the butter with a table knife, it will cool the butter down and then you can use the knife to help distribute the butter in the popcorn.) Toss to mix the butter in and add salt to taste.

Dad sometimes uses "Baby Rice" white popcorn.—Jean

**A Revereware pan works great. After a few times it will be The Popcorn Pan because it will look too bad to be used for anything else.*

McDonald's . . .

It didn't take much to get Dad to stop at McDonald's on the way back from the cottage. Mom appreciated it because she didn't have to cook supper, and Dad must have enjoyed feeding his whole family for under two dollars! The only hitch was Susie, always ordering her hamburger plain, which made the "fast food" into "not-so-fast food."—Jean

Breads and Rolls

"Please pass the butter."

LaFontaine's Bakery made really, really good bread, but Mom's homemade bread was even better. She has always been a natural at baking bread. Hot, fragrant bread, right out of the oven, with the butter melting into it . . . —*Susan*

When you saw Mom's giant stainless steel bowl, it meant delicious bread was not far off.—*Julie*

Breadmaking Tips

▣ **Working with Yeast**: If you haven't made bread before, this is where it's easiest to go wrong. Too cool, and the yeast won't do anything. Too hot, and you'll kill it. The okay range is 110 to 115° ("lukewarm water"), which is a little warmer than your 98.6° finger. If you sprinkle a few grains of sugar on the yeast, you'll be able to see if it's working before you waste all that flour and time. This is called "proofing the yeast." Note that you can also kill the proofed yeast by combining it with anything that is over 115°. (Be sure to check the date on your yeast. Expired yeast won't work.)

▣ **To Make Scalded Milk**: Put milk in a pan over low heat. When small bubbles form all around the edges of the milk, it's scalded. Keep an eye on it. It can bubble over or burn very easily. (Some people define "scalded" as the stage just before it boils.)

▣ **To Measure Flour for Bread**: Our Source Authority (Mom) says she does not pre-sift the flour before she measures it— *unless the recipe calls for it.* She does sift it *after* measuring, before combining it with the other ingredients. Our mother said to tell you to buy good quality flour. (She uses Gold Medal or Robin Hood.)

▣ *Kneading*: Sprinkle countertop with some of the flour you will be kneading in and put the dough on top of it. Letting the dough sit for about 10 minutes will make it easier to handle. (Mom learned this from Aunt Emma.) Using both hands, gather the dough toward you, rotating it a little each time, then push it away firmly downward using the heels of both hands. Repeat and repeat and repeat, adding a little of the specified flour as soon as the previous added flour is kneaded in, until it is all incorporated and dough is smooth and malleable—no longer sticky. For most doughs this will be about 8 to 10 minutes—just don't exceed the specified amount of flour. (Note that *sweet* dough (with sugar and egg) can get tough with too much kneading.)

▣ *To Raise Dough*: Roll the dough ball around in the greased bowl to coat it. Put kneaded dough into bowl, cover with a dish towel, and let rise in a warm place, out of drafts. (*I put a piece of plastic wrap on the bowl, under the dish towel, to keep the dough from drying out.—Susan*)

▣ *"Punch Down"*: Use your fist to punch the dough down to the bottom of the bowl (deflating the air bubbles). This sounds counterproductive, but it improves the texture of the bread. The air bubbles will come back again, but this time they will be smaller.

▣ *How to Tell If the Bread Is Done*: It will be pulling away from the side of the pan and the crust will be golden. A little "thump" with a snapped finger should sound hollow.

White Bread (Mom)

When you see four handsome loaves of bread cooling in your kitchen, you will know it was worth every minute.—*Susan*

MAKES 4 LOAVES

¼ cup sugar

¼ cup shortening (Crisco)

4 teaspoons salt

2 cups scalded whole or 2% milk (Skim milk will not work in this recipe.)

2 packages (½ ounce total) dry yeast

2 cups lukewarm water

10 cups flour, sifted (You might need a little more if the weather is humid.)

In a large bowl, combine sugar, Crisco, and salt. Pour in the hot scalded milk and stir until Crisco is dissolved. Let cool until lukewarm.

Dissolve the yeast in lukewarm water. When first mixture (milk, sugar, shortening, salt) is lukewarm, add yeast mixture. Stir in 5 cups of the sifted flour. Beat well. Gradually beat in 4½ cups flour. (You will have to resort to kneading the flour in at some point.) Let rest in a greased bowl for 10 minutes so it will be less sticky to knead.

Punch down dough. Knead *at least* 8 minutes, incorporating remaining ½ cup flour as you knead, continuing until dough is smooth and elastic. Put dough back into greased bowl (or divide between two greased bowls if not large enough to allow doubling), cover with a dish towel, and let rise in a warm place out of drafts until doubled, about 2 hours.

Punch down dough and divide into four balls. (If you cut the dough with a serrated knife, it will be easier to make the loaves the same size.) Let dough balls rest there on the kneading surface (covered with a towel) for 30 minutes.

Grease bottom and sides of four bread pans. Punch down and shape each of the four sections of dough into a loaf by "making a pillow" of dough the length of the bread pan. Drop the dough into the pan and press down the sides and ends with the side of your hand. Let rise (in the pans) until double in size, about 1 hour. When the bread is nearly doubled, preheat oven to 400°. Bake for 35 to 40 minutes. Bread should be pulling away from the sides of the pan and golden brown on top. Remove loaves from pans and cool on a baking rack.

Mom Note: "I make braided poppy seed bread with this recipe, too. Just before putting in the oven, take an egg yolk mixed with a little water, brush on, and sprinkle with poppy seeds. Braided bread might take only a half hour to bake."

If you bake this bread as regularly as our mother did: "Make a little mark inside your flour canister or some other bowl, so you don't have to measure out 10 cups every time."

Oatmeal Bread

This is a slightly sweet and delicately textured bread, more of a breakfast and toasting bread than a sandwich bread. Rumor has it that a nun sent the recipe in to the *Oshkosh Daily Northwestern*. Mom makes this recipe a lot, and so do I.—*Susan*

MAKES 2 SMALLISH LOAVES

1½ cups old-fashioned (slow-cooking) oatmeal

⅓ cup brown sugar

1 tablespoon shortening (Crisco)

2 teaspoons salt

2 cups boiling water

1 package (¼ ounce) dry yeast

¼ cup lukewarm whole or 2% milk (Skim milk will not work in this recipe.)

1 teaspoon sugar

4 to 4½ cups flour, sifted

Combine oatmeal, brown sugar, shortening, and salt in a large bowl. Pour boiling water over all. Stir and let cool to lukewarm (about 30 minutes).

Dissolve yeast in lukewarm milk. Add sugar.

Pour yeast mixture into cooled oatmeal mixture. Gradually stir in the 4 cups of flour. If the dough becomes too difficult for you to stir at some point, you can knead the rest in. Knead in as much of the remaining ½ cup of flour as the dough will accept without starting to feel dry. This dough will usually take in the extra ½ cup of flour. Knead for about 8 minutes, until no longer sticky.

Rinse out and grease mixing bowl (if large enough to hold doubled dough). Form the dough into a ball and rub the top against greased surface of bowl. Cover and let rise until double in size, 2½ to 3 hours.

Grease two bread pans. Punch down dough and divide in half. Make each half into a "pillow" the length of the bread pan. Place in bread pans, pressing the sides and ends down into the pan, and let rise 45 minutes. Preheat oven to 350°.

Bake bread for 1 hour. Turn bread out of pan and lay on its side to cool on a rack.

I love this toasted, with butter and currant jelly. The loaves are smallish and so good that they go fast. It's worth your effort to double the recipe and have some loaves to put in the freezer. I usually make a triple recipe, curse my greediness as I am kneading that ungainly blob of dough, and thank myself later.—Susan

"Eat your bread crusts and your hair will be curly."

Good Fast Bread (Gail Arne)

This recipe was on one of Mom's recipe cards with the little stove on top. Part of it was printed by Julie, trying to be super neat but stopping in the middle, and the rest was written by me, in a slightly "creative" script. It makes really, really, good rolls, and it's the easiest bread I ever made.

Gail Arne is one of Mom's Homemaker friends. She also taught the 4-H advanced cooking class where Julie learned how to make Swedish Tea Ring (see page 228).—*Susan*

MAKES ABOUT 3 DOZEN RATHER DAINTY SANDWICH ROLLS, ABOUT 2 DOZEN CLOSER TO HAMBURGER-BUN SIZE, OR 3 COFFEE CAKES

This dough can be used for any kind of rolls, coffee cake, kuchen, donuts, stollen, etc.

2 cups warm water

1 cup Spry (or Crisco), melted

¾ cup sugar (Decrease to ⅓ cup if making rolls.)

1 tablespoon salt

2 packages (½ ounce total) dry yeast

½ cup lukewarm water

1 teaspoon sugar

2 eggs, well-beaten

7 cups flour, sifted

1 teaspoon vanilla (Do not use if making rolls.)

In a large bowl, combine water, melted shortening, ¾ cup (or ⅓ cup if making rolls) sugar, and salt. Cool to lukewarm. (This won't take long.)

In a small bowl, combine yeast, lukewarm water, and 1 teaspoon sugar; let stand.

When shortening/sugar mixture is lukewarm, add dissolved yeast mixture and well-beaten eggs. (Stir in vanilla if making dough for a sweet bread.) Add about half the flour and beat well.

Add the remaining flour gradually—mix, but do not knead. Place in a large, lightly greased bowl. Cover and keep in refrigerator overnight or until you feel dough can be handled easily. (Several hours at least.) You don't have to use all the dough at once, but keep it no longer than five days.

To make rolls:

Punch down and shape the portion of the dough you will be using into balls (pressed down about halfway) on greased cookie sheets and let rise in a warm place until light. (*Plain old-fashioned cookie sheets will work best. The sugar in this dough causes the bottoms to get too dark when baked on the "new, improved" cookie sheets.—Susan*) Bake rolls at 375° until golden, 15 to 20 minutes.

Mom says: "This is a wonderful recipe."

Grandma Sanvidge had copied this recipe on one of Mom's cards and noted: "For donuts, use ½ c. sugar." This means reduce the amount of the sugar in the dough from ¾ cup to ½ cup because you will be putting sugar on the outside of the donuts.—Susan

"Toss me a roll."

The Corner Grocery Store

In the '50s, Mom's source of groceries was the neighborhood corner grocery store. Two of them in Oshkosh come to mind: Kubasta's, on the corner of Boyd and Parkway, and Werner's, on Bowen Street and Irving.

They were small, family-owned-and-operated, friendly places, dimly lit, with creaky wood floors and very small grocery carts. There was a butcher behind a big refrigerated glass case and a cashier who rang up our purchases on a (non-electric) cash register.

The '60s brought the "supermarket." Lucky us! A big, new Piggly Wiggly was built just two blocks away on Evans and Murdock! I have fond memories of their grand opening, complete with free yo-yos and miniature loaves of Wonder Bread. It was probably due to us showing up several times that the store policy became "One to a customer!" I'm sure that Mom liked the new, improved "supermarket," since it was close enough to send one of us down there when she needed something.

Although supermarkets are now commonplace, there is still a vestige of the old corner grocery store in White Lake. In our cottage days, it was known as Pomasl's Red Owl. It has changed hands, but it still has one of the swinging-in-and-out doors, the creaky wood floor, and the smell, flavor, and friendliness of the past that can't be erased . . . "Got any Archie comic books?" —*Jean*

Cloverleaf Rolls

All of the company meals roll into view when I think of these. Each roll has three bumps on it, and you can pull the rolls into thirds to eat (and butter) them.—*Susan*

MAKES 2 DOZEN ROLLS

1 cup scalded whole or 2% milk (Skim milk will not
   work in this recipe.)
¼ cup (4 tablespoons) margarine or butter
¼ cup sugar
1 teaspoon salt
1 package (¼ ounce) dry yeast
¼ cup lukewarm water
1 egg, beaten until light
3½ cups flour, sifted

Combine hot scalded milk and margarine (or butter) in a large bowl and let the margarine melt. Stir in sugar and salt. Cool to lukewarm.

Dissolve yeast in lukewarm water. Add yeast and beaten egg to lukewarm milk/margarine (or butter) mixture and stir. Gradually stir in flour to form a soft dough. Beat vigorously. As you add the last of the flour, this will be difficult to stir. You may have to do a little gentle kneading.

Lightly butter the top of the dough, cover with a dish towel, and let rise in a warm place until it doubles. This should take about 2 hours.

To make cloverleaf rolls:

Butter 24 muffin cups. Rub a little butter on your hands (the dough is quite sticky) and roll dough into 1-inch-diameter balls. Put three balls in each muffin cup. (To "come out even," you could pat the dough down, cut it into 24 pieces, and make three little balls out of each piece.) Let the rolls rise again until they puff up a bit, 45 minutes to an hour.

Preheat oven to 375°. Bake cloverleaf rolls for 15 minutes. Rolls should be golden brown.

For plain dinner rolls:

Form into 24 balls and flatten a bit. Put onto greased cookie sheets. Let the rolls rise again until they puff up a bit, 45 minutes to an hour. Preheat oven to 375°. Bake plain dinner rolls until golden brown, about 18 minutes.

Parker House Rolls

What does a Parker House Roll look like? According to our mother: "like a slightly lop-sided hind-end."—*Susan*

MAKES 3 DOZEN ROLLS

2 cups scalded whole or 2% milk (Skim milk will not work in this recipe.)

¼ cup (4 tablespoons) butter, plus more for buttering hands and muffin cups

2 tablespoons sugar

1 teaspoon salt

1 package (¼ ounce) dry yeast

¼ cup lukewarm water

1 egg, slightly beaten

5½ cups flour, sifted

You will also need: a 2½-inch round biscuit cutter

In a bowl large enough to hold all of the ingredients, pour hot scalded milk over butter, sugar, and salt. Stir. Cool until lukewarm.

Dissolve yeast in lukewarm water.

Add dissolved yeast and beaten egg to lukewarm milk mixture. Stir in flour gradually and beat thoroughly. As you add the last of the flour, this will be difficult (for most people), and you may have to knead it in. Handle this dough gently (it can get tough with over-handling) while incorporating all the flour. Cover and let rise until light, about an hour.

Butter the muffin cups, and then butter your hands to deal with this sticky dough. Punch down and toss dough on a lightly floured board. Pat down the dough and then roll out to a scant ½ inch thick. Cut dough into rounds with a 2½-inch biscuit cutter. Using a smooth knife handle, press a deep groove in the top of each round so you will be able to fold up one-third of the round. Fold one-third of each round up. (It should look like a chubby little taco, only one side doesn't come up as high as the other.) Pinch the fold together (and a little way up the curved edges) so the "chubby little tacos" stay folded. Place each roll in a muffin cup, folded side on the bottom. Let rise until nearing the shape of finished rolls, 30 to 45 minutes.

Forming Parker House Rolls

Preheat oven to 400°. Bake rolls until lightly golden brown and pulling away from the side of the pan, 15 to 18 minutes.

This is a lovely soft dough based on a recipe that has been in The Settlement Cook Book *since way back when. If you find the process of forming these rolls too time-consuming (which it is), you can make respectable-looking plain dinner rolls. Pluck off pieces of dough and roll into balls. Place one in each muffin cup. (But then you can't call them Parker House Rolls.)*

"I think I'll have a . . . roll with honey."
—Grandpa Noffke (winking) every single time he went to Kentucky Fried Chicken

For the sake of historical accuracy: Mom says she used to make these Parker House Rolls clustered in a cake pan. How the "little lop-sided hind-end" rolls that are shaped like tacos before they raise fit into a round pan is still a mystery. (I even tried it.) Every time Mom attempts to describe how she did it we start laughing so hard that we never did figure it out.—Susan

Butter Nut Braid (Mom)

If you have ladies coming over for coffee, need to bring something for a potluck buffet, want an after-school snack or something to welcome your new neighbor, this is it. The filling is astoundingly scrumptious (and the recipe has filling to spare). We eat it with our eyes closed in bliss. Mom used to frost this braided bread with the leftover filling (the filling inside soaks into the bread), but now it stays in a bowl to "butter" the slices as we eat them.—*Susan*

MAKES 2 LOAVES

Basic Sweet Dough:

1 cup scalded whole or 2% milk (Skim milk will not work in this recipe.)

½ cup (8 tablespoons, or 1 stick) butter, melted

⅓ cup sugar

½ teaspoon salt

1 package (¼ ounce) dry yeast

¼ cup lukewarm water

1 egg, lightly beaten

4½ to 5 cups flour, sifted

Filling:

1½ cups powdered sugar

¾ cup (12 tablespoons) butter, softened

1 teaspoon vanilla

1½ cups chopped pecans

In a large bowl, combine hot scalded milk, melted margarine or butter, sugar, and salt. Cool to lukewarm.

Dissolve yeast in lukewarm water.

When milk mixture is lukewarm, add yeast/water mixture and beaten egg. Add half of the flour and beat until smooth. Add remaining flour gradually. At some point it will be easier to just knead in the flour, but don't overdo it. Put in a greased bowl and let rise until doubled, about 2 hours.

While dough is rising, make the filling. Beat powdered sugar, butter, and vanilla thoroughly. Beat in nuts.

When dough has doubled, grease two cookie sheets. Punch dough down and divide in half. To make the first braided loaf, divide half of the dough into three parts. Pat each piece into a rectangle about 6 x 14 inches. Spread each rectangle with filling, not quite to the edges. (Note that there will be leftover filling, and you will be happy about this later.) Roll up tightly to make three 14-inch-long rolls and pinch edges together tightly. (It will be easiest to braid the loaf right on the cookie sheet.) Braid three long rolls together for each loaf, making sure to pinch the ends of the rolls together and tuck them under. Repeat for the other loaf. Let rise until doubled, about 30 minutes.

Preheat oven to 350°. Bake loaves until golden brown, 20 to 25 minutes. Use remaining filling to "butter" the bread when you slice it.

Caramel Pecan Rolls (Mom)

These are at their best served warm, but you won't have to force people to eat them if there are any left over.—*Susan*

MAKES 1 DOZEN ROLLS

Rolls:

1 cup scalded whole or 2% milk

3 tablespoons butter

2 tablespoons sugar

1 teaspoon salt

1 package (¼ ounce) dry yeast

¼ cup lukewarm water

3⅛ to 3¼ cups flour, sifted

Filling:

¼ cup sugar

¼ teaspoon cinnamon

Topping:

3 tablespoons butter (plus more for buttering the outside of the rolled-up dough)

1¼ cups brown sugar

2 tablespoons water

¾ cup whole pecans

You will also need: a 10-inch cast-iron frying pan and a heatproof plate to hold the 10-inch-wide cluster of hot-from-the-pan rolls

To make the rolls: Pour hot scalded milk into a large bowl over butter, sugar, and salt. Stir until butter is dissolved. Cool until lukewarm.

Dissolve yeast in warm water. Stir and let it sit for about 5 minutes until you see evidence that it is working (thickening on the surface, for example). Then add yeast mixture to lukewarm milk mixture. Add the flour gradually and beat thoroughly. When the dough becomes too stiff to stir, knead in the rest of the flour until the dough will accept no more. Knead until smooth. Put in a greased bowl, cover and let rise until doubled, about 1 hour.

Make the filling by combining sugar and cinnamon.

When the dough has nearly doubled, make the topping. Melt butter in the 10-inch cast-iron frying pan. Cover the butter with brown sugar and add water. Stir until brown sugar is moistened. Turn the burner to low heat, wait for widely spaced tiny bubbles to form, and then cook for 1 minute to dissolve the brown sugar. Remove from burner. Sprinkle whole pecans over the caramel mixture.

When dough has doubled, punch down and toss dough on a lightly floured board. Pat out the dough into a 9 x 12-inch rectangle (it will be about ½ inch thick). Sprinkle cinnamon sugar evenly over dough rectangle. Starting at one long side, roll the dough up tightly into a tube shape. Pinch the seam together. Use soft butter to grease the outside of the dough roll, and butter the sides of the frying pan above the brown sugar mixture. Cut the roll into 1-inch slices. Lay the little spirals cut-side down in the caramel-pecan mixture. Cover with a dish towel and let rise to the top of the pan before baking, about 1 hour.

Preheat oven to 375°. Bake rolls until evenly brown and pulling away from the side of the pan, 30 to 35 minutes. Turn out onto a large plate, pecan side up, immediately after baking. (Sticky and soggy are the results if you don't do this.)

Believe it or not, we put butter on these rolls when we eat them.—Susan

A Tea Party (circa 1956)

Be sure to drink your "tea" with your pinkie finger up in the air the whole time.—*Susan*

> a little tea set
> lukewarm water from the faucet
> soda crackers
> raisins

Fill the teapot with the lukewarm water. (This will be your tea.) Distribute the soda crackers and raisins evenly among the little plates so there will be no fighting.

Swedish Tea Ring

I was the only one of us who took the advanced cooking class in 4-H, where I learned how to make this delicious recipe. It does take a while to make, but it makes three coffee cakes.—*Julie*

Basic Sweet Dough:

2 cups scalded whole or 2% milk (Skim milk will not work in this recipe.)

1 cup sugar

2 teaspoons salt

2 packages (½ ounce total) dry yeast

½ cup lukewarm water (105 to 110 degrees is called for in this recipe)

8 to 10 cups sifted flour (Note from Mom: In this recipe you sift *before* measuring.)

½ cup (8 tablespoons, or 1 stick) butter, melted and cooled to lukewarm, plus a little extra to grease the bowl

3 medium eggs (Specified in the original recipe, but Mom says it worked fine with large eggs.)

Filling for all three tea rings:

6 tablespoons butter, softened, divided

1½ cups sugar, divided

6 teaspoons cinnamon, divided

1½ cups raisins, divided

Icing:

2 cups powdered sugar

⅓ cup butter, melted

1½ teaspoons vanilla

2 to 3 tablespoons hot water

Garnishes:

candied cherry halves

pecan halves

You will also need: three jelly roll pans or cookie sheets

Pour hot scalded milk over sugar and salt in a mixing bowl. Stir. Cool to lukewarm.

In a small bowl, soften yeast in warm water. Add to the lukewarm milk mixture. Add enough flour (about 4 cups) to make a medium-thick batter. Beat thoroughly. Let stand until light and foamy, 10 to 15 minutes. Add melted butter and eggs. Mix. Add enough flour to make a soft dough that can be handled easily.

Sprinkle a tad of flour on a board or cloth and turn dough onto it. Let it rest while you clean the bowl. Grease the bowl generously with more butter.

Knead the dough until smooth and satiny, 8 to 10 minutes. It will be softer than most bread dough. Put dough into the bowl, turn it to butter all sides, and cover with a clean dish towel. Let rise in a warm, draft-free place until double in bulk, about an hour.

Punch down dough and divide into three portions. Let rest 10 minutes.

Take one portion of the dough and gently roll and stretch it into a thin, 10 x 15-inch oblong—yes, use a ruler so all of your tea rings turn out the same.

Spread one rolled section of dough with 2 tablespoons butter. Combine ½ cup sugar and 2 teaspoons cinnamon and sprinkle over butter on dough. Distribute ½ cup raisins evenly over the cinnamon-sugar mixture. With your hands on the long side of the sheet of dough, tightly roll the dough, pinch the end closed, and form a ring, pinching to seal the joint of the two ends. Place on the jelly roll pan with the sealed edge at the bottom. With a kitchen shears, cut through the ring almost to the center in sections about 1 inch wide. Turn slices partly to one side and overlap them. It will look like a ring of cinnamon buns!

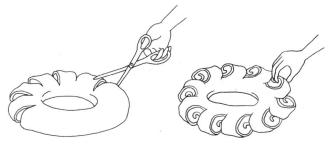

Cutting and turning the dough for Swedish Tea Rings

Repeat the filling and shaping process with remaining dough and filling ingredients to form two more tea rings. Let all rise until doubled.

Preheat oven to 350°. Bake tea rings until light golden brown, 20 to 25 minutes. Remove from pan before completely cool or you will find that the sugar has fused them to the pan. Cool tea rings on racks.

While tea rings are cooling, prepare the icing. Combine powdered sugar, melted butter, and vanilla. Add enough of the hot water so it will pour off a spoon in a thin stream. Mix well. Drizzle on cooled tea rings. If desired, garnish with candied cherries and pecan halves.

NOTE: *You can freeze the baked tea rings without the icing.*

Julie with Swedish Tea Rings made by her and two girls in her 4-H cooking class.

Pumpkin Bread (Mom)

This could also be a dessert. Our mother says you should try a slice of this with ice cream or whipped cream.—*Susan*

If you prefer, you can make this into 24 muffins. Use liners AND grease the pan. Use an ice cream scoop to dole out the thick batter; bake for 25 minutes at 350°. Add some Cream Cheese Frosting (see page 238), and you can call them cupcakes.—*Julie*

MAKES 2 LARGE LOAVES OR 3 SMALLER LOAVES

2 cups sugar

⅔ cup margarine (but Crisco can be substituted)

4 eggs

1 can (15 ounces) pumpkin

⅔ cup water

3⅓ cups flour

2 teaspoons baking soda

1½ teaspoons salt

1 teaspoon cinnamon

½ teaspoon baking powder

¼ teaspoon ground cloves* **

⅔ cup coarsely chopped nuts (optional)

⅔ cup raisins (optional)

Preheat oven to 350° and grease bottoms only of two large loaf pans or three small loaf pans. Mix sugar and shortening in a large bowl. Add eggs, pumpkin, and water. Blend in flour, baking soda, salt, cinnamon, baking powder, and cloves. Stir in (optional) nuts and raisins. Pour into pans. Bake until a toothpick inserted into center comes out clean, about 1 hour and 10 minutes; cool for 15 minutes. Loosen sides of loaves from pans; remove from pans. Cool completely before slicing. To store, wrap and refrigerate no longer than ten days.

*The original recipe calls for 1 teaspoon of cloves, but the Sanvidges are just not that crazy about cloves.—Julie

**News Flash: Mom says she uses a whole teaspoon of cloves. Should we believe her? Is it Julie who isn't that crazy about cloves?—Anonymous

Biscuit Mix (Grandma Sanvidge)

This recipe will save you time and money. Put the money you save into an empty Mogen David bottle with a little slot cut into the cap (like Grandma did). —*Diane*

EACH CUP OF BISCUIT MIX WILL MAKE 6 BISCUITS

8 cups flour

⅓ cup baking powder

8 teaspoons sugar (optional)

2 teaspoons salt

1 cup shortening (Spry or Crisco)

Mix flour, baking powder, sugar, and salt. Using a fork, blend in shortening. Store mixture in an airtight container. This will keep in a cupboard a little while but will last for months in the refrigerator.

To Make Biscuits:

Preheat oven to 425°. For every cup of Biscuit Mix you use (for lighter biscuits, spoon mix into the measuring cup so it doesn't pack down), add ⅓ cup milk or buttermilk. Add the milk all at once. Stir only until flour mixture is moistened. Roll ½ inch thick on a floured board and cut out biscuits. Bake until puffed and golden on top, 10 to 15 minutes.

I used my food processor, mixing 4 cups of the flour with all the other ingredients, then putting it into a giant zip-top bag, adding the remaining flour, zipping firmly, and shaking the bag to mix. Make sure to combine it well. (The biscuits are very good. Now I have a fresh box of Bisquick and this giant bag of Biscuit Mix!)—Julie

Desserts

"Be sure to save some room . . ."

Mom and both grandmas have more desserts than anything else in their recipe files. (In contrast, the "Foreign Foods" section of Mom's recipe box is completely empty.) Preparing the meat-and-potatoes part of a meal is an everyday necessity, and making a dessert is optional—but very satisfying. A dessert is a little celebration, and it makes everybody happy.

Mom made a lot of these "little celebrations" for us. Cinnamon wafting from the oven, the tart fragrance of baking cherries, an oozing apple pie cooling on the countertop, "licking the beaters," and dipping a finger into smooth sweet frosting: desserts even made us happy while they were being made.

We are carrying on the unbalanced-recipe-box tradition of our mom and grandmas with our ample Desserts section (but we discreetly moved the cookies and bars to a separate section so it wouldn't look *too* ample). I make Mom's dessert recipes often, and people always love them. In case you're wondering, we're not huge . . . yet—*Susan*

Apple Betty (Mom)

We don't know who Betty is and we don't care...just make this for us, Mom!
—*Julie*

McIntosh or Cortland apples, peeled and sliced (enough to half-fill a 9-inch
    square baking pan, or about 1 quart)
½ cup sugar
½ teaspoon cinnamon
½ cup (8 tablespoons, or 1 stick) butter or margarine
2 cups bread cubes (½- to ¾-inch cubes)

Preheat oven to 350° and butter a 9-inch square baking pan. (Mom uses a
glass baking dish.) Put apple slices into the pan. Mix the sugar and cinnamon
and sprinkle on the apples. Toss to distribute the sugar and cinnamon.

In a saucepan, melt the butter or margarine. Remove from heat, add the
bread cubes, and stir until well-coated. Fold the bread cubes into the apple
mixture, making certain some cubes stay on top to become crispy.

Bake until apples are done and cubes of bread are light brown, 30 to 45
minutes. Best served warm. (*With vanilla ice cream!—Jean*)

Mom says: Be sure to use good bread for the cubes. (No stale hamburger buns!)

Cherry Cobbler (Mom)

Cherry Cobbler smells so good when it comes out of the oven that it's hard to wait for it to cool off. I have burned my tongue on this lovely stuff many times.
—*Susan*

Preheat oven to 375° and grease a 9 x 13-inch Pyrex cake pan or equivalent size ceramic casserole dish. Spread 2 cans cherry pie filling* in the pan. Put the pan in the oven to get pie filling warm and bubbly.

Meanwhile, prepare Bisquick shortcake dough as described on the box. Drop dough in 12 rounded tablespoons onto the hot fruit. Return to the oven and bake until the dough drops are nicely browned and baked through, 20 to 25 minutes.

Cherry pie filling used to be a softer, more natural-looking red. Our mother often made her own cherry pie filling by buying canned sour cherries and thickening the juice by stirring in cornstarch and sugar to taste. Cook until the sauce thickens and correct the amounts of cornstarch and sugar. (Remember: Don't burn your tongue.)

Tomato Soup Cake (Cile)

This is "Susie, the Picky Eater," here to tell you that I always LOVED this cake. This is a rosy-orange tomato-soup color, moist and succulent spice cake similar to carrot cake. The frosting is the same as for carrot cake, too, and worth making to eat all by itself.—*Susan*

1 teaspoon baking soda

1 can Campbell's tomato soup

2 cups sifted flour

1 cup sugar

2 teaspoons baking powder

1 teaspoon nutmeg

1 teaspoon cinnamon

½ cup (8 tablespoons, or 1 stick) butter, melted

1 egg

½ cup dark raisins

½ cup nuts (*Always chopped pecans.—Susan*)

Preheat oven to 350° and butter a 9 x 13-inch cake pan. Dissolve the baking soda in the soup. Sift the flour, sugar, baking powder, nutmeg, and cinnamon together to distribute the ingredients evenly. Add the melted butter and egg to the tomato soup mixture and beat well. Beat in the sifted dry ingredients gradually. Stir in raisins and nuts. (This will look like too little batter for the pan size, but you can trust Grandma and Cile. The finished cake will be about 1½ inches high.) Bake until a toothpick comes out clean, 25 to 30 minutes. When cake has cooled, cover with Cream Cheese Frosting. (See recipe below.)

Store this cake in the icebox—because we love it when the frosting gets firm like fudge!
—Julie

Cream Cheese Frosting (Cile)

Four stars in the frosting category! Make sure you try it on something.—*Susan*

1 package (8 ounces) cream cheese, softened
2 teaspoons butter, softened
1½ cups powdered sugar

Beat cream cheese and butter together and then gradually beat in powdered sugar until smooth and creamy. Try to frost the cake without eating most of the frosting before you're done.

"Want to split a piece? Want to split a piece? Want to split a piece? Want to . . ."
—Diane and Susan

Date Chocolate Chip Cake (DonnaBelle Heding, our neighbor in Oshkosh)

This is a dense, moist cake with lots of good things in it. We both remember it very fondly. Don't forget the vanilla! (This is noted on the recipe card. It's the last thing you put in, and it's easy to forget.)—*Susan and Diane*

Cake:

1 cup cut-up dates

¾ teaspoon baking soda

1½ cups boiling water

1 cup sugar

¾ cup shortening (Crisco or Spry)

2 eggs, beaten

1¼ cups plus 2 tablespoons sifted flour

1 teaspoon cinnamon

½ teaspoon baking soda

½ teaspoon salt

1 teaspoon vanilla

Vanilla

Topping:

⅓ cup sugar

½ teaspoon cinnamon

⅔ cup chocolate chips

½ cup chopped nuts

Preheat oven to 350° and grease and flour the bottom only of a 9 x 13-inch cake pan. Put the cut-up dates in a bowl, sprinkle baking soda over them, and pour boiling water over all. Let cool. (*This will take a long time.—Diane*)

Cream sugar and shortening. Add beaten eggs and mix well.

Sift together flour, cinnamon, baking soda, and salt. Alternately add flour mixture and cooled date mixture to the creamed shortening mixture. When all is mixed together, mix in vanilla. Pour batter into pan.

Mix together topping ingredients and sprinkle over top of batter. Bake for 30 minutes.

This is good and rich just as it is, but you could serve it with whipped cream or ice cream—if you need to gain some weight.

"It's not good to be too thin, because then if you get sick . . ."
—Mom

Wacky Cake (Grandma Noffke)

It's wacky, all right. No eggs, no bowls, no mixer; just poking holes and pouring things in. All that time you spent in the sandbox will come in handy here. —*Susan*

I found this recipe in a blue hardbound notebook (with *Recipes* on the cover and spine) that came from Grandma's cottage in Three Lakes. Inside the front cover Grandma had written, "From: Mrs. Paul Noffke, Dec. 25, 1935," and on the pages were recipes Grandma had copied down, in pencil (as I often do), from friends, neighbors, and relatives.—*Jean*

1½ cups sifted flour (*Sifting before measuring makes a big difference in this cake.*)

1 cup sugar

3 tablespoons unsweetened cocoa

1 teaspoon baking powder

½ teaspoon salt

5 tablespoons butter, melted

1 tablespoon vinegar

1 teaspoon vanilla

1 cup cold water

Preheat oven to 350°. Sift flour, sugar, cocoa, baking powder, and salt directly into ungreased 8-inch square pan. (*This also works in the skimpy 7.6-inch square pan that some* man *thought would be a good way to save money for his company.*) Blend with a fork. Make three "holes" in the dry ingredients: Put melted butter in one; vinegar in another; and vanilla in the third. Pour the cold water over all. Use the fork to blend ingredients thoroughly (as you would when scrambling eggs). The batter will look like chocolate pudding. Bake until the center springs back when you touch it lightly, about 30 minutes. (It took 38 minutes in that 7.6-inch square pan, in my oven.) Let cool and frost with a half batch of Cake Decorating Frosting (page 259). (No, you don't have to decorate the cake. You can just spread it on—nice and thick.)

Chocolate Cake (also known as Tobacco Cake)

Mom comments: "When we were kids, this was our favorite cake. We observed Uncle Louie Becker spitting tobacco juice and imitated (with the cake!).* That's why we called this Tobacco Cake." It's a wonder Grandma Noffke kept making it.—Susan

"Dissolve 2 sq. chocolate [unsweetened] in 5 tbsp. boiling water, cream ½ c. butter, adding gradually 1½ c. sugar. Add: 4 egg yolks, and beat thoroughly. Add the chocolate, ½ c. cream or [whole or 2%] milk, 1¾ c. flour, 2 rounded tsp. baking powder, 1 tsp. vanilla. Beat the egg whites to a stiff froth and stir carefully into the mixture. Bake in three tins [buttered, then floured] for layer cake or as desired."**

*"I have to tell you that we went outside to do this, not in Uncle Louie's spittoon!" —Mom

**Diane made Tobacco Cake to check the temperature and timing. She used two 8-inch round cake pans and baked the cake at 350° for 30 minutes. She had this comment: I think the real reason this was called Tobacco Cake is that when you add the chocolate squares to the boiling water and stir it up, the liquid looks like it came right out of a spittoon! This cake is not "real chocolatey." It is more the color of German chocolate cake. It would be good if you frosted it with chocolate frosting and sprinkled toasted coconut on top . . . (and you'd get a few laughs, too).—Diane

Cherry Devil's Food Cake (Mom)

Mom says: "This was one of the first cakes I ever made, and it was always a big hit."

1½ cups sifted cake flour*

1 teaspoon baking soda

½ teaspoon salt

1 cup sugar

½ cup shortening (Crisco)

1 egg

1 square unsweetened chocolate, melted

1 cup sour whole or 2% milk**

1 tablespoon maraschino cherry juice

Preheat oven to 350°. Grease and flour the bottom only of an 8-inch square pan. Sift flour, baking soda, and salt together. In another bowl, cream the sugar and shortening thoroughly. Add egg and beat 1 minute. Add melted chocolate and blend. Alternately add dry ingredients, sour milk, and cherry juice to shortening mixture, beating after each addition. Pour into an 8-inch square cake pan and bake until it starts to pull away from the sides of the pan and a toothpick inserted in the center comes out clean, 35 to 45 minutes. (This cake is good with Birthday Cake Frosting, page 262.—*Diane*)

Any time Mom bakes a cake from scratch, she uses cake flour, not regular flour. As she puts it, "When you bake a cake, you need all the help you can get."

**To make 1 cup sour milk: Put 1 tablespoon of lemon juice or white vinegar (either works fine) in a measuring cup and pour in whole or 2% milk until you have 1 cup.*

Spice Cake (Cile, from Modern Priscilla*)

A while back, I was on the phone with Mom, reminiscing about Cile's Spice Cake. Mom found three different spice cake recipes she had copied from Cile when she was in her teens and sent these old recipes to me with the Christmas wreath she makes for us every year. I tried this one, and the moment I put the spices in, my kitchen smelled like Grandma's. (The recipe is here verbatim, with my comments in italic.)—*Susan*

"½ c. butter *[softened]*

¾ c. sugar

2¼ c. sifted cake flour *[Sifting before measuring is very important. My cake might have been better if I had used cake flour!]*

2 eggs

4 tsp. baking powder

¼ tsp. cloves *[ground]*

1 tsp. cinnamon

½ tsp. nutmeg

¾ c. milk *[Note that whole milk was used for baking at this time. Do not use skim milk in this recipe.]*

Cream butter, add sugar gradually, then whole eggs, and beat thoroughly. Sift flour with baking powder and spices and add to first mixture alternately with milk. Bake in two layers. [*Butter and flour the pan. Cile usually used a 9 x 13-inch cake pan, which could affect the timing.*]

The addition of ½ c. currants or chopped raisins [*Yes!*] and ¼ c. coarsely chopped walnuts [*Yes!*] make a good variation.

Time in cooking: 25 min. Temperature 350°.

Recipe makes 2 layers 8 inches in diameter, 2¼" deep. Ten servings."

Baking Tip: The cake may look pale on top, but as long as it meets the "toothpick test" and "spring-back-test," don't keep it in (like I did) and let it get too dry (like I did). The second time I made this, I took it out after 25 minutes, which was an improvement. Next time, I'll obey the Settlement tip! (I bake a lot, but have made very few cakes.) Even though this was an amateur's attempt, my test kitchen taster said, "Don't lose that recipe!" and every bit (a total of four one-layer cakes) was eaten.

Most of the time Cile used Cream Cheese Frosting (see page 238) on her spice cakes, but sometimes she used the Caramel Frosting on the next page.—Susan

*I have seven of Grandma Noffke's issues of Modern Priscilla *from 1921 through 1930. It's a large-format woman's magazine with recipes ("A Homely, Homey Company Dinner"), embroidery and knitting patterns, cleaning advice, room arrangements, and advertisements.—Susan*

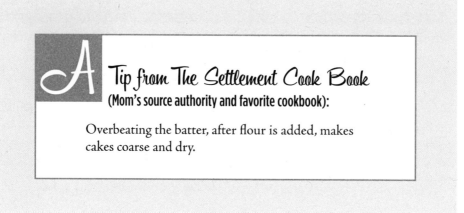

A Tip from The Settlement Cook Book
(Mom's source authority and favorite cookbook):

Overbeating the batter, after flour is added, makes cakes coarse and dry.

Caramel Frosting (Cile)

This frosting is buttery sweet, like vanilla fudge. (Cream Cheese Frosting is much better on Cile's Spice Cake.) This Caramel Frosting is unbelievably delicious on angel food cake. The recipe here is quoted word-for-word from one of the recipe cards our teenaged mother copied from Cile's.—*Susan*

"1 c. light brown sugar

½ c. granulated sugar

⅔ c. water

2 tbsp. butter

½ tsp. vanilla

[In a sauce pan over low heat . . .] Mix the sugars, water and butter. Boil gently and stir frequently until soft ball forms when portion is slowly poured into cup of cold water.* Remove from fire at once. Let stand 15 minutes. Add vanilla. Beat *[with a whisk, not a mixer]* until creamy. Frost top and sides of cake *[while frosting is still warm]*. Chopped nuts can be sprinkled over top of frosting before it stiffens. *[Also good on a spoon!]*"

*Or use that candy thermometer Mom gave you and heat until temperature reaches 235°, the "soft ball" stage. You will be able to check it with a glance and won't waste any of this luscious frosting. (Whatever method you use, this step requires a little patience.)

Gingerbread Cake

Buy Dromedary Gingerbread Cake Mix. (This has been around forever and is still available—if you can't find it at your local store, you should be able to get it online. I have read that it was one of the very first cake mixes.) Make the cake according to the package directions. When the cake is done, sprinkle with powdered sugar. Cut into squares and serve while still warm.—*Susan*

This is really good with whipped cream or vanilla ice cream.—Jean

"You can take as much as you want, but eat all you take."

Other Cakes We Have Known

◻ *Hickory Nut Cake*—A small, square cake from LaFontaine's Bakery in Oshkosh. I remember the cake was a tannish color, almost gray, with dark flecks of hickory nuts. The frosting was white with a faintly sour taste. You wouldn't think it was good from that description, but it was.

◻ *Boston Cream Pie*—A yellow cake split in two horizontally, filled with vanilla pudding, and frosted on the top with chocolate icing (dribbling down the sides). Lucky you! This is a cake mix that is still around. I just saw it at the grocery store.

◻ *Ice Cream Cake Roll*—Devil's food cake and vanilla ice cream rolled together in a little log. (Newly Weds was the brand name.) We drizzled Hershey's Chocolate Syrup over the spiral slices.

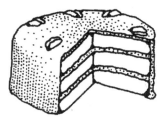

▣ *German Chocolate Cake*—Yum. This was (and is) a layer cake the color of milk chocolate. The frosting was very thick and had coconut and pecans in a thick sugary frosting. Mom always made German Chocolate Cake from a mix (which is still available), but she made the frosting from scratch. (See recipe below.) I would like a piece of this cake right now. —*Susan*

Frosting for German Chocolate Cake:
1 cup evaporated milk
1 cup sugar
¼ cup (½ stick) butter
1 teaspoon vanilla
3 egg yolks, beaten
¾ cup chopped pecans
¾ cup shredded or flaked coconut

Mix evaporated milk and sugar in a saucepan and, stirring frequently, bring to a boil over medium-low heat. Remove from heat. Stir in butter until melted, then stir in vanilla. Let sit 5 minutes and then pour in beaten egg yolks gradually, stirring briskly as you pour. Put back on the stove and cook over medium-low heat for 12 minutes, stirring frequently, until thickened. Stir in pecans and coconut. Let cool slightly. Put some of the frosting between the layers and use the rest to cover the entire cake.

Berry Torte (Grandma Noffke)

A wonderful recipe. If you want to make this ahead, it freezes well without the berries. I love the leftovers for breakfast with coffee. Make photocopies of the recipe if you're planning to serve it to company—they'll be asking for it.—*Julie*

Crust:

1½ cups flour

1 tablespoon sugar

1 cup (2 sticks) margarine or butter

Filling:

2 eggs

½ cup sugar

1 package (8 ounces) cream cheese, softened

1 tablespoon lemon juice

1 teaspoon vanilla

a little salt

¼ cup whole or 2% milk (Do not use skim milk for this recipe.)

Topping:

2 cans of any desired berry pie filling (Grandma wrote: "Blueberries very good" on her recipe card, but she made it most often with cherries, and so do we.)

Preheat oven to 350°.

Make the crust: Combine the flour and 1 tablespoon sugar in a bowl. With a fork, pastry cutter, or food processor, work in margarine or butter until well-combined. Press mixture into bottom and sides of a 9 x 13-inch cake pan to form a crust. Bake until light golden brown, 20 to 30 minutes. Be sure to check on it after 20 minutes.

Lower oven temperature to 325°.

Make the filling: Separate the eggs and save the yolks for the next step. Beat the egg whites until stiff, then beat in ½ cup sugar. Set aside.

Beat the egg yolks. In another bowl, beat the cream cheese and add lemon juice, vanilla, salt, milk, and the beaten egg yolks. Beat until smooth. Fold egg white mixture into cream cheese mixture.

Pour batter into crust and bake for 25 minutes at 325°. It will firm up after removal from oven. Cool on rack.

When cool, put on the berry topping. Chill.

I've also put glazed whole strawberries on top, and it's quite good.—Julie

Blitz Torte (Grandma Noffke)

This was Grandpa Noffke's choice for his birthday cake. Grandpa's birthday cake always had the vanilla filling.—*Julie*

Make this dessert to impress your guests. They will think you spent a lot of time on it. You did. (It's not one of our favorite desserts. *"Grandpa, wouldn't you rather have chocolate cake?"*)—*Diane*

Cake:

½ cup sugar

½ cup (8 tablespoons, or 1 stick) butter

4 egg yolks (save whites in separate bowl to beat later for the meringue)

1 cup sifted cake flour

6 tablespoons whole or 2% milk (Do not use skim milk for this recipe.)

½ lemon, grated rind and juice (or substitute 1 teaspoon vanilla for vanilla filling version)

1 teaspoon baking powder

pinch of salt

Meringue:

4 egg whites saved from above

1 cup sugar

½ cup chopped walnuts

Filling:

¾ cup sugar

5 tablespoons cornstarch

⅛ teaspoon salt

2 eggs, slightly beaten

2 cups scalded whole or 2% milk (Do not use skim milk for this recipe.)

½ teaspoon lemon extract (Substitute 1 teaspoon vanilla for the vanilla filling version.)

You will also need: a double boiler (for the filling)

> "Nobody could make a meringue like Lucille."
> —Mom

Preheat oven to 300°.

Make the cakes: Grease and flour two 9-inch cake pans. Cream sugar and butter. Add egg yolks, flour, milk, rind and juice of ½ lemon (or, if making vanilla filling version, add vanilla), baking powder, and salt. Beat very well until smooth. Pour mixture into cake pans.

Make the meringue: Wash beaters and beat the 4 egg whites until stiff, adding 1 cup of sugar gradually and beating hard after each addition. Spread egg white mixture over batter in each cake pan. Sprinkle with chopped walnuts. Bake for 30 minutes. Cool.

Make the filling: Mix sugar, cornstarch, and salt in a bowl. Stir in the hot scalded milk. Put the slightly beaten eggs in the top of a double boiler and gradually stir in the hot milk mixture a very little at a time (so you don't curdle the eggs), stirring as you pour. Cook until thickened into a pudding, stirring constantly. Cool and beat in lemon extract (or vanilla if you are making the vanilla filling version). (*Grandma's recipe specified only "lemon." So I tried this with lemon juice, then with lemon extract. The extract is better.—Diane*).

Turn one of the meringue-covered cakes upside down on serving plate (meringue down.) Cover with lemon or vanilla filling. Put other layer on. (Meringue up.)

A serrated knife and a gentle sawing motion will be the best way to cut this.

Peach Kuchen (Mom)

I always thought this recipe came from a long-ago Bisquick package, but along with all the butter, cream, and egg yolks in this exquisitely good dessert comes a legend, too. According to Mom, Grandma got this from a Mrs. Halder, wife of one of Grandpa's business associates, and *she* got it from her grandmother, who was a cook in a royal household (unspecified). I think we can presume that the Bisquick shortcut in the crust was a later addition.—*Susan*

Crust:

2 cups Bisquick

2 tablespoons sugar

½ cup (8 tablespoons, or 1 stick) butter

Filling:

6 peaches, skinned and cut in half

1 cup sugar

1 teaspoon cinnamon

2 egg yolks

1 cup cream

Preheat oven to 400°. Mix Bisquick, butter, and 2 tablespoons sugar together until crumbly. Pat into bottom and up the sides of a 9 x 9-inch pan. Place peaches (round side up) on the crust. Combine 1 cup sugar and cinnamon and sprinkle over peaches. Bake for 15 minutes. Turn oven down to 350°. Combine egg yolks and cream well (no dark yellow streaks of yolk, but don't beat it) and pour over the peaches. Bake for 25 minutes. Serve warm (not hot) or cold. Store in the refrigerator.

"Pinapple Desert" (Mom)

The "Pinapple Desert" recipe card was written very neatly, by one of us, probably about nine years old. This dessert was one of the first mentioned by two sisters out of four when we started gathering recipes for this book.—*Susan*

½ pound marshmallows

⅓ cup whole or 2% milk (Do not use skim milk for this recipe.)

1 can (20 ounces) crushed pineapple, drained

1 cup cream, whipped (could be Dream Whip or Cool Whip, but it will be
   sweeter)
unbaked Graham Cracker Crust (see page 268), pressed into the bottom and
   sides of an 8-inch square pan
You will also need: a double boiler

Melt marshmallows in the milk in a double boiler. Remove from heat. Add
drained pineapple. Fold in whipped cream and pour into unbaked graham
cracker crust. Chill. Do not freeze!

Hawaiian Angel Food Cake (Mom)

Greater than the sum of its parts!—*Julie*

Put the oven rack up one notch from the center position. Cut chunky slices
of angel food cake* and place on broiler pan. In a bowl, mix together brown
sugar and enough melted butter to make a soft crumbly mixture. Spread a
little of the brown sugar mixture on each slice of cake. Place one well-drained
pineapple ring on each piece. Turn broiler on to low setting. Broil briefly until
the brown sugar mixture is bubbly. "Watch it like a hawk!" This can burn very
easily. Place each slice on individual serving plates and add a healthy dollop
of sour cream. Sprinkle with chopped nuts. Serve immediately. If making for
company, you can assemble everything but the pineapple a few hours before
and broil at the last minute.

*Make sure the slices are flat, or the topping will slide off.—*Jean*

Pineapple Upside-Down Cake

If Dad does not get this for his birthday, you're going to hear about it!—*Susan, Diane, Jean, Julie*

½ cup (8 tablespoons, or 1 stick) butter

2 cups brown sugar

1 can (1 pound, 14 ounces) sliced pineapple, drained

maraschino cherries

whole pecans

4 eggs, separated

1 cup sugar

1 cup flour

1 teaspoon baking powder

Topping:

1 cup cream (for whipping)

3 tablespoons sugar

You will also need: a 10-inch cast-iron frying pan

Preheat oven to 350°. Melt butter in a 10-inch cast-iron frying pan. Cover bottom of pan evenly with the brown sugar. Place one slice of pineapple in center on top of the brown sugar and fill the rest of the pan with a single layer of slices. (Make this look pretty. This will be the top of the cake.) Put a whole cherry in the center of each pineapple slice and fill the spaces between with whole pecans top side down.

Beat the egg yolks and sugar together until light. In a separate bowl, sift the flour and baking powder. Fold dry ingredients into egg/sugar mixture ⅓ cup at a time.

Beat the egg whites until peaks form. Fold the stiffly beaten egg whites into the batter. Pour the batter over the pineapple slices in the frying pan. Bake about 30 minutes (do the toothpick test). Immediately after it comes out of the oven, put a (heatproof!) serving plate on top of the frying pan and turn upside down. Let it rest for a minute and very slowly pull frying pan off.

To make the topping, chill bowl and beaters. Beat cream until stiff. Slowly beat in sugar to sweeten it. Serve with pieces of warm Pineapple Upside-Down Cake.

"Happy Birthday, Dear Da-a-ad . . . "

Birthday Cake à la Helene

After her cake decorating class, Mom made the most absolutely professional-looking birthday cakes. Better than professional—remember Dad's bakery-made "Neon Blue on Brown" cake? Mom's colors were subdued. Graceful pale green leaves, perfect shell pink roses, and "Happy Birthday" in Mom's own handwriting.—*Susan*

Buy a package of angel food cake mix.* (Duncan Hines was the preferred brand.) Follow directions. Cut a small disk of cardboard to cover the hole (unless you'll be putting a doll into it; see page 261). Get out your cake-decorating kit ... and make the frosting recipe below.

Do not even think of making angel food cake from scratch. The package mix is fine. I once made seven angel food cakes from scratch to get two barely presentable cakes. Dozens and dozens of eggs ... (My oven temperature was off.)—Susan

Mom did not decorate **this** cake.

Cake Decorating Frosting (Mom)

It's not only perfect for making tinted leaves, roses, and ruffles. This lovely frosting can be whipped up in five minutes to frost a simple cake.—*Susan*

**MAKES ENOUGH FROSTING TO DECORATE ONE ANGEL FOOD CAKE
(IF YOU DON'T GO CRAZY WITH THE DECORATING)**

3 cups sifted powdered sugar

¼ cup (4 tablespoons) butter or margarine

¼ cup shortening (Crisco)

¼ cup lukewarm water

1 teaspoon vanilla

¼ teaspoon salt

"**Why is there frosting on Barbie's legs?**"—Diane

Combine all ingredients and beat at high speed for 5 minutes.

Mom decorated birthday cakes for our Noffke cousins, too. Remember the Wilton cake decorating book and watching her make frosting roses?—Julie

Cake Decorating

Mom loved to make birthday cakes.

With the *Baker's Coconut Cut-up Cake Cookbook* as her inspiration, she made her earliest out-of-the-ordinary birthday cakes for us. She would cut up flat cakes to make different animals, frost them, sprinkle coconut all over, and put on the little decorations.

Later Mom took a cake decorating class at the Tech. She made the most delicious buttercream frosting, tinting it to just the right pastel shade (mint green, pale pink, yellow) with little jars of food coloring paste. She stored the food coloring, decorating tips, and frosting bags in a big metal tin with yellow-checked oilcloth pasted on the lid. (A plain version of this tin transports her Famous Granola Bars to lucky recipients.)

Mom made angel food cakes and covered the hole with a cardboard circle before frosting the cake. She trimmed the cake with roses, leaves, and rippled borders. "Who gets to lick the cardboard?"

You would think she would use an angel food cake pan when she made a doll cake, because the hole was already there. But no . . . that sharp edge just wasn't right for a skirt. So she baked the cake in her rounded stainless steel mixing bowl, cut a hole in the center of the cake, and stuck Barbie in up to her waist. She used one of her decorating tips to make a ruffled skirt and heart-shaped frosting bodice. Barbie never looked better.—*Diane*

Julie and the doll birthday cake Mom made for her.

"Birthday Cake Frosting"
(Before cake decorating)

This is an unusual but delicious recipe. It's light and fluffy, but stable. (Too soft to use with decorating tips.)—*Julie*

THIS WILL MAKE ENOUGH TO FROST THE TOP OF A 9 X 13-INCH CAKE. DOUBLE THIS RECIPE FOR A LAYER CAKE.

½ cup whole or 2% milk (Skim milk will not work in this recipe.)
2½ tablespoons flour
½ cup shortening (Crisco)
½ cup sugar (Yes, granulated sugar—it will dissolve.)
½ teaspoon vanilla
¼ teaspoon salt

"What do you think this is? Your birthday?"
—Dad (on your birthday)

Combine milk and flour in a small saucepan and mix together until smooth. Cook over medium heat, stirring until mixture thickens into a paste. Cool. Put cooled mixture into a bowl and add shortening, sugar, vanilla, and salt. Beat until smooth and creamy.

Mom says: "This is good frosting because it's not too sweet. Try it on white cake."

. . . or on Cinnamon Bars (page 316).—Susan

The Birthday Party circa 1955

There were two things for sure about birthdays in our house: Mom would make you a very special birthday cake, and you opened your presents as soon as you got up. Sometimes Mom was too busy to wrap your presents, and you got them in the store bag—those fancy cakes took a lot of time! On special birthdays (I don't know how this was determined) you got to have a party. Neighborhood playmates and kids from school were invited.

The girls arrived dressed in their Sunday clothes: nylon dresses with ruffles and as many petticoats as their mothers would allow, and patent leather "Mary Jane" shoes with lace-topped ankle socks. The boys wore dress pants and good shirts and had their hair slicked down. (But most of the time it was just girls.)

After all the guests had arrived, the games started. Mom had prizes wrapped up for the winners. The Birthday Girl could play the games but could not win a prize.

We started with "Pin the Tail on the Donkey." (Mom bought the game at Woolworth's.) The big piece of paper with the donkey on it was unfolded and taped to the kitchen wall. The tails were in a pile on the mangle with rolled-up tape on the backs. Contestant Number One was blindfolded with one of Dad's red work handkerchiefs and turned around a couple times. (Dizziness evened the field.) He or she walked toward the donkey and stuck the tail on. Placing the tail in the most anatomically correct position won you the prize.

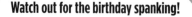

Watch out for the birthday spanking!
"A spank for every year old, a pinch to grow an inch, a sock to grow a block!"—Jean

Next we played "Musical Chairs." For this game: Find enough chairs so that all but one child will have a seat. Line the chairs up in two rows, back to back. Start a record on the record player. All the children walk around the chairs. When Mom stops the music, everyone sits on a chair. The child without a chair is out, one chair is removed, and the music starts again. Repeat this until the biggest child wins and all the other children are crying and saying "_____ cheated!" The cheater wins the prize.

Everyone lines up for "Drop the Clothespin in the Bottle." This could never have been fun. Everyone stands in line to drop five clothespins (from waist height) into a glass milk bottle. The contestant with the most clothespins in the bottle wins.

Everyone perks up for "Farmer in the Dell." We all stand in a circle with the Birthday Girl in the middle. "The farmer in the dell, the

The Little Sisters' Table at Susan's 4th grade birthday party. Diane is making her "picture face," Jean is in the back, and Jean's friend, Mary Lou Lux, little sister of Susan's friend Patsy, is in the foreground. The globe bank must have been a prize.

farmer in the dell, hi-ho-the-derry-o, the farmer in the dell. The farmer picks a wife, the farmer picks a wife, hi-ho-the-derry-o, the farmer picks a wife." The Birthday Girl picks her favorite friend to join her in the middle. "The wife picks a child . . ." The favorite friend picks a favorite friend to join her. This continues on to the last verse: "The cheese stands alone. The cheese stands alone . . ." Nobody's favorite wins a prize.

The prizes have all been doled out: ball and jacks (which nobody knows how to play), paddle ball (not in the house!!!), coloring book, magic tablet, Mexican jumping beans . . .

Now it is time to open the presents. Everyone sits in a semicircle in the living room while the Birthday Girl sits by the fireplace and opens her presents. Paper dolls, colored pencils, potholder-making kit, paint-by-number . . . Wow!

Next, it's time for food. The kitchen table is set with paper plates and crepe paper–covered nut cups filled with pastel dinner mints and Spanish peanuts. Everyone puts on a party hat and eats hot dogs and potato chips.

The birthday cake is brought to the table with the candles lit, and everybody sings Happy Birthday to You. The Birthday Girl makes a wish and blows out the candles. (Make sure you don't talk before you finish eating your cake or your wish won't come true. Everybody will try to make you talk!)

It's time for the guests to leave. I want to play with my new stuff!
—*Diane*

Lemon and Toffee Crunch Cake

This is Mom's version of a German war bride's family recipe. I remember Mom made it one time up north when most of us were up there. She barely got the cake finished and it was wolfed down before she knew it!—*Jean*

Cake:
one yellow cake mix

Lemon Butter Filling:

"If someone skipped dessert for some reason, was that item still theirs? Did they have dibs on it? Or was it fair game?"—Julie

1 small package (2.9 ounces) lemon
   pudding

½ cup sugar

2 cups water

½ cup (8 tablespoons, or 1 stick) margarine

Toffee Crunch Topping:

½ cup sugar

1 cup finely chopped pecans

Bake the cake mix in two round layer-cake pans according to package directions.

In a saucepan, combine lemon pudding mix and sugar. Pour in ¼ cup of the water to dampen the pudding mix and sugar. Mix well. Add the remaining 1¾ cups water. Cook, stirring often, until mixture boils and thickens. Remove from heat. Cool to lukewarm. Stir in margarine while still warm.

Butter a cookie sheet (with sides!). In a frying pan, melt sugar until caramelized. (Be careful it doesn't burn.) Add pecans. Pour onto buttered cookie sheet to cool. When completely cool, roll with rolling pin to break up.

Slice each cake layer in half horizontally to make thinner layers. Cover the first layer with one-quarter of the lemon butter and add one-quarter of the toffee crunch topping. Lay the next layer on top of it and repeat process for each layer to make a four-layer cake. The sides of the cake are not covered. (*Mom says: "When you get to the top layer, hold off putting on the nuts until just before serving so the 'toffee crunch' will stay crunchy."*)

Do not walk too fast when carrying this to the table. It has a tendency to slide.—Susan
You could put a skewer down the center.—Jean

Lemon Pudding No-Bake Cheesecake

Every time this recipe comes up, Mom says the same thing: "The crust never gets soggy!" Sometimes she uses blueberry (or cherry) "pie fill" to top this, but we had it most often plain.—*Susan and Jean*

   1 package (8 ounces) cream cheese
   2 cups cold whole or 2% milk (Skim milk will not work in this recipe.)
   1 package (3¾ ounces) lemon instant pudding
   1 unbaked 9-inch Graham Cracker Crust*

Beat cream cheese with a mixer until well-softened. Add ½ cup of the milk, a little at a time, blending until mixture is very smooth. Add remaining 1½ cups milk and pudding mix. Beat until just blended, about 1 minute. Pour into crust. (Mom always sprinkles a little of the graham cracker crumbs on the top.) Chill until firm, or for at least 1 hour.

This crust can be store-bought or homemade.

Graham Cracker Crust (the way our mother makes it for a 9-inch pie crust):

9 double honey graham crackers (or ⅔ cup graham cracker crumbs)

3 tablespoons margarine, softened

Crush graham crackers with a rolling pin between sheets of waxed paper. Mix with softened margarine and press into a 9-inch pie pan. (No need to bake it for this recipe.)

For a pie that calls for a baked graham cracker crust, put in the oven for 10 minutes at 350°. You could fill this baked crust with any pudding and top with whipped cream.

Cheese Cups

We've seen these delicate little creations disappear directly from the muffin tin. Cheese Cups can be embellished with blueberries, dabs of lemon filling, or whatever, but they really don't need a thing, except maybe an armed guard. —*Susan*

MAKES 3 DOZEN

Crust:
1 cup graham cracker crumbs

butter, to grease tins

Filling:
2 packages (8 ounces each) cream cheese

¾ cup sugar

3 eggs, separated

a very little salt

Topping:
¾ cup sour cream

2½ tablespoons sugar

1 teaspoon vanilla

You will also need: 36 mini muffin cups (cup capacity: 2 tablespoons)

Preheat oven to 350°. Butter the muffin cups very generously. (The butter holds the crumbs to the sides of the cups and forms a little crust. Jean uses a pastry brush and very soft butter.) Sprinkle a little more than a teaspoon of graham cracker crumbs in each cup. (*In a pinch, crushed vanilla wafers will work.—Susan*) Move the pan around or use the handle of a teaspoon to move crumbs up the sides. Every part of the cup should be covered, or you won't be able to get the Cheese Cups out intact.

Combine cream cheese, sugar, egg yolks, and salt. Mix until smooth. (*If you mix the egg whites first, you won't have to wash the beaters twice.—Jean*)

Beat egg whites until very stiff and, still using the mixer—on its slowest speed—blend into cheese mixture. Fill mini muffin cups to top. Bake for 15 minutes. Remove from oven (keep oven on) and cool for 10 minutes. The tops of the cakes will sink in.

Combine topping ingredients and mix well. Spoon some of the topping onto each little cheesecake, spreading it not quite to the edges, and return to the oven for 5 minutes. Cool thoroughly, then run a table knife around the edges before removing from pans. Place Cheese Cups on serving platter and chill before serving. (They will become firmer than the one you could not resist tasting.)

Strawberry Shortcake

This is Mom's favorite. It's what she likes on her birthday and for breakfast the next day. Make this when she visits your house, and she won't even use a bobby pin to check the corners for dust. (Make two quarts of strawberries if you want to be *really sure* there will be enough left for Mom's breakfast.)—*Susan, Diane, Jean, Julie*

Strawberries:
1½ quarts (3 pints) strawberries

sugar, to taste

Shortcake:*
2 cups flour

4 teaspoons baking powder

2 tablespoons sugar

½ teaspoon salt

½ cup shortening (Crisco) or cold butter (1 stick)

¾ cup whole or 2% milk

Hull the strawberries, slice them into a large bowl, and add sugar to taste. Mom uses an old-fashioned potato masher to crush them. The sugar will draw out the juice.

Preheat oven to 450° and grease a 9 x 9-inch square or 10-inch round cake pan—or two 8-inch round cake pans, which will make a much thinner shortcake. (You could even cut this into round biscuits, but that's not how our mother does it.) Mix flour, baking powder, sugar, and salt. Work in shortening or butter (cut into little chunks) with a fork or pastry blender and then add milk all at once. Stir only until dough is formed. Press into pans with fingers or a fork. Bake until slightly golden on top, 10 to 15 minutes for a single pan of shortcake, but only about 8 minutes for two 8-inch round pans.

Cut warm (or not) shortcake and ladle strawberries on top. You could put Cool Whip or half-and-half on top. (We loved the squirt-on whipped cream Reddi-wip, but we always had a little too much fun with it for Mom to buy it very often.)

*You could use the Bisquick package recipe instead. Mom often does.

You can freeze the baked shortcake wrapped in foil. Let it thaw and heat it up (unwrapped) in a 350° oven until warmed through.—Susan

Mom's Birthday Surprise

The first year that we lived up north, we lived in the cottage. Dad was building the new house, and Mom was making do with life in a small house with few conveniences. No dishwasher, no central heat, and no laundry room. When the weather was warm, she had a wringer washer that she ran outside. When the weather was bad, she had to go to the dreaded laundromat. Either way, doing the laundry took considerable effort.

For her birthday that year I decided to make her a beautiful chocolate sheet cake. I planned to write on it in white icing and generally make it very nice. This was the first year without the rest of the girls around for her birthday, and I wanted to keep things cheery in that tiny house! I baked the cake, and as there wasn't any other counter space available, I put it on the smooth right side of the gas stove to frost it. The frosting was so-o-o creamy and I had made so-o-o much of it that it was really fun to swirl it around on the top of the cake. I made one particularly enthusiastic sweep, and the whole cake slid off the stove and fell frosting side down into a basket of clean white laundry.

Sorry, Mom . . . Happy Birthday?
—Julie

No-Crust Apple Pie (Grandma Noffke)

This really needs a catchier name. It is basically a Dutch apple pie without the crust (much less fattening), but you can still cut it like a pie. It's a find.—*Susan*

 6 medium-size tart apples (or 5 Granny Smiths*), peeled and cut

 ½ cup water

 ½ cup sugar

 1 teaspoon cinnamon

 3 tablespoons butter or margarine (*It's even better with 4 tablespoons.—Susan*)

 ¼ cup brown sugar

 ½ cup flour

 ½ teaspoon baking powder

 ½ teaspoon salt

 You will also need: a 9- or 10-inch ceramic or enameled pan (straight-sided is
    best for serving pieces intact)

Mix apples, water, sugar, and cinnamon in a saucepan. Cook until apples are just slightly softened, about 10 minutes. Then turn into pie pan.

Preheat oven to 350°. Cream butter and gradually add brown sugar. In another bowl, sift together flour, baking powder, and salt. Add to creamed mixture and mush together thoroughly with a fork. Sprinkle mixture over apples. (*I squeeze the topping into "Dutch apple pie" size crumbles with my hands as I'm sprinkling it.—Susan*) Bake until apples are tender and top is nicely browned, about 45 minutes. (You might want to put something under this when it's in the oven. It has a tendency to bubble over the sides.) Let the pie cool to lukewarm before you try to cut it. You can serve this with a spoonful of whipped cream or ice cream, but it's just fine without.

I used Cortlands and they were good, too. This is about 7 cups of apples.—Jean

Fast Pie Crust (The One with the Oil)

Before all the ready-made pie crusts became available, this was the crust used most often at our house. It's an odd recipe for pie crust, but it takes very little time to mix up, and you roll it out right away without chilling it. Follow the instructions carefully or it won't work (as three of us found out).—*Susan*

MAKES TWO 8-INCH CRUSTS

2 cups sifted flour
1 teaspoon salt
½ cup vegetable oil
¼ cup cold whole milk (2% *also works. Do not use skim milk!*)

In a large bowl, sift together flour and salt. Using a glass measuring cup, measure the vegetable oil and pour the milk on top of it. DO NOT STIR! Add the liquids all at once to the flour and salt mixture. Stir quickly with a fork. Mix until dough cleans the sides of the bowl. The dough will be in moist crumbs of various sizes. Squeeze into a ball. (Do not chill this dough before rolling.) Divide into two parts and roll out immediately to about ⅛ inch thick between two sheets of waxed paper.

For a double crust pie: Follow baking directions in the pie recipe you are using.

For a single crust (one-half recipe): Bake at 475° for 8 to 10 minutes (empty). Make sure it is pressed tightly to the bottom and sides of the pan. Prick the crust with a fork before you bake it.

Mom says: "This makes a tender and flakey crust."

Good Pie Crust (formerly known as The One with the Paste)

The original version of this recipe could be the reason our mother switched to using pie crust sticks. Somebody had the brilliant idea of making a "paste" out of the water and ½ cup of the flour so you wouldn't have to spend so much time working in the shortening, but that gluey "paste" (literally) is *much* harder to work in than soft shortening. We tried making this crust without the oddball "time-saver," and (drum roll)...it makes a perfect crust! (Our mother taught us to question authority.)—*Susan*

MAKES TWO 9-INCH CRUSTS

2 cups flour
a rounded ½ teaspoon of salt

⅔ cup vegetable shortening (Crisco or Spry)

4 tablespoons cold water

Sift flour and salt together. Work shortening into the flour mixture with a fork or pastry blender. Stir in cold water a tablespoon at a time. Form into two balls, making one of them a bit larger for the bottom crust, and chill. Roll to about ⅛ inch thick between two sheets of waxed paper.

Follow the temperature and timing for whatever double-crusted pie you are making.

Use this crust to make the "pre–pie stick" original version of the Apple Pie below. It makes a perfect pie.—Susan

Apple Pie

Mom used Betty Crocker Pie Sticks to make pie crust for a long time. She used Apple-Tru pie filling until it was no longer available.—*Julie*

More recently, she and Dad both use Jiffy Pie Crust Mix.—*Diane*

Pile unpeeled apples in a 9-inch pie pan to see how many you will need (a little more than 4 cups, about 4 large McIntosh or Cortland apples). Prepare the Jiffy Pie Crust Mix according to package directions. (You will need a top and a bottom crust.)

Preheat oven to 400°. Peel, core, and slice the apples ⅛ to 3/16 inches thick. Put the apples into a bowl and mix them with ¾ cup of sugar, 2½ tablespoons of flour, about a half teaspoon of cinnamon, and a dash of salt. (No piles of sugar, cornstarch, or nutmeg—not the Sanvidge way.) Put the apple slice mixture into the bottom crust. (Optional: Sprinkle with a little lemon juice—we like it a little tart.) Dot with butter. Put on top crust. Crimp edges with your thumb and the first knuckle of your pointer finger. Cut vents in the top or prick with a fork. Bake for 50 minutes.

Mom used to sprinkle cinnamon and sugar on the leftover pie scraps and bake them for us to eat right out of the oven.   Julie

"Apple-Tru" (R.I.P.)

And now Mom would like a moment of silence for the lost and much-lamented "Apple-Tru."

This was a canned "pie fill" of tart, thin-sliced apples (a blend of different varieties listed on the label) without all that gluey jelly that pie fillings have today. Apple-Tru tasted like you had cut up all those apples yourself. It would have saved you a lot of time, but . . . it's gone.—*Susan*

Raspberry Pie

Grandma just brought over raspberries from her garden. Let's make Raspberry Pie!—*Diane*

1 baked 9-inch pie crust
fresh raspberries (about a quart)
1 cup sugar
1 cup water
3 tablespoons cornstarch
half of a 3-ounce package of raspberry Jell-O powder

Cook raspberries, sugar, water, and cornstarch over low heat, stirring constantly, until clear (not cloudy). Pour raspberry mixture into baked pie crust and (while mixture is still hot) sprinkle (1½ ounces) raspberry Jell-O over the top. Let cool before serving.

If your Grandma doesn't have raspberry bushes or it's the wrong time of year, you can use frozen raspberries. Don't thaw or rinse them, just pour them into the saucepan with the sugar, water, and cornstarch, and follow the recipe.—Diane

Lemon Meringue Pie

Mom's Lemon Meringue Pie has a pale crust, and the meringue is high and browned on the tips. This is on the Favorite Desserts List.—*Susan*

1 baked 8-inch pie crust

Lemon Filling:

1 cup sugar

¼ cup cornstarch

1 cup boiling water

1 tablespoon butter

3 egg yolks, lightly beaten (Save the whites for the meringue.)

grated rind of 1 lemon (yellow part only)

juice of 1 lemon (about ⅓ cup)

Meringue:

3 egg whites

¼ teaspoon cream of tartar

6 tablespoons sugar

You will also need: a double boiler

Put water in the bottom part of the double boiler and put on to heat so it will be ready when you need it. Mix sugar and cornstarch in the top part of the double boiler. Add boiling water slowly and cook over *direct* medium heat until mixture thickens and boils. Remove from heat, stir in butter and, gradually, the lightly beaten egg yolks. Put pan over the bottom part of the double boiler and cook until mixture is very thick, stirring constantly. Remove from heat and stir in lemon rind and juice. When cooled, pour into baked crust.

Preheat oven to 300°. To make the meringue, beat the egg whites and cream of tartar until foamy. Gradually beat in sugar until egg whites are stiff and form a peak. Spread meringue on top of lemon filling and bake for 15 minutes. (The low heat will prevent "dew drops" from forming on the meringue.)

Cherry Pie

For Cherry Pie, Mom used "pie fill," as she called it.—*Julie*

Prepare Jiffy Pie Crust Mix according to package directions. You will need a top and a bottom crust. Place the bottom crust in a 9-inch pie pan.

Preheat oven to 400°. The top crust will be a "lattice" crust. Roll out the top crust and cut into ½-inch strips. Pour the cherry pie filling into the bottom crust. Dot with butter. Weave the strips into a top for the pie. (*Mom says: "If you are not making this for your mother-in-law, you can just lay them on top."*) Crimp edges with your thumb and the first knuckle of your pointer finger. Bake for about 50 minutes or so, until the cherries are bubbling and the crust is golden.

Rhubarb Pie

Mom didn't make this pie because she was the only one in our family who would eat it, but Grandma and Cile made it every year and always sent a piece over for Mom. This recipe is here to honor all those pieces of Rhubarb Pie that crossed Bowen Street.—*Susan*

2 unbaked 9-inch pie crusts

5 cups cut-up rhubarb (This is about 20 stalks of rhubarb cut into ¼- to ½-inch pieces, or 1½ pounds.)

1 cup sugar

¼ cup flour

3 eggs, lightly beaten

1 tablespoon butter, cut up for "dotting"

Preheat oven to 425° and place bottom crust in 9-inch pie pan. Put the cut-up rhubarb pieces into the bottom crust. Mix the sugar, flour, and beaten eggs and pour over rhubarb. Dot with butter. Make a lattice crust for the top of the pie by rolling out the top crust, cutting it into ¾-inch strips, and placing them at equal intervals on the pie. Weave strips across in the other direction. Pinch together with the bottom crust. Bake for 30 minutes, then reduce heat to 325° and bake for 30 minutes more.

"Kew-hoo!" (Grandma Noffke is at the back door.)

Mile-High Frozen Strawberry Pie (Mom)

This recipe is made with frozen strawberries. I didn't think Mom would ever "waste" fresh strawberries on anything but Strawberry Shortcake or jam. You can also make this with frozen raspberries.—*Susan*

It's hard to believe so few ingredients would fill two pie crusts, but they do. The pies are really light and fluffy. You could thaw an extra package of strawberries to serve on top for more strawberry taste.—*Diane*

MAKES TWO 8-INCH PIES

1 package (10 ounces) frozen sweetened strawberries, thawed

2 egg whites

1 tablespoon lemon juice

⅛ teaspoon salt

½ cup cream, whipped

1 teaspoon vanilla

2 baked 8-inch pie crusts

Combine strawberries, egg whites, lemon juice, and salt and beat for 15 minutes. Fold in whipped cream and vanilla. Pour into 2 cooled crusts. Freeze several hours or overnight.

Mom says: "I began to worry about uncooked eggs at some point and stopped making this."

Strawberry Pie (like Mom and Julie had at The Mint)

I must be the only person who ever looked forward to appointments at the orthodontist! When I was in high school, I had braces installed by the nearest orthodontist—sixty miles away in Wausau. Mom and I would make a day of it, shopping, eating, and finally having my braces adjusted. We ate at The Mint, a classic little diner, and we almost always ordered strawberry pie. This tastes just like it!—*Julie*

1 cup sugar

1 cup water

3 tablespoons cornstarch

two-thirds of a 3-ounce package of strawberry Jell-O
    powder

1 quart (not too huge) strawberries, hulled

1 baked 9-inch pie crust

whipped cream for topping

Mix sugar, water, and cornstarch in a saucepan and cook over medium heat, stirring constantly, until mixture becomes thick and no longer cloudy. Add Jell-O powder. Stir to blend thoroughly and dissolve the powder. Let cool.

Place strawberries in cooled pie crust and pour Jell-O mixture over all. Chill for four hours or overnight. Serve with big dollops of real whipped cream!

Pecan Pie

This recipe came from Mom's longtime neighbor and friend Joyce Peters.—*Susan*

    1 unbaked 9-inch pie crust

    3 eggs, lightly beaten

    1½ cups Karo dark corn syrup

    ½ teaspoon vanilla

    ¼ teaspoon salt

    ⅔ cup whole pecans

Preheat oven to 450° and put crust into pie pan. Combine beaten eggs, Karo syrup, vanilla, and salt. Mix well. Pour into crust. Place pecans on top of filling. Bake for 10 minutes, turn oven down to 350°, and bake for 25 minutes more.

Baked Apples

The apple skins get a little leathery, but the insides are delicious.—*Susan*

    cooking apples, 1 per person (*I used Cortlands.—Diane*)

    cinnamon

    brown sugar

    butter

    half-and-half or cream for topping

Preheat oven to 375°. Wash the apples and scoop out the cores*, trying not to go through to the bottom. Leave most of peel on, but peel the crown of the apple. Place in a baking dish. Fill center of each apple with brown sugar and cinnamon. Place about a teaspoon of butter in each apple. Cover bottom of pan with about ½ inch of cold water. Cover dish and bake until apples are cooked through and tender (but still look like apples), about 40 minutes. Serve with half-and-half or cream.

I once used a carrot peeler to do this. It wasn't pretty, but it worked.—Susan.

Rice Pudding (Mom)

This is one of Mom's classics. If you bought too much milk, this will help you use it up. Rice Pudding is very easy to make, and this recipe is much better than the gluey, custardy kind. Everybody at my house likes it a lot.—*Susan*

4 cups cooked white rice*

4 cups whole or 2% milk (Skim milk will not work in this recipe.)

1 cup dark raisins

½ cup sugar

¼ cup (4 tablespoons) butter

1 teaspoon cinnamon

Preheat oven to 350° and butter an ovenproof bowl** or 2-quart casserole dish. Combine cooked rice, milk, raisins, sugar, butter, and cinnamon in the bowl and stir. Bake covered for 20 minutes and then give it a stir. Bake uncovered, until top is browned and fairly solid (but there should be a little soupiness), 30 to 40 minutes longer. This is good hot, warm (best), or cold (some think this is best) with maple syrup poured on top. Some people pour on a little half-and-half.

To make 4 cups of cooked white rice: Combine 1¼ cups uncooked rice and 2½ cups water in a saucepan. Bring to a boil, cover, and cook on very low heat for 14 minutes.

**To be Authentic-Mom-Style, use a pale turquoise Pyrex bowl with white drawings of roosters on the sides. Rice Pudding doesn't puff up much, so whatever fits the total ingredients can be used for baking. (Jean says we should remind you to keep this in the refrigerator.)*

Vanilla Pudding with Bananas

1 package vanilla pudding (the kind you cook)
bananas
milk

Make the pudding following directions on package. Lay waxed paper over top to prevent skin from forming as it sets. (But the skin will form no matter what you do. Just eat it. It's good.) Slice bananas over the top and pour on a little milk and serve. (At our house, chocolate pudding had only milk on top—no bananas.)

Just Plain Old Vanilla

This was not our favorite answer to "What's for dessert?" You can see from all these recipes that Mom was no slouch when it came to the dessert category. She did deserve a break now and then.—*Susan*

Ignore whining. Get out ice cream scooper, bowls, and spoons. Go to the freezer and bring up that carton of Brand X Ice Milk you got on sale. Scoop and serve.

Things To Do When Mom Hands You . . . "Just Plain Old Vanilla"

"Hey, Mom, what's for dessert?" (We would be imagining Mom's Lemon Meringue Pie, Cherry Cobbler, German chocolate cake . . .) We'd see her hesitate, and we knew the dreaded answer—"Just plain old vanilla ice cream." We were spoiled by Mom's good baking and expected it every day!—*Jean*

Sprinkle ice cream with Nestlé's Quik.

Slice bananas on it and pour maple syrup on top.

"Who hid the vanilla ice cream under the sprinkled laundry?"

Pour Hershey's chocolate syrup on it and sprinkle it with nuts.

Smush it up until it's like a vanilla shake from Leon's Drive-in.

The Real Thing

When Mom was little, her family used to make their own ice cream and store it in the "ice room" of her parents' coal yard office. (Grandpa sold ice, too.) One summer we were having a picnic on Grandma and Grandpa Noffke's big lawn and everybody took turns cranking the ice cream churn to make homemade ice cream.

I am writing the recipe down just as it was, with little interjections in italics from our mother. (Uncle Hank has that ice cream churn now, so we haven't tried it.) It is interesting that the name of Cile's original recipe is:

Plain Vanilla Ice Cream

"*[In a double boiler . . .]* Blend 3 tablespoons cornstarch, 1 cup sugar and ¼ teaspoon salt. Add 4 cups scalding *[whole]* milk and cook over hot water, stirring until creamy and smooth, about 10 minutes. *[Take off the stove and let cool slightly (so you don't curdle the eggs) . . .]* Add gradually 3 beaten eggs, stirring constantly. Return to double-boiler and cook over hot water for 3 minutes, stirring constantly to prevent lumping. Chill. Fold in 1 cup cream, beaten until stiff and 2 tsp. vanilla. *[See below.]* Freeze."

Mom says: "The ice cream mixture was put into the central sleeve of the ice cream churn, rock salt and ice were put in the outside container, and the paddles were put in. A crank rotated the paddles. After a lot of cranking, the ice cream mixture thickens and coats the paddles and it's ready to eat." Nobody whined about this *plain vanilla ice cream.—Susan*

Do-It-Yourself Desserts

Is your sweet tooth calling? Try one of these.—*Susan*

Beg frosting (when Mom is frosting a cake). Spread begged frosting on a graham cracker.

Spread whipped honey on a soda cracker.

Make a piece of toast. Spread with peanut butter first, then raspberry jam. Eat while still hot and the peanut butter is melting in.

Climb onto the counter. Remove a small amount of chocolate chips from the half-bag hidden on the highest cupboard shelf.

First make sure there are Luden's Wild Cherry Cough Drops in the house (so you won't get the German Potato Salad Cure). Cough a few times, and ask if you can have a cough drop. If you're lucky, Jean will not have eaten them all.

Cookies and Bars

"Who's in that cookie jar?"

You are about to see the real reason we were so fond of the clown cookie jar with its shattered clown-hat lid replaced with the brown top of a Kaukauna Klub cheese crock. (The clink of that heavy lid always gave us away. Mom could hear it from the basement.) Homemade cookies disappeared really really fast; the "boughten" cookies lasted a little longer.

There was nothing at all special about Mom's battered aluminum 9 x 13-inch "cake" pan, but when it was filled with chewy bars made from all our favorite ingredients (nuts, chocolate, coconut . . .), we were irresistibly drawn to it. (Peeling back the tin foil could be done very quietly.)—*Susan*

Crisp Oatmeal Icebox Cookies

We learned how to make these cookies in 4-H, and like several of the 4-H recipes, they were so good that Mom started making them, too.—*Susan*

MAKES 4 TO 5 DOZEN COOKIES, DEPENDING ON SIZE AND THICKNESS

½ cup (8 tablespoons, or 1 stick) butter, softened

½ cup shortening (Crisco or Spry)

1 cup brown sugar

1 cup sugar

1 teaspoon vanilla

2 eggs, beaten until light and foamy

1½ cups flour

1 teaspoon baking soda

1 teaspoon salt

3 cups quick-cooking oats

½ cup chopped pecans

Using an electric mixer, cream the butter and Crisco together. Gradually add the sugars and mix until creamy and fluffy. Add the vanilla. Mix. Add the beaten eggs and mix well.

In another bowl, sift the flour, baking soda, and salt together. Add gradually to butter mixture and blend in thoroughly.

Add the oats ½ to 1 cup at a time, mixing thoroughly each time. The dough will be pretty stiff. Add the nuts and mix again.

Divide the dough in half. On a lightly floured board, shape each portion into a long rectangle about 3 inches across and 1½ inches high. Wrap in waxed paper or plastic wrap to cover and chill for several hours.

Preheat oven to 350° and grease cookie sheets. Slice off the cookies with a thin, sharp knife to about ¼ inch thick and place them on the cookie sheets. Bake until lightly browned, 10 to 13 minutes.

Did you know that . . .

. . . Mom has the most pristine cookie sheets of anyone anywhere? They look brand new after forty years of use. She scours them with SOS. No grease or grime for her!—*Julie*

Now I understand the expression on Mom's face as she made a futile attempt to wash my "seasoned" cookie sheets.—Susan

Grandma Sanvidge's Icebox Cookies

I am writing this recipe just as Grandma wrote it—note "oleo" and "vinilla." I always loved these cookies and looked forward to them. When we would get to Wisconsin, Grandma would always have them ready, sometimes just out of the oven. I also remember her saying Grandpa liked a "crisp" cookie, and I am like him in that regard. I made these several times for my children when they were little, until I figured that they (like my brother Ken) did not even like them! I still stand by them as my favorite cookie and, I think, my favorite Grandma memory.
—*Linda Sanvidge Watts (our cousin)*

"1 cup white sugar

1 cup light brown sugar

2 sticks or one cup of melted oleo

2 eggs (beat)

1 tsp soda disolve in about 2 tbs water

1 tsp vinilla

½ tsp cinnamon (optional)

Flour to form into shape for slicing*

Shape and place in refrig until they hold shape for slicing. Thickness depends on choice. Bake about 12 to 15 minutes in 350° oven. Can unbaked be kept in freezer and baked when needed. I've kept for months and baked a few at a time. To keep crisp I place in plastic bag and put on a twist. That is if you like crisp cookies. Only kind Grandpa would eat. Of course, I put bag in cookie jar. Love, Gran S. Can add 1 tsp B powder if you like them a little lighter. I don't use any."

This means put in just enough flour so you can shape the dough into two loaves for slicing. "B powder" is baking powder. (Grandma Sanvidge always used Blue Bonnet margarine.)—Susan

I added 4 cups of flour when I made Grandma's cookies. Many of us, including our cousin Ken, who didn't like them, remember that Grandma put sliced almonds in her cookies! (Be sure to leave room between the cookies when you put them on the cookie sheets, as they will spread.)—Jean

Grandma Noffke's Icebox Cookies

Our mother remembers "going to Wrchota's grocery store to buy 15 cents worth of walnuts in a little brown paper bag tied with a string." Grandma and Cile wanted to make sure the nuts were fresh, so they bought them only when they needed them.—Susan

MAKES ABOUT 3 DOZEN COOKIES

½ cup shortening (Crisco)

1 cup brown sugar

1 egg, beaten

½ teaspoon vanilla

1½ cups flour

½ teaspoon baking soda

¼ teaspoon salt

½ cup chopped walnuts

Cream shortening. Add brown sugar. Mix. Add beaten egg and vanilla. In another bowl, sift together flour, baking soda, and salt. Add to shortening mixture. Add nuts. Mold dough into a long, flattened roll about 3 inches wide and a foot long.* Wrap and chill in icebox.

Preheat oven to 350° and grease cookie sheets. When dough is firm (after about 45 minutes), slice off ¼-inch-thick cookies and place on cookie sheets. Bake until brown and crisp, about 12 minutes.

If you have two little loaf pans, you can line them with plastic wrap and press the dough into the bottoms. Use the base of one pan to compress the dough in the other. The plastic wrap will allow you to lift the cookies out of the pan. —Susan

Ginger Krinkles (Grandma Noffke)

These were cookie jar regulars at Grandma's, and we loved them. Soft and spicy, they travel well and make a great gift. Several years ago at a yard sale, I stumbled across a whole box full of Vernon Kilns Organdie dishes just like Grandma Noffke's. I made these cookies, put them on those brown and yellow plaid plates, and sent them to my sisters for Christmas. Did they like them? Well, it made them all cry. What do you think? This recipe is just as Grandma wrote it.—*Julie*

MAKES ABOUT 3 DOZEN COOKIES
(*I usually double this recipe.—Julie*)

"⅔ cup shortening (Crisco)
1 egg unbeaten

4 tablespoons *[dark]* molasses

1 cup sugar

½ teaspoon salt

2 teaspoons soda

1 teaspoon cinnamon

1 teaspoon ginger

2 cups sifted all-purpose flour

Mix shortening and sugar thoroughly. Add unbeaten egg and beat until fluffy. Stir in molasses. Sift dry ingredients together and add. Mix well. Chill until firm. Roll teaspoon of dough into ball. Dip in sugar and place on greased baking sheet three inches apart. Bake at 350° *[for 9 to 11 minutes]*. Cookies will crinkle."

Rocks (Uncle Fritz)

"They are good."—*Uncle Fritz (Mom's uncle, Fred Noffke, wrote this at the top of the recipe.)*

Mom says: "These are not called 'Rocks' because they're hard. They have lots of little chunks of dates and walnuts, and they look bumpy—like rocks."

MAKES ABOUT 7 DOZEN COOKIES

1½ cups sugar

1 cup (2 sticks) butter, softened

3 eggs

1 teaspoon baking soda, dissolved in 1 tablespoon hot water

1 teaspoon vanilla

3½ cups flour

1 teaspoon cinnamon

1 teaspoon allspice

¾ pound dates, "chopped fine" (2 cups chopped, about 50 dates)*

1 cup walnuts, "chopped not so fine"

Preheat oven to 325° and butter cookie sheets. Cream the sugar and butter. Add the eggs, baking soda dissolved in water, and vanilla and mix well. In a separate bowl, mix the flour, cinnamon, and allspice. Add dry ingredients to the butter/sugar mixture about a third at a time and mix until blended. Add chopped dates and walnuts and mix until well distributed. The texture of this cookie dough is similar to chocolate chip cookie dough.

Uncle Fritz . . . rocks.

Drop by rounded teaspoonfuls—an inch-plus diameter, pressed down a bit—on the cookie sheets. Bake for 14 minutes. (*Uncle Fritz and his sister, Lena, had an old wood-burning stove, and his baking instructions were "Cook slow," so we had to do some trial runs.*)

Put some butter on your date-holding fingers (and knife blade) while chopping the dates (which don't have to be that fine), and you won't go crazy with the stickiness.

Chocolate Chip Cookies (Our Favorite Cookie)

The "no-raw-eggs" generation will have to exert a little self-control. This dough is as good as the cookies, maybe even better. (Jean and I recently ate one-quarter of a batch of cookie dough—I think we must have built up our immunity by now.)—*Susan*

Go to the store right now and buy a 12-ounce package of Nestlé Semi-Sweet Chocolate Morsels. (*"Morsels?"*) You will find the best chocolate chip cookie recipe (in very small print) right there on that bright orangey-yellow package: "Original Nestlé Toll House Chocolate Chip Cookies." Make sure to get all the ingredients, including REAL BUTTER and pecans.

Some Tips:

- Use real butter. (Yes, we know we just told you that, but it needs to be repeated.)
- Use pecans. (Walnuts aren't as good with chocolate, in Susan's opinion.)
- Form the dough into golf-ball-size blobs for baking. (Get them ready all at once.)
- Do not overbake them. The cookies should be flexible when you take them out of the oven and make you think they are not quite done.
- After you use all the chips, make sure to save the package for the recipe. (You never know when a company will decide to "get with the times" and change a recipe.)

"Hiding Chocolate Chip Cookies in the freezer is not a good way to save them; they are just as good frozen (and easier to sneak)."

—Diane

Our mother is infamous for using only half the chocolate chips specified on the package and tucking away the rest of the bag in her highest cupboard where she thought we would not find them. (We crawled up onto the counter and ate undetectable amounts.) At the very bottom of the clown cookie jar there were always two or three rejects—completely chip-less cookies. We thought this had to do with two things: Mom was thinking about the health of her beloved daughters, and she likes being frugal. But, Julie just found out . . . Mom was eating those chocolate chips (too)!—Susan

Sugar Jumbles

This tiny recipe was written for 4-H cooking classes. Each student would make her own batch during the lesson and bake them. It makes only two dozen yummy, yummy cookies!—*Julie*

MAKES ONLY 2 DOZEN COOKIES!

¼ cup (4 tablespoons) butter, softened

¼ cup shortening (Crisco)

½ cup sugar

1 egg

1 teaspoon vanilla

1 cup plus 2 tablespoons flour

½ teaspoon salt

¼ teaspoon baking soda

Preheat oven to 375° and grease two cookie sheets. Cream together butter, Crisco, and sugar until fluffy. Beat in the egg and vanilla. In another bowl, sift together flour, salt, and baking soda, then add to creamed mixture and mix well. Drop by heaping teaspoonfuls on cookie sheets about 2 inches apart. Bake until very lightly browned, 8 to 10 minutes.

The Little Women 4-H Club

Joyce Misch, who had a daughter Diane's age, and our mother started a 4-H club in Oshkosh. This was unusual because 4-H was associated with farm kids and raising animals to show at the county fair. By a vote of the members, our 4-H club was named "Little Women." (*I hated this name. I was recently reminded that I wanted the club to be called "City Cats." No wonder I forgot.—Susan*) We had regular meetings and learned to cook and sew through 4-H (which stood for head, heart, hands, and health).

In our cooking class we learned how to make really decent muffins ("Yummy Muffins," which are in this book on page 21), Ambrosia (a banana, orange, and coconut fruit salad, page 109), and "Cocoa Sirup" from scratch. We made "Delicious Quick Cake" from scratch, too.

There was information in the recipes that we could apply to making other things. (How to avoid the dreaded muffin tunnels. How to measure ingredients.) When it was time for the fair, we would enter samples of our cooking to be judged (for ribbons!).

Carolyn Jones, our next-door neighbor, who was an expert seamstress, taught the 4-H sewing class. Our first project was an ultra-simple "scarf" that mainly taught us how to find the "straight" of a piece of fabric and that a line of sewing machine stitching would stop fabric from fraying. Other projects were an apron and a "dirndl" (gathered) skirt. Carolyn emphasized neatness, and the judges at the fair were picky about every single detail.

There were food reviews and dress reviews, project books and demonstrations of skill. The meetings were enjoyable get-togethers with the other members and their mothers. These "Little Women" learned a lot in 4-H!—*Jean and Susan (the City Cat)*

"Oh no! This is my third batch of Yummy Muffins, and they are full of tunnels! What else can I make for the fair?"

—Diane

Peanut Butter Cookies (Grandma Sanvidge)

The runner-up for most-likely occupant of Grandma Sanvidge's cookie jar, if it's not filled with Icebox Cookies.—*Susan*

MAKES ABOUT 80 COOKIES, 1 1/2-INCH DIAMETER

1 cup shortening (Crisco or Spry)

1 cup sugar

1 cup brown sugar

2 eggs, well-beaten

1 teaspoon vanilla

3 cups flour

1½ teaspoons baking soda

½ teaspoon salt

1 cup chunky peanut butter

Preheat the oven to 400° and grease cookie sheets. Cream shortening and sugars. Mix well. Add the beaten eggs and vanilla. In another bowl, sift together the flour, baking soda, and salt. Add to the creamed shortening mixture. Add the peanut butter. Mix well and knead. Form into ¾-inch balls and place 1 inch apart on the cookie sheets. Press cookie balls down with fork first lengthwise, then crosswise to form a criss-cross pattern on a 1½-inch diameter cookie. Bake for 10 minutes. (There should be no browning on these cookies.)

"Let's Just Eat Junk!"

Great-Aunt Emma was a favorite with us Sanvidge girls. She was what most grown-ups would call "a real character." To us kids, she was one of us. Aunt Emma wore her gray hair parted in the middle, braided on both sides, with the braids pulled up to the top of her head and pinned down, overlapping each other. She had a kindly face and an ample figure that was usually attired in a dress, often with a cardigan sweater. She traveled admirably light on her overnight trips: a pillow, a pair of underpants, a nightgown, and a toothbrush.

Once in a while, Aunt Emma would join the family for a road trip. She was famous for repeatedly asking: "Is this a town?" on a long-ago trip down south to visit Uncle Cliff and Aunt Millie.

Aunt Emma was *not* known for her healthy cuisine. When she came to take care of us for more than just an evening, she'd say, "Let's just eat *junk!*" and fix us such kid favorites as *homemade* potato chips and *homemade* fried cake donuts! (Do you think maybe it was our very own Aunt Emma who coined the term *junk food?*)

I tried making fried cake donuts several times in an attempt to recapture those wonderful Aunt Emma culinary treasures. I didn't have Aunt Emma's recipe so I used one from a cookbook. The dough was either way too limp or too stiff and the donuts would be tough and dry. I finally put a note next to that recipe, "Jean, you made a mess of these before. Don't try it again!!"—*Jean*

I remember Aunt Emma's donuts fried in lard and done up with powdered sugar in a brown paper bag, and that she ate bacon grease sandwiches! —Julie

I remember her eating lard sandwiches. When the trip included a social event, she tossed a red lipstick into her pillowcase (which also served as her suitcase).—Susan

Aunt Emma with Diane, Jean, and Susan in our Bowen Street living room.

Aunt Emma's Cardamom Cookies

These are soft, dry, very spicy old-fashioned cookies. If you like your cookies crisp or chewy, you might want to try a different recipe.—*Susan*

Cardamom

MAKES ABOUT 5 TO 6 DOZEN COOKIES, DEPENDING ON SIZE

1¼ cups brown sugar

½ cup shortening (Crisco or margarine)

1 egg, beaten

½ cup light molasses

½ teaspoon baking soda, dissolved in ½ cup hot water

4 cups flour

1½ teaspoons ground cardamom*

½ teaspoon allspice

½ teaspoon ground cloves

(Mom recommends adding a scant ½ teaspoon salt.)

Preheat oven to 375° and grease cookie sheets. Cream brown sugar and shortening. Add beaten egg, molasses, and soda dissolved in hot water and beat in.

In another bowl, combine flour, cardamom, allspice, cloves, and salt. Add flour mixture to batter, gradually beating in.

Drop batter onto cookie sheet in teaspoon-size blobs. (No need to flatten them.) Bake for 10 minutes. Store in an airtight container.

*The best cardamom comes in its pod. You will need to shuck the little seeds out and crush them. If you have a mortar and pestle, use that. (But you can also buy it ground.)

Hermits (Grandma Sanvidge, who found it in Household Magazine)

Hermits are biscuit-like cookies that taste like spice cake. After I made them as a test run, I sat down and had some with a cup of hot tea. It wasn't hard to imagine Grandma Sanvidge doing exactly the same thing.* Here is Grandma's recipe as she typed it.—*Susan*

"Cream 3 tablespoons butter. Add ½ cup sugar. Stir in one beaten egg. Sift together 2 teaspoons baking powder and 1 cup flour. Add this mixture alternately with 2 tablespoons milk. Add ½ teaspoon each of cloves and cinnamon. Stir in ¼ cup raisins, chopped finely, and 2 tablespoons chopped nut meats. *[I used walnuts.—Susan]* Drop 2 inches apart on an oiled sheet from a teaspoon. Bake in a moderate oven *[350°]* 20 min. Double Recipe *[because it makes only about two dozen small cookies]*."

*Grandma's tea would be in a Blue Willow cup for sure.—Diane

To Buy for the Cookie Jar

Oreos, Johnson's Chocolate Pinwheels, LaFontaine's huge sugar cookies with the scalloped edges, pecan shortbreads, Marshmallow Puffs, vanilla cream and chocolate cream sandwich cookies, butter cookies (the kind with the hole in the middle), Fig Newtons, ginger snaps ... (Skip those Dutch Windmill cookies and the "boughten" chocolate chip cookies!)

Brownies

These are excellent brownies, much better than the package mixes and not at all difficult to make. This is a very fudgy brownie. For a chewier version, see instructions below. You will be asked for the recipe. Mom found the original in the *Oshkosh Daily Northwestern*. (Don't forget the cup of flour that goes in last!)—*Susan*

4 eggs
2 cups sugar
1 teaspoon vanilla

1 cup butter (2 sticks)

4 squares unsweetened chocolate (or 9 tablespoons unsweetened cocoa
   powder for Chewy Brownies below)

1 cup flour

nuts for topping (whole, or almost whole, walnuts or pecans; chopped pecans
   for Mom's chewy brownies)

Preheat oven to 325° and butter the bottom and sides of a 9 x 13-inch
pan. Using an electric mixer, beat eggs lightly and then beat in sugar and
vanilla. In a saucepan, melt butter over low heat. When almost melted, add
unsweetened chocolate. Stir. Pull off heat as soon as chocolate is melted. Pour
into egg/sugar/vanilla mixture, beating as you pour (so you don't "cook" the
eggs). Add flour and mix well. Pour into baking pan. Sprinkle with whole (or
almost whole) walnuts or pecans. Bake for exactly 43 minutes. If you know
your oven is accurate, just pull them out. It's always okay at 43 minutes. (If
refrigerated, they will be even fudgier.)

For Chewy Brownies (the way Mom usually makes them):
Follow the recipe above but substitute 9 level tablespoons unsweetened cocoa
powder for the 4 squares of unsweetened baking chocolate. Melt the butter
as noted above and mix it into the egg/sugar/vanilla mixture, followed by the
cocoa powder, and then the flour. The batter will be thick—you will have to
spread it in the pan. (Baking time will be the same.) Mom sprinkles ½ cup
chopped pecans on her Chewy Brownies before baking.

*You will be in trouble if you make only one pan of these and you intend to give it away (to
a church bazaar like Mom did). These brownies freeze very well.—Susan*

Mom's Famous Granola Bars

These are very popular with the grandchildren. Mom gives them containers full of her Famous Granola Bars (and Dad gives them frozen jars of his homemade applesauce).—*Susan*

⅔ cup margarine or butter

1 cup brown sugar, firmly packed

4 cups quick-cooking oats

⅓ cup light corn syrup or honey

1 teaspoon vanilla

½ teaspoon salt

½ cup coarsely chopped nuts (usually pecans; walnuts are good, too)

⅓ cup flaked coconut

You will also need: a 15½ x 10½-inch jelly roll pan

Preheat oven to 350° and butter a 15½ x 10½-inch jelly roll pan generously. Melt margarine (or butter) in a 4-quart saucepan. Take off the stove and stir in all other ingredients, nuts and coconut last of all. Blend well. Press the mixture lightly into the well-buttered jelly roll pan.

Bake until lightly browned on the edges, 20 to 25 minutes. (Watch carefully!) Cool 5 minutes, then cut into squares and remove from pan while still warm (or you won't be able to get them out!). A meat cleaver or a large chef knife works best. Start from the outside edges because it cools from the outside in. Store in a tightly covered container.

Mom says: "Don't use raisins or dates. They will turn into little pellets."

Lemon Bars

The recipe Mom gave me says her friend Marge Elst gave it to her.—*Julie*

Crust:

1 cup (2 sticks) margarine or butter, softened

2 cups flour

½ cup powdered sugar

Filling:

4 eggs

2 cups sugar

6 tablespoons lemon juice (fresh is best—about 2 good-sized lemons)

¼ cup flour

1 teaspoon baking powder

pinch of salt

powdered sugar for dusting

Preheat oven to 350°.

To make the crust: Put softened margarine (or butter) in a bowl with the 2 cups flour and ½ cup powdered sugar. Using a mixer, blend well. Press mixture into bottom of a 9 x 13-inch cake pan. (This will be easy to do using a bent-blade metal spatula—the kind you would use to serve a cake from this pan—as a trowel. It will make up for all the time you just spent with the mixer.) Bake for 20 minutes.

While crust is baking, make the filling. Beat eggs until fluffy. Add sugar, lemon juice, flour, baking powder, and salt. Beat until well blended. Pour mixture over the baked, still warm crust. Return to 350° oven until firm, about 25 minutes. When cool, dust with powdered sugar.

On My Own (with Grandpa)

In the summer of 1971, Mom, Dad, and Julie moved up north to live in the cottage while Dad built the new house next door. I had been living at home and going to college, so I rented a third-floor apartment at my friend Rose Palma's house on Amherst Street. There was about a two-week period before I could move into my new place, so Grandma and Grandpa Noffke graciously offered me a place to stay.

I was out on a date one night and returned late and found Grandpa at the table having a "midnight snack." I chatted with him for a few minutes, and he offered me a piece of cheese. It must have been a good date, because I certainly wasn't thinking about what Grandpa had just offered me when I said, "Yes." I hate cold, stinky cheese! As I sat there choking it down, he said, "How about a glass of milk to go with that

cheese?" More like a glass of milk to *wash down* that awful cheese, I thought. "Yes, please," I said and took a huge gulp before I realized it was *buttermilk*! Yuck! About this time I was really missing our good old refrigerator at home. (I guess all those years of "at least try it" were helping me to choke down that combo without embarrassing myself.) Finally, Grandpa said, "How about a graham cracker?" This time I thought first, wracking my brain . . . Is there any way these could be screwed up? They were the real deal—normal old reliable honey graham crackers, thank goodness!
—*Jean*

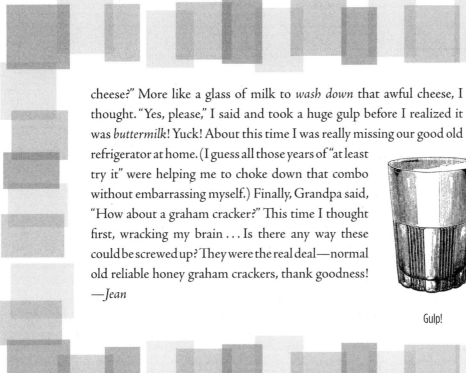

Gulp!

California Dream Bars

Don't just dream about these. Make 'em!—*Jean*

Crust:

1 cup flour

½ cup brown sugar, firmly packed

½ cup (8 tablespoons, or 1 stick) butter, melted

Filling:

4 eggs, beaten until light

2 cups brown sugar, firmly packed

2 cups flaked coconut (Mom uses Baker's Angel Flake.)

2 cups pecans (Use the kind that are broken into small pieces.)

¼ cup flour

1 teaspoon baking powder

½ teaspoon salt

Preheat oven to 375°. Mix flour, sugar, and melted butter with a fork until blended, and press firmly into the bottom of a 9 x 13-inch cake pan. (Use a bent-blade spatula as a trowel.) Bake until somewhat browned, 10 to 12 minutes. (Leave oven on.)

With a mixer, beat together beaten eggs, brown sugar, coconut, pecans, flour, baking powder, and salt. Spread over baked crust. Bake until set, not wobbly, 30 to 35 minutes. When completely cool, slice into bars.

Mom contributed this recipe to her Homemakers Club cookbook. It is knock-you-out delectable, but very rich. The California Dream Bars that our health-conscious mother made for us had half the filling! To make sensible Wisconsin Dream Bars: Make the crust the same way, but bake it for 13 minutes. Halve all the filling ingredients and bake the filled crust for 15 to 20 minutes until firm, not wobbly. We loved these, and never knew what we were missing.—Susan

Cookie Bars (also known as Hello Dollys)

If you know Joyce Peters's sister-in-law, could you thank her for us?—*Susan*

½ cup (8 tablespoons, or 1 stick) butter

1½ cups graham cracker crumbs

1 small bag (6 ounces) semi-sweet chocolate chips

1 cup chopped pecans

1⅓ cups flaked coconut

1 can (14 ounces) Eagle Brand sweetened condensed milk

"No, I don't want to split a piece. I want another piece!"—Jean

Preheat oven to 350°. Melt butter in a 9 x 13-inch pan. Sprinkle graham cracker crumbs evenly over bottom of pan, soaking up butter, and pat down gently to form a crust.* Sprinkle (in this order): chocolate chips, nuts, and coconut evenly over crust. Drizzle sweetened condensed milk evenly over all. Bake until top is lightly browned, about 25 minutes. Cool thoroughly before cutting. Store at room temperature. (You can also freeze these. Reheat slightly before serving.)

Somebody didn't want to dirty a dish. This would be much easier to do in a bowl. Use a bent-blade spatula to press it into the pan.—Susan

Cinnamon Bars (Mom)

These are delicious! You probably already have everything you need to whip them up.—*Julie*

I always thought if you called something a "bar," it would be chewy. Cinnamon Bars are more like a not-very-high, moist spice cake.—*Susan*

1 cup brown sugar
¼ cup shortening (Crisco)
1 egg
1 cup hot coffee
1½ cups flour
1 teaspoon baking powder
½ teaspoon cinnamon
¼ teaspoon baking soda
¼ teaspoon salt
½ cup raisins
¼ cup chopped pecans or walnuts

Preheat oven to 350° and grease a 9 x 13-inch pan. Cream sugar, shortening, and egg. Stir in coffee. In another bowl, sift together flour, baking powder, cinnamon, baking soda, and salt. Stir into creamed mixture. Blend in raisins and nuts. Spread in pan. Bake until a toothpick poked into the center comes out clean and it is pulling away from the sides of the pan, 20 to 25 minutes. Cool.

Mom says: "Birthday Cake Frosting (page 262) is good on Cinnamon Bars."

Holidays

The only time there's candy in the house.

For Easter we had new white or patent leather shoes with stiff straps and slippery soles, flower-sprigged hats that clamped on our heads (giving us headaches), and dainty purses (holding a nickel and a Kleenex). It was really nice to have new outfits, but our focus was on the scrumptious contents of our Easter baskets. Candy was our favorite part of Halloween, too. (Thanksgiving was just "the holiday between Halloween and Christmas.")

Christmas was by far the biggest holiday for us. Our mother has always loved Christmas, and no effort was too much. The delicious aroma of cookies, and more cookies, baking in the oven; Christmas carols on the radio; the smell of the Christmas tree coming into the house; the cookie decorating and filled candy dishes; and last, but not least, that growing pile of presents under the tree.—*Susan*

Baked Ham

Dad says: "Buy a Hillshire Ham. I've never been disappointed in one." Bake a ham and you will have food for a week.
—*Susan*

Buy an uncooked whole smoked ham with a bone.

Follow the instructions on the ham package. If there aren't any instructions with your ham, these are the general rules:

Preheat oven to 325°. Wipe the ham and put it in a shallow pan with a little water in the bottom, fat side up. Bake until a meat thermometer inserted into the ham reads 160°, 18 to 20 minutes per pound.

"My Easter hat fell off, and it's on my legs! How can I pick it up with my hands folded?"
—Diane (to herself, still kneeling after taking Communion on Easter Sunday)

Here Comes Peter Cottontail . . .

We almost always gave up candy for Lent and looked forward to our Easter baskets.

The week before Easter we colored eggs at the kitchen table. Mom covered the table with newspapers and mixed the boiling water, vinegar, and color tablets in coffee cups. The wire egg dippers were bent, and six eggs were submerged. While we waited for the color to intensify, we punched out the spinning tops and egg holders printed on the box and used the wax crayon to claim an egg in the next batch. Six eggs out, six more eggs in, stains everywhere. By the last batch (we usually dyed three dozen eggs), we had begun to experiment with multiple dipping. The resulting eggs were an unappetizing grayish purple.

On Saturday afternoon, we took baths and got our hair set in pin curls with bobby pins and put our Easter baskets outside our bedroom doors.

We woke up extra early Easter morning, eager to see what the Easter Bunny had brought us. Caramel jelly beans, fruit-flavored colored jelly beans, fluffy "potato" eggs with pastel-colored hard shells, and malted milk balls were nestled in the cellophane grass! Bubbles, a jump rope, or a paddle-and-ball game were bonuses. In 1958, when our little sister Julie was born one week before Easter, Dad was the Easter Bunny. He made one stop: Hughes' Home Maid Chocolates in Oshkosh. (Yes, that's how they spell "made." They sell their delicious chocolates only from September through Easter.) He bought chocolate-coconut nests with jelly bean "eggs," chocolate bunnies, and chocolate-filled eggs. We started eating the candy right away and don't remember what else (besides candy) we had for breakfast. Our mother says we always had fresh cut-up pineapple, which we love, so we must have eaten some. (It was whiter-looking then, not so yellow.)

We dressed in our new frilly dresses with petticoats and lace, matching hats and purses, white gloves, and new shoes. We had spring coats, but often it was too cold to wear them and we had to cover our new springy dresses with our old winter coats.

Easter dinner was at noon, and both grandmas and grandpas came. There was a big ham and scalloped potatoes baking in the oven while we were all at church. Often there were baked beans in the oven, too. Mom says she always made them with Great Northern beans and used the recipe in *The Settlement Cook Book*. Sometimes we had peas and carrots served in the Petite Bouquet divided vegetable dish. Lime Cottage Cheese Salad (a Jell-O mold; see page 81) and homemade Cloverleaf Rolls (page 219) or Hoska (page 347) completed the menu.

For dessert, Mom often made an angel food cake with fluffy white Seven-Minute Frosting (page 323).

In the afternoon the adults sat and visited while we ate candy, played inside, ate candy, played outside, and ate candy. The Easter season ended for us the next weekend. Our Easter candy was long gone, and we finally ate the leftover grayish purple eggs for Saturday lunch—after peeling them with our eyes closed.—*Diane*

Jean and Diane in their Easter outfits on Grandma Noffke's lawn.

Baked Beans for Easter

This is Mom's version of a recipe from *The Settlement Cook Book*. Mom makes her baked beans in a brown ceramic bean crock that sits on a plug-in burner.
—*Diane*

1 quart Great Northern beans (two 16-ounce packages)

½ pound unsliced bacon, cut into 1-inch cubes

3 tablespoons brown sugar (Mom uses brown sugar, but white sugar can be substituted.)

2 tablespoons light molasses

1 tablespoon salt

1½ teaspoons dry mustard (but Mom usually leaves this out)

1 cup boiling water

You will also need: a 4-quart kettle and a 4-quart casserole dish or roasting pan

Rinse the beans and pick out any bad ones (or stones). Put the beans in a pan or pot. Pour in enough cold water to cover the beans and let them soak overnight.

The next morning, rinse the beans again and put in enough fresh water to cover the beans. Cover and heat slowly on the stove. Cook the beans just below the boiling point. Our mother says this is called "parboiling." After 1 to 1½ hours, check to see if the beans are cooked. Put some on a spoon and blow on them. If they're done, the skins will burst. When the beans are cooked, drain them and put them in the bean crock or a 4-quart baking dish.

Preheat oven to 325°. Fry the cubed bacon until it is starting to get transparent and lose some of its fat. Drain the bacon and stir it into the drained beans.

In a bowl, combine the sugar, molasses, salt, and optional mustard. Pour in the boiling water and stir to blend. Stir this mixture into the beans and bacon. Add enough water so the beans are just covered. Cover and plug in your (one-gallon!) bean pot, or bake in a covered casserole dish for 6 to 8 hours, removing the cover for the last hour.

The Voice of (Bad) Experience Speaks: I didn't have a 4-quart casserole, so I divided the beans between a heavy enameled cast-iron pot and a ceramic casserole dish. At 6 hours, I had burnt beans in both pots! (The beans in the ceramic casserole dish were more burnt.) So, cook your beans all in one pot.—Susan

Seven-Minute Frosting (also known as Boiled Frosting)

Making this light-as-air frosting feels like magic, and it is perfect on angel food cake. (Use a package mix for the angel food cake and spend the time you save buying Easter Bunny candy.) You can swirl this lustrous, spun-satin frosting, make peaks, or you can sprinkle shredded coconut over it after you frost the cake. It's like eating marshmallows, but softer.—*Susan*

1 egg white, thoroughly chilled

1 cup sugar

½ teaspoon vanilla

"Are we sure there are no more Easter eggs hiding in Uncle Hank's couch?"—Diane

¼ teaspoon cream of tartar

½ cup boiling water

Combine egg white, sugar, vanilla, and cream of tartar in the bowl of an electric mixer. Add boiling water and beat at high speed for about 7 minutes. The frosting is done when it will hold a stiff peak.

Trick or Treat

We never got a costume from the store. Store-bought costumes came in a box with the face of the hard plastic mask showing through a cellophane window. A shiny nylon suit to wear over your clothes was folded behind it. The details of Mighty Mouse or Roy Rogers body were printed on the suit. Neato! We envied the kids who got these costumes. They looked so authentic. As the night wore on, the legs of their suits ripped, and they had to take baby steps. Then their masks got flipped to the tops of their heads and they couldn't see. Halfway through trick-or-treating, they couldn't run from house to house anymore. (Maybe these store-bought costumes weren't so great after all.)

We *did* get to create our own costumes from things we had at home. An old sheet and scissors made us into a ghost; a flowered skirt, summer top, Aunt Dorie's Mexican jacket, lipstick, and a "beauty mark"—a gypsy; blue jeans, Dad's work shirt, and a bandana tied to a stick—a hobo.

There were masks sold separately at the dime store. They were made of a starched, coarse material. They smelled terrible. By the end of the night the mask was soggy around the mouth and our lips were stained red.

One year I colored a brown paper bag, cut eyes out, and wore it over my head. The Unknown Comic stole my idea twenty years later.

St. Mary's School made us wear *saint* costumes to school for Halloween. (The mothers must have hated having to come up with two costumes for each kid.) Susie was St. Helen in a dark purple Grandma-leftover velvet dress with a silver paper crown on her head. I was St. Theresa, the Little Flower, in a dress made from a sheet, with a blue ribbon tied around my waist, holding a bunch of flowers from an old Easter hat.

Susan in her first-grade Halloween costume, as St. Helen. (The nuns made us dress as our patron saint for Halloween, and Mom let Susan borrow her saint. We didn't have those fat missals with the lives of saints in the back yet, so we didn't know there actually was a St. Susanna.)

On Halloween night we headed out to make our rounds as soon as supper was over. We met Patsy and Mary Lou outside and started the door-to-door ritual. We covered three or four blocks running between houses.

At home we dumped our loot on our beds and began sorting it. Our favorites were Butterfinger and Baby Ruth candy bars, Mr. Goodbars, Tootsie Rolls and Tootsie Pops, Pixy Stix, Bit-o-Honey and Slo-poke suckers. Grandma Noffke, who cared about our health, always gave us little boxes of raisins. We found peanut butter kisses in orange and black wrappers and candy corn without wrappers; strawberry, chocolate, or banana Kits candies, three squares wrapped together; two-packs of Chiclets gum and five candy cigarettes in a box. At the bottom of the bag there was always a beat-up apple that we didn't want. We traded a few things and then started eating the candy.

We loved candy and couldn't control ourselves . . . in two days we had eaten every bit of it. Months later we would be playing at Patsy and Mary Lou's, and *their* trick-or-treat bags were still full of candy.
—*Diane*

Susan and Diane in bed with bags of Halloween candy.

Skull Face Marshmallows

One year we had a Halloween party, and along with the classic "bobbing for apples" in an old washtub (go for one with a stem), we served these eerie marshmallows in mugs of hot cocoa.—*Susan*

> a very small brush (the kind you use to paint a picture) or a toothpick
> marshmallows (the big ones)
> blue food coloring

Use the brush or toothpick to paint skull faces on the flat sides of the marshmallows with blue food coloring: little vertical lines for the eye and nose sockets; a row of vertical lines for the teeth. The marshmallow skulls will melt, ghoulishly, when placed (face up) in the "swamp" of hot cocoa. (*See recipe for Hot Cocoa on page 205.*)

Popcorn Balls

Dad makes these Popcorn Balls. These are much, much better than the (stale-tasting) kind you can buy.—*Susan*

MAKES ABOUT 18 POPCORN BALLS, DEPENDING ON SIZE

4 to 5 batches of popcorn, unbuttered (1½-quart pan two-thirds filled with
    popped corn, roughly 6 quarts)* **

¾ cup brown sugar

¾ cup sugar

½ cup light corn syrup

½ cup water

1 teaspoon salt

1 teaspoon vinegar

¾ cup butter, softened

You will also need: a candy thermometer and waxed paper

> **"Joan, mix me an alloy."**
> —Dr. Weinzierl (our dentist)

Make the popcorn and put it all in a large bowl. In a large saucepan, combine the sugars, corn syrup, water, salt, and vinegar. Heat to 260° (check with a candy thermometer). Whisk in butter. Pour over popcorn and stir until all popcorn is coated. Let sit for 10 minutes, butter hands, and start forming into balls (about the size of a baseball). Wrap in waxed paper, twisting sides.

To make Popcorn à la Dad, follow the recipe on page 207.

**Shake the popcorn so the "old maids" (unpopped kernels) fall to the bottom (and don't use them in the popcorn balls).—Jean*

The Holiday without Candy or Presents

The week before Thanksgiving was "make some room in the refrigerator" time. On Thanksgiving morning, Mom and Dad would work together in the kitchen (all I remember us doing is sometimes making place cards or setting the table), with Dad up to his elbows in his famous stuffing and Mom making the fancier things. There was a huge pile of pots and pans for this extravaganza. Both sets of grandmas and grandpas would be at our house for Thanksgiving, and sometimes one of the grandmas would bring mincemeat pie. (Yuck.)

Dad would stand up to carve the turkey at the table, and everyone passed their plate for turkey as he cut it. "I want a leg!" The Petite Bouquet (our good dishes) salt and pepper shakers were so tiny that Dad always brought the battered salt and pepper shakers from the stove to the table. (Picture Mom's face when he did this.) The dainty gravy boat was so tippy on its (matching) plate that every pass of the gravy was accompanied by "Be careful!," and the Cranberry Sauce always stained the tablecloth.

Everybody always groaned about how full they were, but when the table was cleared and the pies came out, nobody ever said no. As everyone waited for dessert, Mom whipped cream for the pies, adding a little powdered sugar, watching carefully so it wouldn't turn into butter.

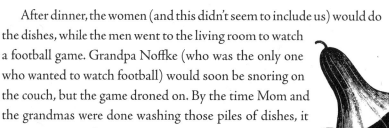

After dinner, the women (and this didn't seem to include us) would do the dishes, while the men went to the living room to watch a football game. Grandpa Noffke (who was the only one who wanted to watch football) would soon be snoring on the couch, but the game droned on. By the time Mom and the grandmas were done washing those piles of dishes, it was time to start all over again—with turkey sandwiches, and everything coming back out of the refrigerator. —*Diane*

Cranberry Sauce

I think it has to be a holiday before you are allowed to make this.—*Susan*

2 cups water
2 cups sugar
4 cups fresh whole cranberries, washed

Mix the water and sugar together in a large saucepan over medium heat. Cook until you have a clear syrup, about 10 minutes. Add the cranberries. Cover and cook until the cranberries are translucent and have popped open. Serve cold with turkey or chicken.

Pumpkin Pie

Does anybody remember having this when it wasn't Thanksgiving?—*Susan*

1 unbaked 10-inch pie crust
3 eggs, lightly beaten
1 cup sugar
1 teaspoon salt
1 teaspoon Mixed Spices*
1½ cups scalded whole or 2% milk (Skim milk will not work in this recipe.)
½ cup cream
2 cups canned pumpkin
whipped cream

Preheat oven to 450° and put pie crust in pan. In a large bowl, combine beaten eggs, sugar, salt, and Mixed Spices. Gradually stir in hot scalded milk and cream, and then stir in pumpkin. Pour into pie crust. Bake for 10 minutes. Reduce heat to 350° (while pie is still in the oven) and bake until a knife in the center comes out clean, about 25 minutes longer. Serve with a dollop of whipped cream.

To make Mixed Spices: Combine 1½ teaspoons cinnamon, ½ teaspoon ground cloves, ½ teaspoon mace, ½ teaspoon allspice, ½ teaspoon nutmeg. (Save the rest for next Thanksgiving.)

Christmas Eve

We always opened our presents on Christmas Eve night. During the day, people came by to drop off presents and eat cookies, and Uncle Keith would always bring a huge box of Hughes' Chocolates. Mom says Grandma Sanvidge used to make oyster stew on Christmas Eve, but at our house macaroni and cheese was the traditional supper.

For quite a few years, we would go across the street to Uncle Hank's house after we had finished (trying to eat) our supper. As the parents calmly sipped their drinks, our little Noffke cousins were whipping themselves into a frenzy (behind the kitchen door), *and we just couldn't wait*... Is that a noise I hear at the door? It's Santa!!! (Thanks, Dr. Graber!) Santa in person comes in with a bag of presents! The wrappings are flying everywhere! The squealing! The chaos! (Meanwhile, we still haven't opened our presents, except the ones directly from Santa's bag.) More drinks. "Dad, can you see if Santa came to our house yet?" (Amazingly, every time he checked, Santa *had* already been there.)

Julie opens her presents on Christmas Eve. (A whole set of pots and pans! She also got a little stove.)

So . . . we all go back to our house, and there is an absolute *mountain* of presents under the tree! We open our presents (trying to keep our little cousins from "helping" us) and eat Christmas cookies under the Christmas tree lights. Then everybody goes home. Christmas Eve almost always ended with us walking around in our underwear (those pretty nylon dresses were scratchy!) or putting on brand-new pajamas made by Grandma Noffke. (One year Grandma made matching pajamas for our dolls.)

Christmas Day was usually celebrated with a big dinner at our house, with both sets of grandparents and often Grandma Great (bringing in her Suet Pudding). We loved seeing our skinny Grandpa Sanvidge next to our fat Grandpa Noffke! The mountains of mashed potatoes, the Carrot Pineapple Jell-O, the cookies . . . —*Susan*

Christmas Eve Macaroni and Cheese

We thought we must have had "the real kind" at some point, but Mom herself says: "Kraft was always in charge of the macaroni and cheese." —*Susan*

Buy Kraft Macaroni and Cheese.* Follow directions on package.

It was the original kind that now says "The Cheesiest" on the box.

Macaroni and Cheese on Christmas Eve

No one could accuse *me* of being a "Picky Eater" when I was a kid. But I do remember that I wasn't too fond of macaroni and cheese until Dad picked up the phone and threatened to call Santa and tell him not to come unless I'd eat it. Needless to say, I ate it!—*Jean*

"What's that, Neil? She's not eating her macaroni and cheese?"

Oyster Stew on Christmas Eve

Grandma Sanvidge, whose family background was mostly English, traditionally made oyster stew on Christmas Eve. When Mom and Dad were first married, Mom made this at Christmas for a few years. Dad would bring the fresh oysters (as fresh as they could be in Oshkosh) home in a little white cardboard carton. Mom remembers cleaning the oysters and cooking them gently in milk and butter. Helen Nancy (Dad's cousin who was raised with him and his brothers as a sister) remembers that Grandma always served this with little oyster crackers (which Helen Nancy ate instead of the oysters).—*Susan*

Spiced Apple Slices

Grandma Sanvidge served these bright red Spiced Apple Slices at Christmas. Mom knew roughly how she made them, but we never had a real recipe for them, so I experimented a bit. This is what I came up with.—*Jean*

4 cups of water

4 ounces cinnamon red hots (Yes, that is what Grandma used to flavor the apples!)

1 teaspoon liquid red food coloring (It takes a lot because it is coloring water.)

4 Delicious apples (about 2½ inches in diameter)

In a medium saucepan, combine water, cinnamon red hots, and red food coloring. Bring to a boil, stirring to dissolve red hots.

Peel and core apples. Cut into slices a little thicker than ¼ inch (across the apple—you will be making "rings" out of the cored apple). Turn down the heat under the water/cinnamon mixture and place apple slices in the water. Cover and simmer apple slices on low heat for 45 minutes to an hour. Stir gently from time to time so color will soak evenly into the apple slices. Slices are done when they can be pierced easily with a fork (but are not falling apart). Drain slices and put them in a tight, non-metal container that you don't mind staining (or line it with plastic wrap). Chill until ready to use.

Use drained slices as a garnish. Grandma put them on the meat platter, surrounding the meat.

You might want to use a DARK *platter. These very red apple slices leave a "footprint!" Mom remembers that one year Grandma Sanvidge made the apple slices green. Do you think Grandma used mint extract flavoring and green food coloring?—Jean*

Skillet Surprises (also known as Coconut Balls)

It's just not Christmas without these little gems!—*Julie*

These were always one of my favorite Christmas sweets. I liked them best when they started getting a little dried-out and chewy, but they usually went too fast. —*Susan*

MAKES ABOUT 2 DOZEN COOKIES

2 eggs, beaten
1½ cups chopped dates (8 ounce package)
¾ cup sugar
2 cups Rice Krispies
1 teaspoon vanilla
coconut (the flaked kind works best)

Mix beaten eggs, dates, and sugar. Put into a cold, lightly buttered frying pan. Cook over low heat, stirring constantly, until the mixture becomes golden brown and thick, about 10 minutes. Remove from heat. Stir in the Rice Krispies and vanilla. Drop by teaspoonfuls onto flaked coconut. Roll into ball-shaped candies, about the size of a walnut. Let cool until firm. Keep in an airtight tin.

Christmas Cookies (the cut-out and decorated ones)

Mom made these every year for Christmas (and now I do, too). As kids, we would always get together to frost and decorate them, sometimes getting a little too creative. One year some gingerbread-man-shaped cookies had those little chocolate sprinkles in their "armpits."

This is an unusually good recipe, not at all like the thick and dry cut-out cookies you see everywhere. You can freeze the dough and bake the cookies when you have time. And you can freeze the unfrosted cookies until you have time (and helpers) to decorate them. You probably should double this. It's just not enough. I make four to six times this recipe every Christmas.—*Susan*

A BATCH OF FROSTED, DECORATED COOKIES IN A VARIETY OF SHAPES MADE WITH THE FOLLOWING RECIPE WILL LOOSELY FILL ONE HALF-GALLON TIN.

1 cup shortening (Crisco)
⅔ cup sugar
2 eggs, unbeaten
2 teaspoons vanilla
1¼ teaspoons salt
2½ cups flour

Combine shortening, sugar, eggs, vanilla, and salt and beat thoroughly. Add the flour a little at a time and mix the dough well. Divide dough in half and wrap in plastic wrap, flattening and compressing the dough into a flat rectangle—a good shape for rolling out. CHILL UNTIL FIRM. (This is very important. You won't be able to roll out the dough if it is not thoroughly chilled.)

Preheat oven to 375°. Get your cookie cutters ready. Roll out a chunk of dough (the rest should stay cold in the fridge) on a floured surface to ⅛ inch thick*, using a light sprinkling of flour to keep the rolling pin from sticking. (Don't re-roll too much—the dough can get tough.**) Cut out the shapes. Bake on ungreased cookie sheets until only slightly browned on the edges, 8 to 10 minutes. Watch the first batch closely for timing. While the first batch is baking, cover a surface with dish towels and then with waxed paper. Lay the hot cookies on the waxed paper to cool. Cookies must be completely cool before frosting and decorating.

*To keep the thickness of these cookies uniform, I have a cut-in-half yardstick (most are exactly ⅛-inch thick) that I use as a guide for the rolling pin. Put one stick on each side of the dough and the rolling pin rides on top of the yardstick pieces, keeping the dough uniformly ⅛ inch thick.—Susan

**I just go ahead and bake the tough ones, and eat them right away (to keep up my strength).

Cut-out Cookie Icing:

2 cups powdered sugar
½ teaspoon vanilla
pinch of salt
water

Combine powdered sugar, vanilla, and salt and slowly add a little water as you stir with a fork, stopping when it looks like icing. (I use about 2 tablespoons, but this will vary with the brand of sugar you use.) If it's too thin, add more powdered sugar. Too thick? Add a little more water. Decorate before the icing sets. (*Mom uses hot water in this frosting to help the icing dry faster. I use cold water because I don't like the taste of hot tap water.—Susan*)

What We Used for Decorating:

Colored sugars, cinnamon dots ("red hots"), pecans, walnut pieces, silver balls (now we hear you weren't supposed to eat them), coconut, multicolored little sprinkles, those leftover chocolate chips, the chocolate sprinkles (mentioned above), and raisins (not popular, but useful for creative decorating).

"Only the first three Christmas cookies are fun to decorate."

—Diane

Spritz Cookies

This is the recipe you use for the cookie press. It's what most people think of when they hear "Christmas cookie."—*Jean*

MAKES ABOUT 9 DOZEN COOKIES

1 cup shortening or margarine

1 cup sugar

2 egg yolks, beaten

½ cup sour cream

4 cups sifted flour

1 teaspoon nutmeg

½ teaspoon salt

½ teaspoon baking soda

1 teaspoon vanilla

colored sugars for decoration

Cream shortening (or margarine) and sugar together well. Add beaten egg yolks and sour cream. In another bowl, sift together flour, nutmeg, salt, and baking soda. Add dry ingredients to creamed mixture a little at a time, mixing well after each addition. Add vanilla and mix in. It helps to chill the dough for a bit before proceeding.

Preheat oven to 400°. Shape dough by using a cookie press and place cookies directly on ungreased cookie sheets. Sprinkle with colored sugars before baking. Bake just to the point of browning, 8 to 10 minutes. Keep an eye on them.

These are pale yellow, tender cookies with a fine crumb.

All I Want for Christmas is . . . at the Piggly Wiggly

I remember age five being the point at which I could walk the three blocks to the Pig by myself and that I made my first gift purchase there . . . a blue plastic clip-on butterfly that I remember thinking was very beautiful. It was for Mom, and it cost 3 cents. Find a penny on the ground? Run to the Pig and get one piece of Bazooka gum! At Christmas time they put large-scale, expensive toys on the ledge above the produce section. I *begged* Mom for either the beauty shop or the vanity table for probably five years in a row. I got flashcards and math workbooks instead. Today, I'm not very good at math, but I'm hooked on hair highlights, and my Estée Lauder lady waves when she sees me coming. Parents, there's just so much influence you can exert.—*Julie*

If I use the two dollars I got for tying Grandpa's shoelaces, the 8 pennies I found, and the 73 cents in my bank, I'll only need . . .

Ribbon Cookies (Mom)

For years, these were the only Christmas cookies I made! One year, I gave some "bricks" of Ribbon Cookie dough to a friend who had recently had a baby. She and her seven-year-old sliced them up and baked them together for some no-fuss, no-muss quality Christmas time! It's nice to have this dough in the fridge over the holidays so you can bake up fresh cookies any time guests drop in.—*Julie*

MAKES ABOUT 9 DOZEN COOKIES

2 cups (4 sticks) salted butter

2 cups sugar

2 eggs, beaten

1 teaspoon vanilla

4½ cups flour

2½ teaspoons baking powder

¾ teaspoon salt

3 tablespoons poppy seeds

1 cup candied cherries, sliced (or each one chopped into a few pieces)

½ cup finely chopped pecans

2 squares unsweetened chocolate, melted

Cream butter and sugar. Add beaten eggs and vanilla. In another bowl, combine flour, baking powder, and salt. Mix into creamed mixture. Divide dough into three parts. Put each in a separate bowl.

In Bowl One, add poppy seeds; in Bowl Two, add cherries; in Bowl Three, add pecans and melted chocolate. Mix each.

Line two loaf pans with enough plastic wrap to hang over the sides of the pan. Press one-half of the cherry mixture firmly into the bottom of each pan. Then press one-half of the chocolate mixture into each pan. Then press one-half of the poppy seed mixture into each pan. Chill 24 hours, tightly covered.

Preheat oven to 400°. Slice loaf lengthwise,* then slice off ¼-inch to ⁵⁄₁₆-inch cookies. Place on ungreased cookie sheet and bake 4 minutes. Rotate cookie sheet in the oven and bake until set but not browned, about 4 more minutes.

*Like this:

Cutting lines for cookies

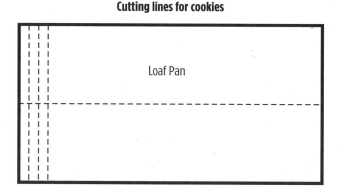

Loaf Pan

Cut Cookie

Cherry mixture   Chocolate mixture   Poppyseed mixture

"Ball" Cookies (Mom)

There has to be another name for these! They're a little like those crescents with almonds, but they're balls, with walnuts or pecans.—*Susan*

MAKES 4 TO 5 DOZEN COOKIES

1 cup (2 sticks) butter, softened (*No skimping! Nothing else works as glue.—Susan*)

4 heaping tablespoons sugar

2½ cups flour

1½ cups finely chopped pecans or black walnuts

1 teaspoon vanilla

3 to 4 teaspoons milk (optional, use only if dough feels too dry to form balls)

powdered sugar for rolling

> **"Don't sit around or Mom will find something for you to do."**
> —Jean to Diane, Susan to Julie . . .

Grease cookie sheets. Cream butter and sugar. Gradually mix in flour, then nuts and vanilla. If dough does not hold together when you squeeze it, add milk a little bit at a time until it does. (*I had to add 2 teaspoons of the "optional" milk.—Susan*) Chill dough for about 30 minutes before forming balls.

Preheat oven to 400°. Squeeze this very crumbly dough into balls about 1 inch across. Bake until barely golden, 5 to 10 minutes. Remove from oven and roll immediately in powdered sugar. Using a pair of teaspoons as if you were mixing a salad will be very helpful. (These cookies can be frozen.)

Pecan Fingers (Mom)

They melt in your mouth . . . —*Jean*

MAKES ABOUT 4 DOZEN COOKIES

1 cup (2 sticks) butter
¾ cup powdered sugar
2 cups flour
2 cups coarsely chopped pecans
1 tablespoon ice water
1 teaspoon vanilla
⅛ teaspoon salt
powdered sugar for rolling

Preheat oven to 325° and grease cookie sheets. Cream butter and sugar. Add the rest of the ingredients and mix well. Roll with palms of hands into finger lengths and place on cookie sheets. Bake until barely golden, 20 to 25 minutes. Roll in powdered sugar while still warm.

Hoska

 Hoska is a slightly sweet braided bread with yellow raisins and sliced almonds that was made by our Bohemian great-grandmother, Augusta Ringsmuth Sanvidge. We grew up thinking of Hoska as an Easter bread that we also had for Christmas but have since found out it's a Czechoslovakian Christmas tradition. Like my mother and great-grandmother, I make Hoska every Christmas—a triple batch (6 loaves).

 Mom substituted her sweet dough recipe for the bread part, but she did keep those raisins and almonds! We like it toasted and buttered for breakfast during (any) holiday season. It's too good to have only once a year.—*Susan*

MAKES 2 LOAVES

Basic Sweet Dough:

1 cup scalded whole or 2% milk (Skim milk will not work in this recipe.)

½ cup (8 tablespoons, or 1 stick) margarine or butter, melted

⅓ cup sugar

½ teaspoon salt

1 package (¼ ounce) dry yeast

¼ cup lukewarm water

1 egg, lightly beaten

4½ to 5 cups flour, sifted

Filling:

⅔ cup yellow raisins

⅓ cup sliced almonds (with the skins)

flour enough to coat raisins and almonds

In a large bowl, combine hot scalded milk, melted margarine or butter, sugar, and salt. Cool to lukewarm.

Dissolve yeast in lukewarm water.

When milk mixture is lukewarm, add yeast/water mixture and beaten egg. Add half of the flour and beat until smooth. Add remaining flour gradually. At some point it will be easier to just knead in the flour, but don't overdo it. This is a sweet dough and can get tough with over-kneading. Work in the full 4½ cups, and keep adding the remaining flour until the dough is starting to become a little stiff, then stop. Put in greased bowl to rise until doubled, about 2 hours.

To make the filling, mix the golden raisins and sliced almonds with just enough flour to coat them.

When dough has doubled, grease two cookie sheets. Punch dough down and divide in half. To make the first braided loaf, divide half of the dough into three parts. Pat each piece into a rectangle about 6 x 14 inches. Sprinkle each rectangle with one-sixth of the raisins and almonds, not quite to the edges. Roll up tightly (to make three 14-inch-long rolls) and pinch edges together tightly. (It will be easiest to braid the loaf right on the cookie sheet.) Braid 3 long rolls together for each loaf, making sure to pinch the ends of the rolls together and tuck them under. Repeat for the other loaf. Let rise for 30 to 45 minutes or until doubled.

Preheat oven to 350°. Bake loaves until golden brown, 20 to 25 minutes. This bread freezes well.

Peanut Brittle (Mom)

I think I'll take this chance to thank Mom for her diligence in searching for raw peanuts and burning her hands making this great stuff all these years. It's the best. Mom said to tell you to be sure to buy a *Very Good Quality* candy thermometer: "It has to be accurate, or all of your work will be in vain!"—*Susan*

2 cups sugar

1 cup light corn syrup

1 cup water

3 cups raw Spanish peanuts

¼ teaspoon salt

1 teaspoon butter

1 teaspoon baking soda

You will also need: a candy thermometer and a 15½ x 10½-inch jelly roll pan

Butter a 15½ x 10½-inch jelly roll pan lavishly. In a large saucepan, cook sugar, syrup, and water over medium heat to "hard ball stage." (This is marked on the candy thermometer—and will take a while.) Add peanuts and salt. Cook to "hard crack stage."(Also marked on the candy thermometer.) Remove from heat. Add butter, then baking soda, stirring until it foams thoroughly, and then pour while still foaming into buttered jelly roll pan. Cool 10 minutes. Put mixture on a buttered, heatproof surface and, working from the outside in (the outside will be cooler), stretch and prod the peanut brittle out, little by little, to a relatively uniform ¼ inch thick. (Process is similar to stretching lumpy dough into a flat rectangular shape, or blocking out a sweater.) Let cool. When cool, break into pieces and store in an airtight tin.

Althea's Caramel Corn (Dad)

Mary Jo Peters taught Dad how to make this. Althea is her second cousin, in case you were wondering.—*Julie*

Remember Cracker Jack? This is like Cracker Jack, but you don't get the peanuts and you don't get the prize. What you do get is fresh, homemade, crispy caramel corn, and lots of it.—*Susan*

6 quarts popped popcorn, unbuttered

2 cups brown sugar, firmly packed

½ cup light corn syrup

1 cup (2 sticks) butter or margarine

1 teaspoon salt

1 teaspoon baking soda

Preheat oven to 250° and butter cookie sheets. In a large pan, combine brown sugar, corn syrup, margarine, and salt. Boil 5 minutes. Remove from heat. Stir in baking soda. Put the popcorn in a large (turkey size) roaster pan and pour sugar mixture over the popcorn. Stir well to distribute the caramel. Pour caramel-covered popcorn onto buttered cookie sheets. Bake for 1 hour, stirring every 15 minutes.

Sugared Walnuts (Mom)

Sugared Walnuts would look nice in your antique candy dish.—*Susan*

MAKES ABOUT 2 CUPS

1½ cups sugar
½ cup sour cream
2 cups walnut halves
1½ teaspoons vanilla
You will also need: a candy thermometer and waxed paper

Combine sugar and sour cream in a heavy saucepan. Cook over low heat, stirring constantly, until a candy thermometer registers 225°. Stir in nuts and vanilla, making sure all nuts are coated. Spread on waxed paper (which you've placed on a dish towel—or you will be scraping melted wax off your counter), trying to make sure the nuts are separated and top side up. This will be easier if you spoon the nuts out of the pan and use two forks to help you spread them out before they cool. Cool thoroughly. Store in an airtight container. (A *hidden* airtight container—until you're ready to put them out. It's hard to stop eating them.)

How about an After-Dinner Mint Instead?

Grandpa Noffke amazed the grandchildren one Christmas when after dinner he took a match from his pocket, struck it on the zipper of his pants, and lit his pipe. "H.A.! Is something burning?" He had also lit his pants!—*Diane*

Peanut Clusters

One year, on the way up north for Christmas, we stopped in to see Cile at the house she shared with her brother. She gave us Peanut Clusters, made with dry-roasted peanuts and semi-sweet chocolate. They were salty-sweet and delicious.—*Susan*

MAKES ABOUT 3 DOZEN

8 ounces semisweet chocolate (or 1⅓ cups semisweet chocolate chips)

½ pound Spanish peanuts (*Cile used dry-roasted peanuts to make hers. Both are very good.*)

You will also need: a double boiler

Cover 2 cookie sheets with waxed paper. Melt chocolate in a double boiler. While still over the heat, stir in the peanuts, and coat well. Drop clusters of coated peanuts from teaspoon onto cookie sheets. Cover and chill for about 12 hours or overnight. Remove from refrigerator, put peanut clusters into a covered container, and keep in a cool place.

Suet Pudding

Grandma Great (Myrtle Ingersoll Safford) would bring a little packet of this every year to Christmas dinner. After Grandma Great died, no one had the recipe. One Christmas, Mom gave each of us a copy of *The Tritt Family Cookbook* (relatives on Dad's side). And there it was. Dad's cousin Joyce Dexter had sent in the recipe (as plum pudding). She noted: "This recipe was originally used by Julissa Hubbard Tritt, wife of William Tritt *[our great-great-great grandparents]*, and was sent to me by Madaline Roycraft, daughter of Leon Tritt."

The next Christmas, Mom and I bought some suet and made this old, old recipe. Mom added the notes in italics. We made half of this recipe. Half of this is still a lot of pudding—a little over 2 quarts. (Don't forget to make the batter the day before you steam it.)—*Susan*

"Beat 6 eggs, then add:

2 lbs. sugar *[4½ cups]*
1 tsp. salt
2 tsp. grated nutmeg

1½ c. sweet milk [*This means plain milk, not sour milk. Use whole milk in this recipe.*]

2 lbs. raisins [*a little over 6 cups*]

1 lb. currants [*a little over 3 cups*]

1 lb. suet, ground fine [*4 cups packed*]

Flour [*See below.*]

Use enough flour [*about 5 cups*] to make a batter so stiff a spoon will stand up straight. [*Chill overnight.*] Put into bags* the next morning, leaving room for it to swell. Then put bags into a kettle of boiling water and boil for 4 hours. Use a saucer in the bottom of the kettle to keep bags from sticking.

[*If you don't happen to have muslin cooking bags in your cupboard, try this: Mom put a colander in a big soup pot with water at the bottom and put a bowl (buttered) of pudding in the colander. Cover to hold in the steam. Cooking a half-batch of pudding this way took 6 hours. Make sure you check the water level periodically.*]

Sauce for Pudding:

In a pan:

1 c. brown sugar

4 T. flour

1 tsp. vanilla

Dash of nutmeg and salt

Pour over this 1¼ c. boiling water and cook to thicken. Add 1 tablespoon of butter last. May be made using white sugar which results in a whiter sauce, and this may be used on any pudding."

The white sugar sauce version would be prettier on the dark pumpkin-colored pudding. The brown sugar sauce is almost the same color as the pudding.—Susan

This looks like the Leftovers Supper after Christmas Dinner. The candles, the glass plates with the little "hobnails," and the coffee in the carafe are definite signs that this is a holiday meal. The ketchup bottle and the milk bottle are out there in plain sight and Mom (facing camera) is so relaxed—this is definitely not the main meal! (Where are we? At the Kids' Table, of course!)

The Christmas Party for "The Men"

A table covered in avocado green . . . young ladies eager to wait on the guests . . . dinner served on white china with tiny rose buds . . . spirits served in bumpy green glasses . . . the arrival of "the men" (who worked for our Dad, Neil V. Sanvidge, Builder) and their wives . . .

One of the fondest of the Sanvidge family holiday memories is the Christmas party that our parents threw annually for "the men" and their wives. I can remember the special event like it was yesterday . . . it was a huge deal! The table would be moved into the den and covered with an avocado green lace tablecloth and matching napkins. (Almost forty years later, these napkins are still in circulation and somehow are without stains or wrinkles!)

The dishes were set—the white china with tiny rosebuds (Petite Bouquet), along with two sets of matching salt and pepper shakers and the double vegetable dish. Placed at the settings were the Americana Star "silverware" and the bumpy green glasses. The table was complete when the centerpiece—a white-painted metal candleholder, decorated with stones that looked like jewels—was placed in the middle of the table.

The guests arrived to the wonderful aroma of Mom's Prime Rib and Twice-Baked Potatoes as the young sisters anxiously awaited their waitress duties. Roy Carpenter was a favorite guest, as he always tipped us . . . once it was five whole dollars!

The evening ended with a platter of the most scrumptious Christmas cookies you have ever seen! Everyone enjoyed themselves . . . maybe there was a Manhattan in the bumpy green glass?

Can "the men" and their wives come over again? We'll waitress!
—*Diane*

Prime Rib

Mom made prime rib for most of the "Christmas Parties for the Men," and she kept track of the amounts and timing.—*Susan*

For six people, buy nearly 9¾ pounds of prime rib ahead of time (so you don't have to worry about finding one) and freeze it. The night before the party, take the prime rib out of the freezer and put it in the refrigerator. For dinner at 7:30 p.m., take the prime rib out of the refrigerator at 10:30 a.m., and unwrap it at noon. Put the meat in a shallow pan and put it into a 325° oven at 2:30 p.m., and the prime rib will be ready to serve at 7:30 p.m.*

Mom served frozen peas with "carrots added for color." The recipe for Twice-Baked Potatoes is on page 121. Mom's prime rib was always roasted to "medium" (of course). If you like your meat rare, the timing would be about 3¾ hours for a prime rib this size.

Steamed Cranberry Pudding (Mom)

A very good choice for the winter holidays. The cranberries look festive, and it's kind of like plum pudding (but lighter in color) with its moist, cakey texture and buttery sauce. When the whole family gets together for the holidays, Mom often makes cranberry pudding for a New Year's Eve dessert.—*Susan*

Pudding:

2 cups cranberries, cut in half lengthwise

¼ cup light molasses

¼ cup Karo light corn syrup

1½ cups flour

2 teaspoons baking soda

⅓ cup hot water

pinch of salt

Sauce:

1¼ cups cream, half-and-half, or evaporated milk

½ cup (8 tablespoons, or 1 stick) butter

½ cup sugar

Grease a 1½-quart Pyrex bowl. In another bowl, combine cranberries, molasses, and syrup, then flour and salt. In a small bowl, mix hot water and baking soda. Add to cranberry mixture and stir well. Put mixture in greased bowl. Put a rack or colander at the bottom of a soup pot (or a spaghetti cooker with a steaming basket) and pour in some water. Put bowl on rack.

Cover pot and steam for 1½ hours. If a toothpick inserted in the center comes out clean, it's done. (Leftovers can be reheated by steaming the same way.)

To make the sauce, combine cream, butter, and sugar in a saucepan and heat slowly. To serve, scoop servings of warm pudding and ladle hot sauce over it.

Time to Clear the Table!

How this book came about . . .

In late October of 2003, Diane had the idea of doing a family cookbook as a Christmas present for our parents. We started out to make a family cookbook, and the recipes evoked all kinds of memories for us, so we wrote them down.

Surprisingly, each of us had collected different recipes. When we couldn't find a recipe, it was difficult to keep our project a secret with our parents just a phone call away! Once we began writing down our little stories, we filled in each other's memory gaps. (Sometimes our memories were a little different!) We had a lot of fun working together on this book. There was a flurry of e-mails, phone calls, and faxes . . .

- "Do we have the Cheese Cups yet? Those have to be my favorite things."

- "I'm going out to buy the beans and molasses and try this right now!"

- "I just bought the most incredible chafing dish for $33 at Costco . . . Diane, you need this."

- "Remember Kinker's Korners and Josef's?" (*Grandma Sanvidge's favorite restaurants*)

- ⊞ "Uncle Hank makes the liver sausage for his kids. I called Aunt Marion, and she's going to mail you the recipe."

- ⊞ "33 tablespoons of cinnamon? On MEAT?"

- ⊞ "None of us oldies remember Apricot Nectar Chicken." (*Julie was right. We should have put this in. It is now.*)

- ⊞ "I talked to Marlene, and she doesn't have Aunt Emma's donut recipe. She's going to ask Cyndi."

- ⊞ "I stood in the aisle of the grocery store and looked at the recipe on the cocoa tin."

- ⊞ "Susan, do you have the [potato dumplings/sweet-sour cabbage] recipe? I've tried to wing it over the years and it's just not the same."

- ⊞ "I'm going to get that potato dumpling/sweet-sour cabbage recipe from Dad . . . he's pretty hard to pull one over on and I'm a lousy actress . . . I really *do* want to try it."

- ⊞ "Can you pull one over on Dad? You've got to be kidding!"

We gave Mom and Dad the cookbook for Christmas in 2003 and made copies for ourselves, the grandchildren, and great-grandchildren, too. We did three more printings of the book to give to family and friends. Diane's idea was a really good one.

For this version of the cookbook, we were able to ask questions, test questionable recipes, correct our errors, get the recipes we were missing, and add even more.

We are all really happy to have done this book. It's nice to know that these recipes and memories have been gathered together, and at the same time spread around!—*Susan, Diane, Jean, and Julie*

The four of us in Diane's kitchen on Congress Street in Oshkosh, from left to right: Diane, Julie, Jean, and Susan.

Each of us has some people to thank . . .

First of all, a HUGE THANK YOU to "Test Kitchen Mom," who hunted for long-lost recipes and found herself making (and eating) a lot of things she hadn't made in years!—*Susan, Diane, Jean, and Julie*

Mom and Julie Make a Deal

If I know how to cook at all, it is because I had great 4-H cooking teachers and because Mom and I struck a deal that encouraged me to cook.

"Julie," Mom said, "I've been cooking every day for many years, and I'm pretty tired of it. If you want to cook dinner or anything else, that's just fine with me— I'll clean up after you."

Cook I did. The first whole meal I made the family was spaghetti. I used a recipe that called for two cloves of garlic. When I bought my ingredients at the Piggly Wiggly, I bought what I thought were two cloves of garlic. Actually, they were two HEADS of garlic. Mom had no instructions for me on how to cut up a head of garlic, so I guessed and probably dug out 50 percent of the pulp. The spaghetti sauce turned out so potent, I don't think anybody liked it very much. But Mom let me keep cooking.

I watched Graham Kerr on TV and emulated him. He drank wine from a wine glass, so I drank milk from a wine glass while I cooked. Noodles, strudels, cookies, cakes, a whole summer of pie experiments . . . whatever I wanted to make, Mom cleaned up after. It was a wonderful way to learn to cook. Thanks, Mom!
—*Julie*

Kudos to Mom and Dad . . .

I'd really like to thank Mom and Dad for teaching us to be capable people. Mom was always willing to turn over the kitchen to us to experiment with our 4-H recipes. (Just don't leave all the cupboard doors open!) Mom gave us the opportunity she didn't have when she was little. Dad not only taught Mom what he had learned about cooking from his mother, but he kept cooking, because he enjoyed it and it gave Mom a break from the kitchen. Mom, you sure were a good student and turned out to be a great cook! Dad was also generous with his carpenter tools and wood scraps. I sure do appreciate what we learned at home.—*Jean*

Diane's Thank You

Susie . . . Who would have thought that the pickiest eater ("pudding skin" "I'll take mine minus the onions." "I ran out of room for kidney beans under my plate.") would become a collector of cookbooks, an adventurous chef, and the main driving force behind this project! Thanks for all of the time and effort you put into this cookbook/family memoir. I am truly overwhelmed by this—it is AWESOME! And to Jean and Julie . . . your stories and memories amaze me! Your contributions brought up so many happy and forgotten memories for me . . . thank you! Now . . . someone make me some of Cile's famous beans!—*Diane*

"Thanks for the Memories . . . "

When I started thinking of the food we ate growing up—what it looked like, how it tasted, how it smelled, the dish or pot it was on or in, the table, the scraping of the chairs, "Please pass the salt"—it didn't take long before I was *there*. Right there. In the safe world created by Mom and Dad—looking under the rocks in the driveway, packing our little suitcases to go to the cottage, ice skating in the back yard, buying our summer clothes from the catalog, playing with Patsy and Mary Lou, practicing for our "circus," making doll furniture from the scrap wood in the garage and doll clothes on my little Singer sewing machine, enjoying the time around the 4th of July with our Georgia cousins every year, pushing the old green Chevy with Uncle Jimmy weak with laughing, playing baseball on Grandma's lawn . . . Thanks to *everyone* who gave us a childhood to remember.—*Susan*

"Time to do the dishes. It's my turn to dry!"

Much of the clip art in this book appears with the permission of Dover Publications, Mineola, New York; doverpublications.com. From *Food and Drink*, edited by Jim Harter (1980): pages 12, 22, 25, 56, 57, 63, 137, 139, 155 (both images), 165, 171, 172, 190, 198, 209, 303, 318, 335, 356. From *Plants*, edited by Jim Harter (1998): pages 59, 78, 80, 89 (both images) 99, 108, 111, 112, 145, 232, 236, 272, 280, 330, 349, 351. From *Goods and Merchandise*, edited by William Rowe (1982): pages 10, 11, 35, 38, 72, 97, 131, 147, 161, 166, 244, 257. From *Victorian Goods and Merchandise*, edited by Carol Belanger Grafton (1997): pages vii, 34, 69, 191, 203, 213, 214, 285, 291, 313, 342. From *Plants and Flowers*, edited by Alan E. Bessette and William K. Chapman: pages 23, 32, 81 (top), 103, 104, 114 (right), 115, 132, 183, 250, 317, 337. From *Montgomery Ward & Co. 1895 Catalog*: pages 70, 113, 117, 149, 178, 182, 219. From *3,800 Early Advertising Cuts, Deberny Type Foundry*, edited by Carol Belanger Grafton (1991): pages 33, 74, 102, 114 (left), 125, 206, 273. From *Harter's Picture Archive for Collage and Illustration*, edited by Jim Harter (1978): pages 122, 284, 287. From *An Old-Fashioned Christmas*, edited by Clarence P. Hornung (1975): pages 334, 343, 359. From *Early American Design Motifs*, edited by Suzanne E. Chapman (2003): page vi. From *Animals*, edited by Jim Harter (1979): pages 154, 205. From *Big Book of Old-Time Spot Illustrations*, edited by Hayward Cirker (2001): page 185

Index

Bold-faced numbers refer to photos.